PIERS PLOWMAN

GARLAND REFERENCE LIBRARY
OF THE HUMANITIES
(VOL. 121)

PIERS PLOWMAN
An Annotated Bibliography of Editions and Criticism, 1550–1977

A.J. Colaianne

GARLAND PUBLISHING, INC. • NEW YORK & LONDON
1978

PR
2015
C64

Library of Congress Cataloging in Publication Data
Colaianne, A   J
    Piers Plowman.

    (Garland reference library of the humanities; v.
121)
    Includes indexes.
    1. Langland, William, 1330?–1400. Piers the
Plowman—Bibliography. I. Title.
Z8482.4.C64 [PR2015]   016.821′1   78–7631
ISBN 0–8240–9822–6

Printed on acid-free, 250-year-life paper
Manufactured in the United States of America

CONTENTS

v

INTRODUCTION

The purpose of this bibliography is, first, to provide a comprehensive review of scholarship and criticism concerning William Langland and the three versions of his alliterative masterpiece *Piers Plowman* and, second, to suggest some directions for future studies of this mysterious and problematic work.

This bibliography is divided into four chapters and an epilogue essay. Each chapter opens with a review of the basic problems in a specific area of *Piers* studies and a general summary of relevant criticism. Next, individual studies are listed and annotated. Items of lesser significance are included but are not annotated. This bibliography does not seek to evaluate the criticism it discusses beyond indicating where the discoveries of later scholarship have corrected the inaccuracies of earlier writers.

Chapter One concerns the evidence for a biography of Langland and problems related to the authorship of the texts. It focuses on J.M. Manly's theory of the "lost leaf" and the subsequent controversy which dominated *Piers* criticism from 1904 to approximately 1940. Chapter Two reviews the problems of establishing texts of the three versions and describes all editions of the poems from Robert Crowley's 1550 printing of the B-text to the recent critical editions published by the Athlone Press. This material also includes selections from the texts printed in anthologies and collections, as well as translations of all or part of the poem. The third chapter encompasses interpretive studies of *Piers Plowman*, and the fourth, studies of the poem's language, style, and meter. The Epilogue examines remaining problems in *Piers* criticism and suggests directions for the future. An Appendix provides a list of studies not included in Chapter One that comment incidentally on the question of authorship.

This bibliography is selective, with special emphasis on critical studies published from 1875 to 1977, although significant items written prior to 1875 have been included as well. It lists studies written in English, German, French, Italian, Czech, Polish, and Japanese. All items deal substantially with *Piers Plowman*: while literary histories and general discussions of medieval literature which deal directly with *Piers* have been listed, no attempt has been made to include passing references to *Piers Plowman* or allusions to *Piers* in early literature. Bibliographical descriptions of *Piers* manuscripts such as those in the *Index of Middle English Verse* (1943) have not been included. This bibliography lists review articles but includes only a few book reviews which have some special value. Dissertations have not been systematically listed, although a substantial number of important English, American, and German dissertations have been included.

The title *Piers Plowman* has been uniformly italicized in all bibliographical citations. Textual citations have also been standardized: Text. Passus, line numbers: *e.g.*, B.XIII, 115–118. Because of the publication of several anthologies of critical essays on *Piers Plowman*, as well as the interrelatedness of much *Piers* criticism, numerous cross-references appear in this bibliography. It is hoped that this cross-referencing will aid the scholar who is interested in tracing the controversies concerning the authorship of the texts as well as the much-debated interpretive cruces. Separate author and subject indices have also been included. In the latter, all scenes, characters, passages, and proper names mentioned in the annotations are listed.

The principal sources used in compiling this bibliography are as follows:

Bloomfield, Morton W. "The Present State of *Piers Plowman* Studies." *Speculum*, 14 (1939), 215–239.

Cambridge Bibliography of English Literature. Ed. F.W. Bateson. 4 vols. Cambridge: Cambridge University Press, 1940.

Cambridge Bibliography of English Literature. Vol. V, Supplement: A.D. 600–1900. Ed. George Watson. Cambridge: Cambridge University Press, 1957.

Dissertation Abstracts of Dissertations and Monographs in Microform (DA), 1961–June, 1969. *Dissertation Abstracts International (DAI),* July, 1969–1977.

Hussey, S.S. "Eighty Years of *Piers Plowman* Scholarship: A Study of Critical Methods." Unpublished M.A. Thesis, University of London, 1952.

Modern Humanities Research Association. Annual Bibliography of English Language and Literature, 1920–1973.

Proppe, Katherine. *"Piers Plowman*: An Annotated Bibliography for 1900–1968." *Comitatus,* 3 (1972), 33–90 [Selective].

Publications of the Modern Language Association Annual Bibliography, 1921–1968. *MLA International Bibliography,* 1969–1976.

Wells, J.E. *A Manual of the Writings in Middle English,* with Supplements i–viii. New Haven: Yale University Press. 1916–1941.

The Year's Work in English Studies, edited for the English Association, 1919–1975.

Although *Piers Plowman* has been, at least for the past fifty years, one of the most popular Middle English poems, no previous attempt has been made to list and annotate *Piers* scholarship and criticism in a systematic fashion. Morton Bloomfield's landmark essay, "The Present State of *Piers Plowman* Studies" (1939), summarizes most of the critical literature produced during the authorship controversy, but it is not comprehensive. Katherine Proppe's *"Piers Plowman*: An Annotated Bibliography for 1900–1968" (1972) is selective and inaccurate. David C. Fowler's *"Piers Plowman"* (in *Recent Middle English Scholarship and Criticism: Survey and Desiderata,* ed. J. Burke Severs [Pittsburgh, Pa.: Duquesne University Press, 1971], pp. 9–27) discusses only the most innovative studies published between 1940 and 1970.

Students of *Piers Plowman* now face a massive amount of scholarship and criticism. In the past fifteen years alone, three substantial collections of essays, twenty book-length studies, and several hundred articles on *Piers* have been published. Presently, in terms of all Middle English critical studies, Langland studies are second in volume only to Chaucer scholarship. This bibliography is designed to serve as a guide to this material and to facilitate future research in *Piers Plowman*.

I would like to thank the librarians of the University of Cincinnati, Xavier University, Virginia Polytechnic Institute and State University, and the University of Pittsburgh for their help in locating research materials. Special thanks are due to Professors Nancy L. Harvey, John P. McCall, and W. L. Godshalk who read this work in its original form as a doctoral dissertation at the University of Cincinnati, and to my parents. To my wife, Kate, without whose loyalty, support, and patience this project could not have been completed, this study is dedicated.

Virginia Polytechnic Institute
and State University
Blacksburg, Virginia

ABBREVIATIONS

ABR	*American Benedictine Review*
AnM	*Annuale Mediaevale*
Archiv	*Archiv fur das Studium der Neueren Sprachen und Literaturen*
CE	*College English*
CP	Skeat, W.W., ed. *The Vision of William concerning Piers the Plowman in Three Parallel Texts together with Richard the Redeless.* London: Oxford University Press, 1886.
DA	*Dissertation Abstracts*
DAI	*Dissertation Abstracts International*
ELH	*Journal of English Literary History*
ELN	*English Language Notes*
ES	*English Studies*
HLQ	*Huntington Library Quarterly*
JEGP	*Journal of English and Germanic Philology*
MLN	*Modern Language Notes*
MLQ	*Modern Language Quarterly*
MLR	*Modern Language Review*
MP	*Modern Philology*
MS	*Mediaeval Studies* (Toronto)
N & Q	*Notes and Queries*
NM	*Neuphilologische Mitteilungen*
PMLA	*Publications of the Modern Language Association*
PP	*Piers Plowman*
PQ	*Philological Quarterly*
RES	*Review of English Studies*
SP	*Studies in Philology*
TLS	*Times Literary Supplement*
WL	William Langland

I. BIOGRAPHICAL STUDIES AND THE
PROBLEMS OF AUTHORSHIP

The poet of *Piers Plowman* has been the subject of biographical
investigation since the mid-sixteenth century and the search for
clues to his identity continues today. He has been known as William
or Robert Langland (De Langlonde, Langley), John Malvern, and even
Piers Plowman.[1] Of these names, only two, William and Robert
Langland, have made serious claims to the attention of modern
scholars. Most contemporary critics follow Skeat's choice of
William Langland, although his proofs for this choice are by no means
conclusive.[2]

The standard biography of Langland is necessarily sketchy,
given the lack of solid documentation concerning the authorship of
the poem. Most scholars now agree that the poem was written by a
single poet, William Langland, the son of Stacy de Rokayle. Born
c. 1332 at Cleobury Mortimer in Shropshire, Langland was probably
educated at the monastery of Great Malvern, and at one time lived in
London. This is actually all that may be said on the matter with
any degree of certainty. There is, however, some additional biographical material that may be best termed "inferential" since it
is based not on factual data but on information drawn from the poem
itself.

The following account of the poet's life by J. F. Goodridge,
for example, is based on information that Will, the first-person
narrator, gives us concerning himself:

> Langland seems to have wandered a good deal from
> place to place and mixed with all kinds of people.
> He knew London well and worked on his poem there.
> He tells us that he lived with his wife Kit and
> his daughter Colette in a cottage on Cornhill,
> and made a meagre living by singing the Office
> of the Dead for wealthy patrons. He certainly
> knew poverty at close quarters. We also hear his
> nickname, Long Will, and he frequently refers to

1

his own tallness and leanness. He sometimes lived
an unconventional life, dressed like a beggar; he
was inclined to treat self-important people with
little respect; he was constantly preoccupied with
writing verses and some people thought him mad.[3]

Although the poet is not referred to in contemporary records,
a few pieces of external evidence clearly name him.[4] The most
significant of these is a note found on the verso of the last leaf
of a C-text manuscript, Trinity College, Dublin, D.4.1:

Memorandum quod Stacy de Rokayle pater Willielmi
de Langlond qui Stacius fuit generosus, et
morabatur in Schypton Vnder Whicwode, tenens
domini le Spenser in comitatu Oxon., qui predictus
Willielmus fecit librum qui vocatur Perys Ploughman.[5]

This ascription has recently been dated c. 1400:[6] as Professor
Kane notes, it was possible for the writer of the note to have had
firsthand knowledge of the authorship of the poem. Although the
authority of this note was attacked in the debate over authorship,
it stands as the most important document in favor of the name
William Langland. Next, we have the testimony of John But, who, in
his addition to the twelfth passus of an A-text manuscript, records
the following:[7]

Wille þurgh in wit [wiste] wel þe soþe,
þat þis speche was spedelich, and sped him wel faste,
And wrouȝ the þat here is wryten and oþer werkes boþe
Of peres þe plowman and mechel puple also.
And whan þis werk was wrouȝt, ere wille myȝte aspie,
Deþ delt him a dent and drof him to þe erþe
And is closed vnder clom, crist haue his soule.
                                      (A.XII, 99-105)

The last piece of external evidence is an explicit found in the
Liverpool University Library MS F.4.8. (c. 1425) which reads simply:
Explicit liber Willielmi de petro le plowȝman[8].

In spite of these ascriptions--one to William Langland and two
to "William"--there has been serious disagreement regarding the name
of the poet. There was, in fact, until fairly recently, support for
the first name Robert, based on the probable misreading of the first
line of Passus VII in the B-text, "Thus yrobed in russet, I romed
aboute" as "& y Robert in rosset gan romed abowhte" or something
similar.[9]

The name "Robertus Langelande" was recorded by John Bale in his
Index Britanniae Scriptorum and *Scriptorum Illustrium Maioris
Britanniae*.[10] Robert Crowley, the first editor of *Piers Plowman*,
probably derived his information from Bale. In the preface to his
1550 edition, Crowley states:

> Beynge desyerous to knowe the name of the Autoure
> of thys most worthy worke, (gentle reader) and the
> tyme of the writynge of the same: I did not onely
> gather togyther suche aunciente copies as I could
> come by, but also consult such men as I knew to be
> more exercised in the studie of antiquities, then
> I my selfe haue ben. And by some of them I haue
> learned that the Autour was named Roberte langlande,
> a Shropshere man borne in Cleybirie, aboute viii
> miles from Maluerne hilles.[11]

In spite of the early tradition which favors the name Robert,
however, it is now almost certain, in light of Kane's thorough discussion of the problem, that the poet's name was William.

Apart from this sparse external evidence, there is a substantial amount of apparently "personal" information in the poem's
narrative which is often read as valid biographical data. Much of
the information which the fictional character Will gives concerning
himself was read by Bright, Jusserand, and others as pertaining to
Langland,[12] and Mensendieck read the text as the poet's spiritual
autobiography.[13] Autobiographical inferences from the text may be
correct in some respects but they are, of course, fallacious in
principle since they blur the necessary distinction between the poet
and his fictional creation.

Until the present century, it was generally assumed that a
single author was responsible for *Piers Plowman*,[14] and the major
critical dispute centered on his identification. In 1906, however,
J. M. Manly noted several differences in the three versions of the
poem, and postulated his famous theory of multiple authorship. To
this day, all students of *Piers Plowman* are affected by the con-
torversy that grew out of his initial reading.[15]

It is now commonplace to disparage the issues raised in the
authorship controversy but it is significant that since Manly's
initial publications, the question has never completely disappeared.
Professor Kane, in his evaluation of the issues, *Piers Plowman: The*

Evidence for Authorship (1965), attempted to conclude the controversy by proving that the multiple authorship contention was not viable. Yet in spite of his efforts, the speculation continues.[16]

While the authorship debate was not always conducted in a completely admirable fashion, its effect was ultimately salutary. At its height, the debate became a very personal battle, marred by partisan and frequently deceptive argumentation. Apart from this, the overall effect of Manly's discovery and the subsequent controversy was quite positive for it focused critical attention on a poem that had for too long been ignored and misunderstood. Although the debate was initiated by Manly's perception of differences in poetic technique in the versions of the poem, it eventually led to the larger considerations of unity and coherence in the poem's narrative. These questions continue to be the major concern of critics today.

The items listed below constitute the main body of criticism concerning the life of the poet and the question of single versus multiple authorship. The latter topic has, of course, been discussed elsewhere in studies which focus on other aspects of the poem. A partial listing of the most important of these studies according to their position on the issue appears in an Appendix.

[1]John Stowe suggested that the poet was John Malvern, a fellow of Oriel College, Oxford. See W. W. Skeat, ed., *The Vision of William concerning Piers the Plowman in Three Parallel Texts together with Richard the Redeless* (London: Oxford University Press, 1886, Rptd., 1954), II, Introduction, xxxviii. William Webbe, in *A Discourse of English Poetrie* (1586), notes: "The next of our auncient Poets, that I can tell of, I suppose to be Pierce Ploughman . . . ." See Skeat, EETS, o.s. 81, p. 867.

[2]Skeat, *CP*, II, xxvii-xxxviii.

[3]J. F. Goodridge, trans., *Piers the Ploughman* (Middlesex: Penguin, 1966), 9-10. For problems with such biographical readings, see n.12, below.

[4]Professor Kane, in his *Piers Plowman: The Evidence for Authorship* (London: Athlone Press, 1965), discusses three kinds of evidence--external, internal, and signature. He necessarily dismisses the inferential biographical information. See n.12 below. The signatures of the poem, especially the cryptogram in B.XV, 148 are discussed pp. 52-70.

[5]Quoted by A. H. Bright, *New Light on Piers Plowman* (London: Oxford University Press, 1928), Appendix F, p. 83.

[6]Kane, *Evidence*, p. 27, n.5. Manly believed that it was written "not early" in the fifteenth century. See *"Piers the Plowman* and Its Sequence," *CHEL* (Cambridge: Cambridge University Press, 1908), II, p. 34.

[7]The identity of But has been discussed by Henry Bradley, "Who Was John But?" *MLR*, 8 (1913), 88-9, and Edith Rickert, "John But, Messenger and Maker," *MP*, 11 (1913), 107-116. The extent of But's addition is a matter of dispute. See R. W. Chambers, "The Original Form of the A-text of *Piers Plowman*," *MLR*, 6 (1911), 302-23. Cf. Kane, *Evidence*, pp. 32-34.

[8]Kane, *Evidence*, p. 34.

[9]This was Skeat's explanation. This reading occurs in Corpus Christi College, Oxford MS 201. See Skeat, *CP*, II, xxviii. A subsequent discovery of a similar reading of this line, "þus Roberd in Russet I Romyd abowtyn," in Library of the Society of Antiquaries MS no. 687 confirms Skeat's explanation. See Kane, *Evidence*, p. 43.

[10]See Bright, *New Light*, Appendices B and E, pp. 79, 82-83. Discussed by Skeat, *CP*, II, xxviii and Kane, *Evidence*, 37-45.

[11]Quoted by Skeat, *CP*, II, lxxiii.

[12]Bright, *New Light, passim*; J. J. Jusserand, "*Piers Plowman*: The Work of One or Five," *MP*, 6 (1908-1909), 271-329. Cf. Jusserand's reply to J. M. Manly, *MP*, 7 (1909-1910), 289-326 and *Piers Plowman, A Contribution to the History of English Mysticism*, revised ed., trans. M.E.R. (New York: Russell and Russell, 1894), *passim*. Autobiographical readings of the poem were often a feature of arguments for single authorship. Professor Kane notes that such readings required "an assumption that the autobiography of Will the Dreamer suggested in the poems necessarily corresponded in some considerable degree to that of the actual poet" (*Evidence*, p. 4).

[13]Otto Mensendieck, "The Authorship of *Piers Plowman*," *JEGP*, 9 (1910), 404-20.

[14]There are at least two exceptions to this. Thomas Wright, in his edition of the B-text (1842, rptd., 1856), believed that B and C were the work of two poets, as did George P. Marsh (*Lectures on the English Language*, 1860). See M. W. Bloomfield, "The Present State of *Piers Plowman* Studies," *Speculum*, 14 (1939), 215-32. Also discussed by J. M. Manly, "The Authorship of *Piers Plowman*," *MP*, 14 (1916), 315-16.

[15]The major critical commentary on the authorship controversy to 1936 is summarized by Bloomfield, "Present State." The controversy is also reviewed in the following: Samuel Moore, "Studies in *Piers Plowman*, I," *MP*, 11 (1913), 177-93 and "Studies in *Piers Plowman*, II," *MP*, 12 (1914), 19-50; J. R. Hulbert, "*Piers Plowman* After Forty Years," *MP*, 45 (1948), 215-25; S. S. Hussey, "Eighty Years of *Piers Plowman* Scholarship: A Study of Critical Methods" (Unpublished University of London M.A. Thesis, 1952); Nevill Coghill, *Piers Plowman*, Writers and Their Work Series, 174 (New York: Longmans, Green and Company, 1964), pp. 7-18; Kane, *Evidence*, pp. 9-23.

[16]The question of multiple authorship has been raised most recently by Sister Francis D. Covella in her unpublished dissertation, "Formulaic Second Half-lines in Skeat's A-text of *Piers Plowman*: Norms for a Comparative Analysis of the A-, B-, and C-texts" (New York University, 1972). Cf. her "Grammatical Evidence of Multiple Authorship in *Piers Plowman*," *Language and Style*, 9 (1976), 3-16.

1. Adams, M. Ray. "The Use of the Vulgate in *Piers Plowman*."
    SP, 24 (1927), 556-66.

     Explores WL's ecclesiastical connections by examining
    his use of the Vulgate, especially as related to ecclesias-
    tical ritual. WL, who was probably a priest in lower orders,
    addressed his poem to the common people. He intended to
    make the Bible more intelligible to the laity, and accordingly
    translated Latin passages and interpreted them in the vernac-
    ular. Of the 450 quotations from the Vulgate in the three
    versions, 318 are from separate passages in the Vulgate;
    seven, from the creeds of the Church; seven, from Latin
    hymns in the ritual; eighteen, from the Church Fathers; and
    the remainder from Latin prose writers. Most of the Vulgate
    quotations are from the "more devotional" Books of the
    Bible--Psalms, Matthew, Mark, and John. WL was also familiar
    with the Breviary Psalter.

2. Bannister, Arthur T. "William Langland's Birthplace." *TLS*,
    21 (Sept. 7, 1922), 569.

     Bannister suggests that WL's birthplace was on the
    western slope of the Malvern and provides evidence that
    certain topographical allusions in *PP* correspond to this
    locale.

3. Bayley, A. R. "Langland at Great Malvern." *N&Q*, Contin-
    uous Series, 181 (1941), 181.

     Answers Peregrinus's query (66) concerning Bright's
    reference to a popular belief that WL lived over the Abbey
    Gateway of Great Malvern. Traces this to James Nott's *Church
    and Monastery of Moche Malverne* (1885), p. 93.

4. Bloomfield, Morton W. "Was William Langland a Benedictine
    Monk?" *MLQ*, 4 (1943), 57-61.

     Based on Bright's conclusions concerning WL's identity
    (10). WL was Willemus de Colewell who was ordained December
    20, 1348, by John de Trillek, Bishop of Hereford. WL used
    both the name of his parish (Colewall) and that of Longland
    or Langland, a large field near his home. Bloomfield suggests
    that a reference in the proceedings of Uhtred of Boldon's
    visit to Whitby monastery pertains to WL--"Willelmus Colvill"
    was fined for his part in a disturbance. Bloomfield feels
    that WL could have been a Benedictine monk. WL's attack
    on the Friars (especially William Jordan in B. XIII, 21-201)
    appears to support this conclusion.

5. Bradley, Henry. "The Authorship of *Piers the Plowman*."
    MLR, 5 (1910), 202-7. Rptd. EETS, o.s. 139 f. (1910).

     Reviews Chambers' comments (16) on Bradley's contention
    that there is a misplaced leaf. Bradley maintains his view:

"whatever his [Langland's] design may have been, it was intended to be accomplished by showing all the seven sins in order." Although withholding final judgement, favors plurality of authorship.

6. _____. "The Lost Leaf of *Piers the Plowman*." *Nation* 88 (April 29, 1909), 436-7.

Answers Carleton Brown (14). Brown's contention is inadequate for three reasons: 1) Brown leaves untouched the matter of Covetousness's promise to deal honestly in the future without mention of restitution; 2) it is impossible that Robert the Robber could replace one of the sins; 3) Brown's reading involves a major contradiction in that Robert says in l. 251 that he can never replace what he has stolen but three lines later promises restitution.

7. _____. "The Misplaced Leaf of *Piers the Plowman*." *Athenaeum* (April 21, 1906), p. 481. Rptd. EETS, Extra Issue 135 B (1908).

Bradley accepts Manly's view that A.V, 236-259 does not properly follow Sloth's confession (58), but proposes a different explanation: "Professor Manly has failed to perceive that the proper place of lines 236-259 is after line 145 at the end of the confession of Covetousness. In this position they not only fit perfectly, but actually improve the sense." Bradley contends that the author wrote his text on loose sheets and that one or more (containing the confession of Wrath and the end of the confession of Envy) were lost and that another (containing lines 236-259) was misplaced. Furnivall endorses this theory in his "Foreword" to the offprint of Manly's *"Piers the Plowman*," EETS, Extra Issue, 135 b (1908), iii. Jusserand concurs (46, p. 287). The theory is answered by Carleton Brown (14).

8. _____. "Who was John But?" *MLR*, 9 (1913), 88-9.

John But was a king's messenger whose death was recorded in the Patent Rolls of 1387. If we assume that the C-version could not have been written before 1387 and if it is true that the A-poet was dead at the time of But's addition, the C-poet could not have been the same person as the A-poet.

9. Bright, Allan H. "Langland and the Seven Deadly Sins." *MLR*, 25 (1930), 133-39.

A biographical reading of the Seven Deadly Sins passages in the three versions. Bright concludes that different attitudes towards the sins in each version represent WL's own attitudes at various stages in his life.

10. _____. *New Light on Piers Plowman*. London: Oxford University Press, 1928. Preface by R. W. Chambers, pp. 9-26.

Bright constructs a biography of WL and maintains single authorship. WL was born at Ledbury c. 1332 and first composed his poem at the priory at Great Malvern. He was ordained in 1348 under the name of Willelmus de Colewell. The braggart who threatens to rob Piers (A.VII) may be William de Conley. Clergy is identified with James de Brockbury. A.XII refers to a time when WL was a tutor at Brockbury, c. 1355. The B-text was written c. 1377 when the poet was living in London. WL was the poet of all three versions: differences in the poems do not reflect multiple authorship but rather a single poet whose vision of reality shifted as he grew older. Includes maps of the Malvern area in WL's time. Appendices provide a text of the Introduction to Crowley's 1550 edition and Bale's notes from the *Scriptorum* and *Catalogus*.

11. _____. "William Langland's Birthplace." *TLS*, 24 (March 12, 1925), 172.

Bright supports Bannister's suggestions that WL was born on the Western slope of the Malvern. WL was born at Ledbury, not Clibery. "Clibery" is twenty-three miles from Malvern Hill, whereas "Lidberry" is only eight miles away. Bright adds that WL's house was in Ledbury parish.

12. _____. "William Langland's Early Life." *TLS*, 24 (November 5, 1925), 739.

1) WL was probably the son of Stacy de Rokayle, but he was illegitimate and for this reason could not take his father's name. (See Cargill, 15)
2) WL once lived on the "Longlands," four miles from Malvern Priory. This gave him both "shelter and a name."
3) The "W" after WL's name in MSS is an abbreviation for "Wycliffanus," added by later readers anxious to identify the poet as a religious reformer.

13. _____. "William Langland's Early Life." *TLS*, 25 (September 9, 1926), 596.

Three entries in the Patent Rolls include references to WL. The poet is the son of Stacy de Rokayle. A Eustace, son of Peter de Rokyale, is evidently the "Stacius" of the Dublin MS note--*i.e.*, WL's father. Bright favors single authorship and contends that But added the lines on WL's death sometime after 1399 when news reached him. WL did not die after writing the A-text.

14. Brown, Carleton. "The Lost Leaf of *Piers the Plowman*." *Nation*, 88 (March 25, 1909), 298-9.

    A suggestion of a "simpler" theory than that offered by Manly (lost leaf) or Bradley (misplaced leaf). All agree that some displacement of the text has occurred following A.V,235. Brown agrees with Manly that the lines seem to belong to Robert the Robber, but urges that 11. 236-41 form a conclusion to Robert's prayer if they are shifted to their proper place following 1. 253. There is neither a lost nor misplaced leaf. Rather, a careless scribe mistakenly placed 11. 236-41 72 lines earlier than they belonged. A similar problem occurs in II, 35-9 and III, 266-9. Theophilus Hall (33) reached the identical conclusion independently. Reply by T. A. Knott (51).

15. Cargill, Oscar. "The Langland Myth." *PMLA*, 50 (1935), 36-56.

    There is little probability that the author was either Robert or William Langland. Rather, the common name "William Longlonde" was used by the poet in order to avoid positive identification. Possibly, he was really William de Rokayle, son of Stacy de Rokayle (Rokell). The lines "'By Marie,' quod a mansed prest of the march of yronde,/'I counte namore conscience bi so I cacche silver'" (B.XX, 220-1, C. XXIII, 221-2) refer to an Irish priest, Walter de Brugge. Brugge was insulted by the reference and tried to locate the author. In the marginal note in the Trinity MS D.4., which may have been Brugge's personal copy, the author is identified as William Langland, the son of Stacy de Rokayle. Brugge was probably informed of the poet's real identity, but included both names.

16. Chambers, R. W. "The Authorship of *Piers Plowman*." *MLR*, 5 (1910), 1-32. Rptd. EETS, o.s. 139 e (1910) in abridged form.

    A summary of previous authorship criticism and a thorough attack on the theses of Manly and Bradley. Chambers disagrees with Manly's contention that Robert's confession is more appropriate to Covetousness and demonstrates that Robert would more logically be related to Sloth, an idle apprentice fallen into wanhope. Chambers discusses alleged incoherencies in the A-poet's treatment of the Seven Deadly Sins and argues that WL did not intend to present a standard procession of the sins, but to reveal the social and economic problems of his day. Thus the omission of Lust and Wrath is not an error since these sins have little bearing on WL's concerns. In spite of some minor incoherencies, the A-text does make sense. Regarding Manly's belief that dialect differences indicate multiple authorship--Manly has not considered scribal variation and he has not examined the MSS. A final answer regarding the authorship question will depend upon a critical edition.

17. _____. "Incoherencies in the A- and B-texts of *Piers Plowman* and Their Bearing on the Authorship." *London Mediaeval Studies*, 1 (1937-1939), 27-39.

Chambers attacks Manly's contention that the B-poet mis-understood the A-text. Rather, Chambers argues, only the B-poet could really understand what was implicit in the A-poet's work and he is constantly refining A's ideas. Ex-amines two parallel scenes to demonstrate this: the Pardon scene in the A-text in which the priest is rebuked and Imaginitif's rebuke of Will in the B-text. The search for Truth has been stopped in the A-text because of problems the poet raised with Clergy concerning the salvation of the heathen. In B, Imaginitif directs Will and reaffirms the truth of God by invoking what was stated explicitly in the Pardon scene of A--*si ambulavero in medio umbre mortis*. Chambers then discusses the difficulties of the Pardon scene. When Piers tears the Pardon, he is tearing only the paper, not the meaning. Concludes that the same poet is responsible for the A- and B-texts.

18. _____. "The Original Form of the A-text of *Piers Plowman*." *MLR*, 6 (1911), 302-23.

Chambers argues against Manly's contention that John But's allusion to the poet's "other works" refers to the "in-stallments" of the A-text (A_1 and A_2). Chambers demonstrates: 1. that the A-text does not lend itself to a division into in-stallments; 2. there are serious chronological objections to the idea that circulation in installments was still prevalent during the reign of Richard II when But added his lines; 3. that evidence points to But's additions being very late and appended to one MS only. In an appendix, Chambers discusses the extent of But's additions: there are five possible points at which the original might end. Chambers feels that either But wrote the whole of Passus XII or that he wrote only from line 89 onwards. Maintains single authorship.

19. _____. "Robert or William Longland?" *London Mediaeval Studies*, 1 (1937-39), 430-62. [Plates of Huntington MS D.4.1.]

A synthesis of earlier notes by Bright, Jusserand, and Chambers himself. The line "I have lyved in londe . . . my name is long wille" (B.XV,148) is indeed a cryptogram for William Langland. Discusses the observations of Crowley and Bale. Argues for the acceptance of the name William by re-viewing Skeat's grounds for choosing this name.

20. Coulton, G. G. "*Piers Plowman*, One or Five." *MLR*, 7 (1912), 102-4.

Coulton notes a parallel to WL's treatment of Robert the Robber in the *Lay Folk's Catechism* (EETS, o.s., 118, p.

93, 1. 1352)--a person guilty of covetousness is therefore guilty of sloth.

21. Covella, Sister Francis A. "Formulaic Second Half-lines in Skeat's A-text of *Piers Plowman*: Norms for a Comparative Analysis of the A-, B-, and C-texts." Unpublished N.Y.U. Dissertation, 1972. Abstracted, *DAI*, 33: 2887 A.

    There are significant differences in the occurrence of formulaic second half-lines in the three versions, suggesting different idiolects of the same poetic language. There is no support for Manly's contention of separate authorship for A_1 and A_2 but strong support for a different B author.

22. Day, Mabel. "The Alliteration of the Versions of *Piers Plowman* in Its Bearing on Their Authorship." *MLR*, 17 (1922), 403-9.

    Day examines the alliteration of the three versions and concludes that the poem is by five different authors. The greatest difference among the versions is between the two poets of the B-text (B_1 and B_2)--the rewritten A-text and the B continuation. Only in one part, B_2, did the poet "consider himself free to change the alliterating syllable in a single word"--this is not done in A, B_1, or C. Also, there is substantial alteration in the use of alliterating prepositions among the versions.

23. _____. "The Revisions of *Piers Plowman*." *MLR*, 23 (1928), 1-27.

    In revising B, C collated with A. The B- and C-texts are revisions undertaken on different lines. The former is a repetition with certain additions and a sequel; the latter is a thorough-going revision based on a good B-text and an A-text of a different type from that used by the B reviser. At first, the C reviser relied on A more than B, but later reversed this practice. Neither reviser was the original author. This is shown by: 1. differences in treatment of subject matter; 2. correction of alliteration in C but not in B; 3. obscuring in C of the Scotist theology of B and differences in the significance of Piers in the three versions. Evidence favors multiple authorship.

24. Deakin, Mary. "The Alliteration of *Piers Plowman*." *MLR*, 4 (1908-1909), 478-83.

    Deakin decides that Manly was incorrect to believe that there are enough significant changes in the alliteration of the three versions to suggest multiple authorship. There are some changes--A is most consistent in alliteration while B and C are careless--but the poems appear to be the work of a single poet who became more interested in theme and subject matter and less concerned with poetic technique.

25. Dobson, Margaret. "An Examination of the Vocabulary of the 'A. Text' of *Piers the Plowman*, with References to its Bearing on the Authorship." *Anglia,* 33 (1910), 391-6.

Undertaken at Manly's suggestion that an examination of the vocabulary of the two parts of the A-text (A_1 and A_2) would substantiate his theory of multiple authorship. Examines the "richness" of the vocabulary, particularly the frequency of adjectives, use of synonyms, and the use of the same word for different meanings. Concludes that the poem is the work of a single author.

26. Donaldson, E. Talbot. *"Piers Plowman*: Textual Comparison and the Question of Authorship." *Chaucer und seine Zeit: Symposion für Walter F. Schirmer.* Ed. Arno Esch. (*Buchreihe der Anglia, Zeitschrift für englische Philologie* 14). Tübingen: Max Niemeyer, 1968.

27. Fowler, David C. "About the Author." Chapter 7, pp. 185-205 in his *Piers Plowman: Literary Relations of the A and B Texts.* Seattle: Univ. of Washington Press, 1961.

The B-text could not have been written by the A-poet. A is oriented toward social revolt whereas B ascribes to revolution within the individual. The B poet may have been John Trevisa. In his translation of Ranulf Higden's *Polychronicon,* Trevisa frequently expresses sentiments similar to the ideas of the poem, especially concerning the salvation of the heathen. Like the poet of B, Trevisa despised Friar William Jordan. The supposed names of the *PP* poet, Malvern and Wilhelmus W., are associated with the *Polychronicon*--early investigators knew only that the *PP* poet had something to do with this work. B.XI, 332-53 is almost certainly derived from the Cornish play *Origo Mundi.* Trevisa, who was of Cornish ancestry, was one of the few individuals outside Cornwall who knew the language.

28. _____. "John Trevisa and the English Bible." *MP,* 58 (1960), 81-98.

Reviews the tradition claiming that Trevisa translated the Bible and suggests that Trevisa did work on the Wycliffite translation before his translation of the *Polychronicon.* Discusses Trevisa's antifraternalism and his concern with the salvation of the heathen, likening his views to the *PP* poet.

29. _____. "New Light on John Trevisa." *Traditio,* 18 (1962), 289-317.

A biography of Trevisa, discussing his residence at Oxford and his ordination. Fowler recapitulates his theory that Trevisa is the author of the B-text.

30. _____. "Poetry and the Liberal Arts: The Oxford Background of *Piers the Plowman*." *Arts libéraux et philosophie au moyen age: Actes du quatrième congrès international de philosophie médiévale*. Montréal: Institute d'Etudes Médiévales; Paris: J. Vrin, 1969.

The apocalyptic conclusion of *PP* reflects a knowledge of the events of 1382 at Oxford where a battle on the issue of academic freedom was fought between the seculars and the regulars. The debate concerned the condemnation of Wyclif. The secular faculty aligned themselves against the friars in Wyclif's defense. The author of the B-text was a "deeply committed member of the arts faculty in their struggle with the friars for control of Oxford. The Barn of Unity is not just Holy Church, it is also . . . the University" (p. 718).

31. Görnemann, Gertrud. *Zur Verfasserschaft und Entstehungsgeschichte von Piers the Plowman. Anglistische Forschungen*, 48 (1915).

Disagrees with the views of both Manly and Jusserand. The A-, B-, and C-texts and all intermediate texts descend from a single original MS written by Robert Langland between 1370 and 1376. After his death, various scribes copied and extended his work, altering it as they wished, and producing several variations. Three main forms can be distinguished. Differences between the MSS of one version are as great as those among the three versions. Criticized by Krog (54).

32. Hales, J. W. "Langland." *Dictionary of National Biography*, 11 (1885-), 545-9.

33. Hall, Theophilus D. "The Misplaced Lines, *Piers Plowman* (A) V, 236-41." *MP*, 7 (1909-1910), 327-8.

Concerning the Robert the Robber passage: "the lines in question are no more fitted to form part of the confession of Wrath than that of Sloth." The lines were an addition to Robert's confession written by the author apart from the text--they were to be incorporated in the confession of either the Robber or Coveitise but a scribe misplaced the lines. Corroborates the independent conclusion of Brown (14).

34. _____. "Was 'Langland' the Author of the C-text of the *Vision of Piers Plowman*?" *MLR*, 4 (1908-1909), 1-13.

By examining omissions in the C-text of B material, C's insertions of new matter, and interfering structural changes in C, Hall concludes that the C compiler was a man of somewhat different temperament and convictions from his predecessor or predecessors. The C compiler is a schoolman and a moralist with little imaginative sensibility. Much of Hall's proof is based on dialect variations in C MSS, and he assumes that such variations are authorial rather than scribal. Hall reached his conclusions independent of Manly but recognizes the affinities of their theories.

35. Hopkins, E. M. "The Character and Opinions of Langland." *Kansas University Quarterly*, 2 (1894), 233-99. [Here and in 36, 37, and 38, Hopkins reviews Skeat's biographical sketch of WL and speculates on various aspects of the poet's character, especially his hatred of political and ecclesiastical corruption.]

36. _____. "The Education of Langland." *Princeton College Bulletin*, 7 (1895), 41-45.

37. _____. "Notes on *Piers Plowman*." *Kansas University Quarterly*, 8 (1899), 29-36.

38. _____. "Who Wrote *Piers Plowman*?" *Kansas University Quarterly*, 7 (1898), 1-26.

39. Hulbert, J. R. *"Piers the Plowman* After Forty Years." *MP*, 45 (1948), 215-25.

A reexamination of the authorship debate, particularly the arguments of Manly and Chambers. Criticizes Chambers for his attempts to ignore the obvious differences between the A- and B-texts. It is clear that B spoils A and that C spoils B. The structure of A is unlike anything that can be found in B. Hulbert believes that the poem represents not merely one man's views but views that any number of writers might share.

40. Huppé, Bernard F. "The Authorship of the A and B texts of *Piers Plowman*." *Speculum*, 22 (1947), 578-620.

After examining five B-text revisions of A material, Huppé concludes that the reviser fully understood A's meaning and was careful to extend and complete that meaning-- this manifests itself in changes in the confession of the sins, in Meed's parentage, and in passages dealing with the concept of charity. WL experienced thematic difficulties in A, XI: he allowed the poem to lie fallow and resumed work on the problem later. Defends the continuity of the A- and B-texts.

41. Jack, A. S. "The Autobiographical Elements in *Piers the Plowman*." *JEGP*, 3 (1901), 393-41.

Autobiographical elements in *PP* must be read as fiction. The time references on which Skeat frequently bases his conclusions are not specific references but "definite alliterative expressions for indefinitely long periods of time." The references to wandering are conventional. The poet's description of his own laziness and beggary are inconsistent with the moralist we know him to be. We can know only a few things about him: he was probably a student or a priest, he led a quiet, meditative life, and he may have been to London.

42. James, Stanley B. *Back to Langland*. London: Sands and Company, 1935.

James examines WL's reactions to his age through the attitudes of Will. WL was a social rebel who desired reform, but was essentially orthodox concerning religion. WL clings to a glorious past symbolized by the figure of the plowman. He is both a preacher and a poet of the people. WL is the true voice of England and the modern world needs to rediscover his spirit.

43. _____. "The Mad Poet of Malvern." *Month*, 159 (1932), 221-7.

44. _____. "The Neglect of Langland." *Dublin Review*, 196 (1935), 115-23.

45. Jusserand, J. J. "Observations sur la Vision de Piers Plowman." *Revue Critique*, 8 (November, 1879), 313-19.

46. _____. *"Piers Plowman*: The Work of One or of Five." *MP*, 6 (1909), 271-329. Rptd. EETS, o.s. 139 b (1910).

A valid biographical interpretation may be based on autobiographical elements in the poem. Concerning the revisions: "The poet let copiests transcribe his work at various moments when it was in the making." Manly's discovery of the Robert the Robber passage displacement is correct but his conclusions are not. Rather, the A-poet also wrote B and noticed the incongruity of his A version. He wrote out some appended passages but the B scribe, misunderstanding this, kept the misplaced passage in the same place. The changes in the versions were not made by different authors but by one man as he aged and learned.

47. _____. *"Piers Plowman*, The Work of One or of Five-- A Reply." *MP*, 7 (1910), 289-326. Rptd. EETS, o.s. 139 d (1910).

A reply to Manly's criticism of Jusserand's earlier essay. Manly's argument rests on assuming that no single author could produce as many variations as exist in the three texts, but these variations are due to Manly's

misunderstanding and the carelessness of scribes. It is
highly unlikely that five poets, so much alike, could have
existed at one time. Jusserand offers thirty-seven points
of dispute and attacks both Manly (59) and A. S. Jack (41).
Contends that a biographical reading of the text supports
single authorship.

48.   Kane, George. *The Autobiographical Fallacy in Chaucer and
      Langland*. Chambers Memorial Lecture. London: Uni-
      versity College, 1965.

      Discusses Chaucer's relation to WL. Warns against
attempts to construct a biography from the text itself--*PP*
is a fiction and should be read as such.

49.   _____. *Piers Plowman: The Evidence for Authorship*.
      London: Athlone Press, 1965.

      Kane reviews issues raised in the authorship contro-
versy. Examines external and internal evidence, as well as
signatures in the texts. There is no argument from antecedent probability against single authorship--the differences
in the three versions may best be explained by "what we know
of the processes of literature and the growth of a poet's
mind" (p. 25). Kane examines the supposed differences in
personality and poetic ability between the A and B versions.
There is no genuine difference in the "visualizing capa-
bility" of the poets. Manly's belief that the A-text must
have originally included a confession of Wrath was based
on a false impression of symmetry in the confessions of
A.V. Evaluates external evidence, finding that the MS
memorandum is, in all probability, genuine. Discusses newly
discovered references to a de Longelond family in the
muniments of the Chide family. The poet reveals himself
indirectly and slowly in the work by means of signature.
The cryptogram in B.XV, 148 is a positive affirmation of his
identity. These signatures appear in all three versions and
this suggests that the author of each was named William, and
therefore indicates a strong case for single authorship.
"The direction of the evidence is that the three forms of
the poem are records of a single writer's successive attempts
to realize an imaginative and creative experience" (p. 72).

50.   Knott, Thomas A. "Observations on the Authorship of *Piers
      the Plowman*." *MP*, 14 (1917), 531-58, and "Observations
      on the Authorship of *Piers the Plowman*--Concluded." *MP*,
      15 (1917), 23-41.

      Contains a list of contributions to the authorship
controversy and a summary of criticism. Defends Manly's
position and indicates that more evidence is forthcoming.
Attacks Chambers's view that Robert the Robber is a victim
of sloth. Maintains that the Robert passage is confused.

51. _____. [Letter to the Editor]. *Nation*, 88 (May 13, 1909), 482-3.

Reply to Brown's article on the lost leaf (14). Favors Manly's theory against Bradley and Brown. There is no doubt that A.V, 236-241 belong before the confession of Robert, not after it. Argues against Bradley's theory of the misplaced leaf.

52. Koziol, H. "Zur Frage der verfasserschaft einiger mittelenglischer Stabreimdichtungen." *E. Studien*, 67 (1932), 165-73. [*PP* discussed briefly pp. 168-9].

53. Krog, Fritz. "Autobiographische oder typische Zahlen in *Piers Plowman?*" *Anglia*, 58 (1934), 318-32.

Krog discusses the use of conventional numbers in *PP*, arguing against Mensendieck's reading of the poem as the poet's spiritual autobiography (60). Numerical references in the fiction are not reliable guides for dates in the poet's life. Also discussed by Jack (41).

54. _____. *Studien zu Chaucer und Langland. Anglistische Forschungen*, 65 (1928). [WL discussed pp. 116-74].

A refutation of Görnemann's individual arguments for a single original MS from which all forms of the three texts descend. Krog demonstrates, for example, that A and C are not closer than A and B or B and C. See 31.

55. Macaulay, G. C. "The Name of the Author of *Piers Plowman*." *MLR*, 5 (1910), 195-6.

Using tradition to back his argument, Macaulay states that the poet's surname was Langland not Langley (see Pearson, 65). "William" is a literary character. Robert is the poet's first name.

56. Manly, J[ohn]. M[atthews]. "The Authorship of *Piers Plowman*." *MP*, 7 (1909), 83-144. Rptd. EETS o.s. 139 c (1910).

A reply to Jusserand (46). Manly recapitulates his hypothesis concerning the lost leaf (59). The C-poet used an A-text MS. Had he been the author of all three texts, he would certainly have chosen a B MS.

57. _____. "The Authorship of *Piers the Plowman*." *MP*, 14 (1916), 315-16.

Manly notes that he was not the first to believe in multiple authorship. In his 1842 edition of the B-text, Thomas Wright indicated that multiple authorship was likely (82).

58. _____. "The Lost Leaf of *Piers the Plowman*." *MP*, 3 (1906), 359-66. Rptd. EETS, Extra Issue 135 b (1908).

Five authors, one of whom was John But, were responsible for *PP*. The other authors are nameless but one may have been WL. A_1 (Passus I-VIII), A_2 (Passus IX-XII), B, and C are by different poets. In A.V there is a lacuna in the text between lines 235 and 236, which Manly explains by means of a missing leaf which would account both for the disruption in thought and the omission of Wrath from the confession of the Seven Deadly Sins. There are 129 lines missing which would fill four pages (a single leaf of a quire). T. A. Knott, Manly's student, suggests that the concluding lines of Envy's confession may have been included on the missing leaf. "It will be observed at once that while ll. 222-35 are thoroughly appropriate to Sloth, ll. 236-41 are entirely out of harmony with his character and could never have been assigned to him by so careful an artist as A, who in no single instance assigns to any character either words or actions not clearly and strictly appropriate" (p. 362). B noticed the omission of Wrath and the confusion of the Sloth passage and attempted to rectify the problem, but his additions are "confused, vague, and entirely lacking in the finer qualities of imagination, organization and diction shown in all A's work" (p. 365). The poets clearly differ in mental qualities, constructive ability, vividness of diction, and versification. Manly's theory is refuted by Kane (49, see esp. pp. 16-22).

59. _____. "*Piers the Plowman* and Its Sequence." *Cambridge History of English Literature*. Cambridge: University Press, 1908. II, 1-42. Rptd. EETS, Extra Issue, 135 b (1908).

Differences in diction, meter, sentence structure, organization, rhetorical devices, visual ability, and topics of interest among the versions indicate the probability of multiple authorship. The first two visions of the A-text are distinguished by unity of structure, directness of movement, and freedom from digression. A_1 also has the greatest visualizing and descriptive powers. This poet's sympathies are with Parliament against the wasters. In the third vision, the logic of the poem breaks down. Passus IX-XII, or A_2, are clearly the work of another poet who misunderstood the work of his predecessor. B likewise misunderstood the work of the earlier poets. He tends to be rambling and vague, cannot think logically, and appears to work by the association of ideas. The inner dreams are structural errors--the author forgets that Will is asleep and already dreaming. B had "no skill in composition, no control of his materials or his thought" (p. 28). C was a man of learning, "But unimaginative, cautious and a very pronounced pedant" (p. 31).

60. Mensendieck, Otto. "The Authorship of *Piers Plowman*." *JEGP*, 9 (1910), 404-20.

Argues for single authorship of A and B by means of an autobiographical reading of the texts. The poems contain "experiences and confessions of the author in autobiographical chronology, where the different periods appear disguised as allegorical figures and following each other . . . in the same order as they had followed each other in the actual life of the author" (p. 405). Thought represents the poet himself in maturity, Wit, the poet in his childhood.

61. Meroney, Howard. "The Life and Death of Longe Wille." *ELH*, 17 (1950), 1-35.

Agrees with H. H. Gluntz's suggestion that B is the poet's original work (350). The A-text is an abridgement by a redactor of the B version who "abandoned his project when the poem became too esoteric" (p. 23). Merony disagrees with Sister Carmeline Sullivan's conclusion that the B-poet perfected A's use of Latin quotations (572). Instead, A explains the full context of the vague quotations in B. A also omits obscure Latin tags unrelated to the context of a passage. He omits the belling of the cat episode because it is irrelevant. A also avoids B's use of obscure Romance borrowings. When But notes that Will is dead, he is thinking of the fictive Will who reaches Unity at the end of B.XX, not the poet.

62. Moore, Samuel. "Studies in *Piers the Plowman*, I." *MP*, 11 (1913), 177-93.

Discusses the question of "the burden of proof" in the authorship controversy. There is no antecedent probability or tradition in favor of single authorship. Examines the tradition of ascription of the poem, focusing on Crowley, Ritson, and Price. Reviews Skeat's proofs for single authorship.

63. _____. "Studies in *Piers the Plowman*, II." *MP*, 12 (1914), 19-50.

Reviews manuscript evidence for single or multiple authorship. At least two poets were involved--Rokayle and Robert Langland. Includes a detailed discussion of Bale's notes on Langland and their derivation from the earlier notes of Brigham, Sparke, and Wysdom. These notes derive from a common original. There is no argument from tradition that William is the correct name of the poet.

64. Orsten, Elizabeth M. "'Heaven on Earth': Langland's Vision of Life Within the Cloister." *ABR*, 21 (1970), 526-34.

There is little evidence that WL was a Benedictine monk
(see Bloomfield, 4). Examines B.X, 300-303 where the
cloister is likened to a peaceful heaven on earth. WL's
view of the monastic way of life is idiosyncratic. Compares
his view to Thomas Brinton's Sermon no. 25: Brinton sees
the "claustrum" not as a refuge for a man seeking a serene
life but rather as a call to a genuine asceticism. WL's
view, on the other hand, is sentimental and does not seem to
indicate genuine firsthand knowledge of monastic life. WL
may have been familiar with the Worcester Diocese monks who
were noted for their learning.

65.   [Pearson]. [Review of Skeat's EETS edition of *PP*]. *North
      British Review*, 12 (1870), 240-5. Note 18, "Contem-
      porary Literature."

      Argues that the surname "Langley" is most probable.
The Langley family was prominent in Shipton-under-Wychwood
as early as 1278 and as late as 1362. Skeat dismisses this
suggestion as being based on insufficient evidence. See
Skeat's "General Preface," *CP*, II, xxiv-xxvi.

66.   Peregrinus. "Langland at Great Malvern." *N&Q*, Continuous
      Series, 181 (1941), 121.

      Requests additional information concerning Bright's
reference (10) to a popular belief that Langland occupied
a room over the Abbey Gateway of Great Malvern. Answered
by Bayley (3).

67.   *The Piers Plowman Controversy*. EETS o.s. 135 B (1908) and
      139 b, c, d, e, f. (1910). [Essays by Bradley, Manly,
      Jusserand, Chambers--listed separately above; 135B
      includes 7, 58, 59; 139 b-f includes 5, 16, 46, 47, 56].

68.   Rickert, Edith. "John But, Messenger and Maker." *MP*, 11
      (1913), 107-16.

      Argues that John But was a king's messenger mentioned
in the 1387 Patent Rolls. Agrees with Bradley (8) that if
But actually died in 1387, the C-poet could not have been
the A poet. Examines A.XII, 78-82, which contains an accurate description of the duties of a messenger.

69.   Silverstone. *"The Vision of Pierce Plowman."* *N&Q*, First
      Series, 6(1858), 229-30.

      A transcription of annotations written on the fly-leaf
of a copy of the 1561 edition of *PP*: the note bears the date
1577. "Robertus Langland" is named as the poet.

70.   Skeat, W. W. "John of Malvern and *Piers the Plowman*."
      Academy, 43 (1893), 242.

71. Skeat, W. W., ed. *The Vision of William concerning Piers the Plowman in Three Parallel Texts together with Richard the Redeless*. London: Oxford University Press, 1886. Rptd., 1924, with an addition of bibliography 1954, 1961, 1965, 1968. II, Introduction, Section 10, "The Author's Name," xxvii-xxxii, and Section 11, "The Author's Life," xxxii-xxxvii. Revised and enlarged from his earlier discussion of the author's life in Part IV of his EETS edition, o.s. 67, xxii-xxxiii.

Reviews the evidence concerning the name of the poet, choosing William over Robert. Reviews and dismisses Pearson's suggestion that the poet's surname was Langley, maintaining that Langland is more likely. WL was born c. 1332 at Cleobury Mortimer. In 1362, when he was approximately thirty years old, he wrote the A-text. He moved to London and lived in Cornhill with his wife Kitte and his daughter Calote (based on C. VI, 1-2; XVII, 286; VIII, 304; XXI, 473; B.XVIII, 426). In 1377, he began work on the B-text. The C-text was composed between 1393 and 1398. WL composed *Richard the Redeless* in September, 1399 when he was at Bristol. Concerning the authorship of the texts: "The various texts of the poem are so consistent, the revision is of so close and minute a character, and the numerous transpositions of the subject matter in the latest version are managed with such skill, that we may well believe him to have been his own scribe in the first instance, though we cannot now certainly point to any MS as an autograph" (p. xxvi).

72. _____. "William Langley or Langland." *The English Poets*. Ed. Thomas Humphrey Ward. 4 vols. London: Macmillan, 1880. I, pp. 91-95.

73. Stroud, Theodore A. "Manly's Marginal Notes on the *Piers Plowman* Controversy." *MLN*, 64 (1949), 9-12.

In his personal copy of Bright's *New Light*, Manly made marginal notes which indicate that he never abandoned his theory of multiple authorship, although he ceased to argue publicly for it. He annotated Chambers's preface, criticizing weaknesses in the argument for single authorship. Basically, Manly's arguments remained unaltered by new evidence.

II. EDITIONS AND TEXTUAL STUDIES:
SELECTIONS AND TRANSLATIONS

Piers Plowman offers serious problems for its editors and
textual critics. The poem exists in fifty-two manuscripts which
fall into three distinct types or versions, but several of the
manuscripts represent composite texts in which one type is sup-
plemented by sections of one or both of the other versions. All
the manuscripts demonstrate excessive scribal corruption and contamination.

The earliest version, the A-text, is approximately 2,500
lines long. The second version, the B-text, contains about 7,200
lines: it expands the 2,500 lines of the A-text into 3,200 lines
and includes 4,000 new lines. The final version, the C-text, is
only about one hundred lines longer than B, but it contains many
extensive revisions--changes in wording, as well as omissions and
insertions of material. The A-text is divided into a prologue and
eleven passus; the B-text, into a prologue and twenty passus; and
the C-text, into twenty-three passus. Many critics, following
J. M. Manly, contend that the A-text is actually composed of two
separate poems, the prologue and eight passus of the *Visio*, and the
prologue and two passus of the *Vita* (Manly's A_1 and A_2).[1]

Skeat suggested 1362 as the approximate date for the composition of the A-text. The poem mentions the Norman campaign of
Edward III and the Treaty of Brittany (1360),[2] and V, 14 may refer
to a storm which occurred in January, 1362. More recently, however,
B. F. Huppé and J. A. W. Bennett have argued convincingly for a
later date, c. 1370-73.[3] Skeat dated the B-text to 1377, on the
basis of allusions to contemporary events in the B-Prologue's
episode of the "rat parliament." According to Skeat, the allegory
of this episode referred to the period between the death of the
Black Prince in 1376 and 1377 when Richard II was heir to the

throne.[4] Huppé and Bennett have suggested a later date, c. 1378-79.[5] The dating of the C-text is more problematic. Skeat believed that an allusion to the country's dissatisfaction with the King (IV, 210) referred to the civil disorders of 1392, but recent scholarly opinion favors an earlier date between 1377 and 1387.[6]

Until the nineteenth century, readers apparently did not recognize that the poem existed in more than one version. Joseph Ritson, in 1802, first noted the differences between the B- and C-texts. T. D. Whitaker, the first editor of the C-text, in 1813, also distinguished the texts but believed that C was earlier than B. In 1824, Richard Price first noticed the existence of the A-text, and believed that it preceded the B- and C-texts.[7] Skeat, in his monumental EETS edition of the texts, first grouped the manuscripts into the three separate versions and established the arrangement, A, B, and C.

Because of the large number of manuscripts and the dialect variations of the copyists, it is clear that *Piers Plowman* was exceptionally popular and widely disseminated in the late four- teenth and early fifteenth centuries. It first became available in printed form in 1550 when Robert Crowley published an edition of the B-text in three separate impressions. This edition was designed explicitly for the sixteenth-century reading public: in his preface and gloss on the text, Crowley stressed the topical- ity of the poem. He amended problematic readings and conven- tionalized the Latin passages in order to make the text more accessible to his audience.[8] Because Crowley's edition was based on a B-text manuscript which is now lost, it is extremely valuable to modern editors.[9] While the B-text was well known in print in the Renaissance, there is evidence to suggest that the A-text circulated widely in manuscript throughout the sixteenth century.[10]

After Owen Roger's 1561 reprint of Crowley's third impres- sion, no edition of *Piers Plowman* was printed for more than two hundred years. In 1813, T. D. Whitaker published an edition of the C-text[11] and in 1842, Thomas Wright published a two-volume edition of the B-text. It was not until Skeat brought out his

EETS edition of *Piers Plowman*, however, that the poem gained the exposure it deserves. In 1866, Skeat published a proposal for the edition along with parallel extracts from the twenty-nine manuscripts to which he had access. A few years later, he reissued the pamphlet with extracts from sixteen more newly discovered manuscripts. In the present century, several more manuscripts have been found.

Skeat described all the known manuscripts in separate prefaces to the volumes of the EETS edition, but he collated only those he thought were most valuable. His basic editorial method was to locate the single best manuscript of a version and to reproduce it with as few emendations as possible. He chose the Vernon MS as the copy-text for his A-version, Laud Misc. 581 for B, and MS Phillipps 8231 for C. Skeat, himself, came to question his choice of the Vernon MS and subsequent editors have favored Trinity College Cambridge MS R.3.14 as the best copy-text for A. But his choice of the Laud MS 581 as a basis for the B-text has been retained by J. A. W. Bennett, one of the most recent editors of that version.[12] Skeat's belief that Langland was also the author of the poem which he called *Richard the Redeless* has been refuted.[13]

Inadequacies in Skeat's texts were noticed early by Teichmann who called for a consideration of all known manuscripts to determine readings. The problems raised by J. M. Manly's contention of multiple authorship contributed significantly to the need for new editions since his arguments rested primarily on determining the poet's original: *e.g.*, whether the B-reviser misunderstood the work of his predecessors, the authors of A_1 and A_2.

Thomas A. Knott began work on a new edition of the A-text in 1908. Knott favored the establishment of a genealogical tree to determine the facts of manuscript tradition. He completed a critical edition of A_1 to VIII, 126, and his work was continued by David C. Fowler who published their edition in 1952. In 1909, R. W. Chambers and J. H. G. Grattan began their important textual studies by reexamining Skeat's texts. Like Knott, they believed that Skeat's choice of the Vernon MS was poor and argued that Trinity College Cambridge MS R. 3. 14 better represented the poet's original. But unlike Knott, they felt that the establishment of a genealogy was an impractical editorial method in a manuscript tradition where extensive cross-copying had occurred. Chambers and Grattan were to be the editors of a new EETS critical edition. Chambers died in 1942 and Grattan in 1951, and the project was temporarily abandoned.

When complete, the definitive edition of *Piers Plowman* will be the four-volume Athlone Press edition under the general editorship of Chambers's student, George Kane. Volume I (the A-text, edited by Kane) and volume II (the B-text, edited by Kane and E. Talbot Donaldson) have already appeared. Volume III (the C-text, edited by G. H. Russell) is forthcoming. Volume IV will contain notes and glossary.

NOTES

[1] See *Piers the Plowman: A Critical Edition of the A-Version* (Baltimore: Johns Hopkins Press, 1952), pp. 3-7.

[2] A, III, 174-193.

[3] B. F. Huppé, "The A-text of *Piers Plowman* and the Norman Wars," *PMLA*, 54 (1939), 37-64; J. A. W. Bennett, "The Date of the A-text of *Piers Plowman*," *PMLA*, 38 (1943), 566-72.

[4] Skeat, *CP*, II, xii.

[5] B. F. Huppé, "The Date of the B-text of *Piers Plowman*," *SP*, 38 (1941), 34-44; J. A. W. Bennett, "The Date of the B-text of *Piers Plowman*," *Medium Aevum*, 12 (1943), 55-64.

[6] See Knott and Fowler, p. 4. Sister Mary Aquinas Devlin, in her unpublished University of Chicago dissertation, argues that the allusions to royal unpopularity may be a reference to the last years of Edward III and that the text may be dated as early as 1377. Furthermore, the poet's failure to mention the Peasants' Revolt suggests that the text was completed before 1381. See "The Date of the C-text of *Piers the Plowman*," *Abstracts of Theses, University of Chicago, Humanistic Series*, iv, 1925-26 (Chicago, 1928), pp. 317-20. For problems with the date of the C-text, see Donaldson, pp. 18-19.

[7] See Skeat, *CP*, II, vii-viii, and Morton W. Bloomfield, "The Present State of *Piers Plowman* Studies," *Speculum*, 14 (1939), 215-16.

[8] See J. A. W. Bennett's facsimile edition of Crowley's first impression: *The Vision of Pierce Plowman*. London: Paradine, 1976.

[9] See George Kane and E. Talbot Donaldson, eds., *Piers Plowman: The B Version* (London: Athlone Press, 1975), pp. 6-7.

[10] See Marie J. Hertzig, "The Early English Recension and Continuity of Certain Middle English Texts in the Sixteenth Century." Unpublished University of Pennsylvania Dissertation, 1973.

[11] Whitaker's edition is evaluated by Skeat, *CP*, II, lxxxi.

[12] J. A. W. Bennett, ed., *Piers Plowman: The Prologue and Passus I-VII of the B Text as Found in Bodleian MS. Laud Misc. 581*. Clarendon Medieval and Tudor Studies, 1972.

[13] Mabel Day and Robert Steele, eds., *Mum and the Sothsegger*, EETS, o.s. 199, 1936.

Editions of the Poems

The A-text

74. Kane, George, ed. *Piers Plowman: The A Version. Will's Visions of Piers Plowman and Do-well*. London: Athlone Press, 1960.

> Description of A-text MSS, pp. 1-18. Trinity College Cambridge MS R.3.14 is the copy text, corrected from other MSS. This MS determines the linguistic form of the edited text. "Recension is not a practicable method for the editor of the A-manuscripts. Nor is the creation of a hierarchy, with some one copy elevated to a role of authority: while some of these manuscripts are clearly more corrupt than others, all are corrupt to an indeterminate but evidently considerable extent" (p. 113).

75. Knott, Thomas A. and David C. Fowler, eds. *Piers the Plowman: A Critical Edition of the A-Version*. Baltimore: Johns Hopkins Press, 1952.

> A-text MSS listed and described, pp. 22-25. MSS genealogy, pp. 26-28. Copy text is Trinity College Cambridge MS R.3.14. Skeat's choice of the Vernon MS was incorrect--this MS represents an inferior tradition. A$_1$ is based on Knott's studies (127). A$_2$ is based on Fowler's unpublished dissertation (146).

76. Skeat, W. W., ed. *The "Vernon" Text; or Text A*. Part I of his EETS edition. EETS, o.s. 28, 1867. See 86.

The B-text

77. Crowley, Robert, ed. *The Vision of Pierce Plowman now fyrste imprynted by Robert Crowley*, dwellyng in Ely rentes in Holburne. Anno Domini, 1505 [1550]. "Cum priuilegio ad imprimendum solum." Facsimile edition: J. A. W. Bennett, ed., *The Vision of Pierce Plowman*. London: Paradine, 1976.

> Earliest printed edition of *PP* exists in three different impressions printed in a single year. Discussed by Skeat (*CP*, II, lxxii-lxxvi) who also reprints Crowley's preface.

78. Kane, George and E. Talbot Donaldson, eds. *Piers Plowman: The B Version. Will's Visions of Piers Plowman, Do-Well, Do-Better, and Do-Best*. London: Athlone Press, 1975. Review Articles: Stanley, E. G., "The B Version of *Piers Plowman*: A New Edition." *N&Q*, 23 (1976), 435-47; Fowler, David C., "A New Edition of the B text of Piers Plowman," *Yearbook of English Studies*, 7 (1977), 23-42.

Basic text is Trinity College Cambridge MS B.15.17, with variants from other MSS. Introduction includes a description and classification of MSS (pp. 1-69). Reviews the descent of the text from the A through C versions with a discussion of the distinction between original readings and unoriginal variants. Includes a brief discussion of the C-text's composition: it is likely that WL worked from a scribally corrupt copy of B in his revision of the C-text.

79. Rogers, Owen, ed. *The Vision of Pierce Plowman, newlye imprynted after the authours old copy with a brefe summary of the principall matters set before euery part called Passus. Wherevnto is also annexed the Crede of Pierce Plowman, neuer imprynted with the booke before.* London, 1561.

Reprint of Crowley's third issue. Discussed by Skeat, *CP*, II, lxxvi.

80. Skeat, W. W., ed. *The "Crowley" Text; or Text B.* Part II of his EETS edition. EETS, o.s. 38, 1869. See 86.

81. _____., ed. *Piers Plowman (Versione B).* Introduzione, scelta, note e glossario a cura by Sabino Casieri. Milan: Cisalpino-Goliardica, 1973.

Text is Skeat's B-text with notes and gloss in Italian. Introduction includes a brief biography of WL, a list of A-, B-, and C-text MSS, and a brief discussion of ME phonology and syntax.

82. Wright, Thomas, ed. *The Vision and Creed of Piers Ploughman; Newly Imprinted.* 2 Vols. London: William Pickering, 1842. Second ed., 1856. Revised, 1895.

Text is based on Trinity College MS B.15.7. Introduction, pp. v-xl, includes summaries of each passus, a brief history of the poem's reception, and a discussion of fourteenth-century society. Notes and Glossary, II, 505-620.

The C-text

83. Haselden, R. B. and H. C. Schulz, eds. *The Huntington Library Manuscript* (HM 143). San Marino: Henry E. Huntington Library, 1936.

Manuscript is reproduced in photostat. Introduction by R. W. Chambers, technical examination by Haselden and Schultz.

84. Skeat, W. W., ed. *The "Whitaker" Text; or Text C*. Part III of his EETS edition. EETS, o.s. 54, 1873. See 86.

85. Whitaker, Thomas Dunham, ed. *Visio Willi de Petro Plouhman* [sic], *Item Visiones eiusdem de Dowel, Dobet, et Dobest Or The Vision of William concerning Piers Plouhman* [sic] *and the Visions of the same concerning the Origin, Progress, and Perfection of the Christian Life*. London: John Murray, 1813.

   Introductory discourse includes a discussion of the dialect and meter of the poem, and an abstract of the argument. Editorial methods are criticized by Skeat, *CP*, II, lxxx-lxxxi.

The Three Versions

86. Skeat, W. W., ed. *The Vision of William concerning Piers (the) Plowman together with Vita de Dowel, et Dobest, secundum Wit et Resoun*. EETS o.s. 28, 38, 54, 67, 81. 1867-84. 5 parts, 4 volumes: I (1867), *The "Vernon" Text; or Text A*: II (1869), *The "Crowley" Text; or Text B*: III (1873), *The "Whitaker" Text; or Text C*: IV (1877-84), General Preface, Notes and Indexes. Later Skeat edited the poems for the Clarendon Press with the three texts printed in parallel form: *The Vision of William concerning Piers the Plowman in Three Parallel Texts, together with Richard the Redeless*. London: Oxford University Press, 1886. 2 volumes. Rptd. 1924. Bibliography expanded in 1954, 1961, 1965, 1968.

   The A-text is Vernon MS to Passus XI, 80. The remainder of Passus XI is based on Trinity MS R.3.14. MS Rawlinson Poet 137 provides Passus XII. Following Tyrwhitt (Advertisement of his Glossary to Chaucer), Skeat dates A- c. 1362. See *CP*, II, ix. The B-text is Laud Misc. 581, corrected from other MSS. Dated 1377. Skeat originally believed this to be the poet's holograph. The C-text is MS Phillipps 8231. Dated 1393-1398. Introduction includes descriptions of each version, a listing of additional passages in the C-text, and a classification of MSS.

Studies of the Texts

87. Allen, B. F. "The Genealogy of the C-Text Manuscripts of *Piers Plowman*." University of London M.A. Thesis, 1923.

Phillipps MS 8231 which Skeat chose as the copy text for his edition of the C-text is far removed from the original C. It is a sophisticated recension. Discusses the groupings of C-text MSS in order to determine the characteristics of the original text. F. A. R. Carnegy's *An Attempt to Approach the C-Text of Piers the Plowman* (96) is based on Allen's findings.

88. [Anon.] "The First Edition of *Piers Plowman*, 1550. Notes on Sales." *TLS* (May 11, 1922), 312.

89. Bennett, J. A. W. "The Date of the A-text of *Piers Plowman*." *PMLA*, 58 (1943), 566-72.

Bennett accepts but modifies Huppé's suggestion of a later date for the A-text (120). Bennett agrees with Huppé that Lady Meed might be identified with Alice Perrers. Alice must cheer Edward just as Lady Meed must cheer the king. A reference to "Romerunners" in A. IV, 109-16 suggests that this passus must have been composed sometime after 1367 when the papacy returned to Rome from Avignon. Bennett favors 1370 as the date of composition. Cargill's suggestion of 1376 is ill-founded, since his main source, the *Chronicon Angliae*, is highly unreliable (95).

90. _____. "The Date of the B-text of *Piers Plowman*." *Medium Aevum*, 12 (1943), 155-64.

Skeat's date of 1377 for the B-text is disputable. Bennett agrees with Huppé's suggestion that it must be later (121). B-, Prologue, 107-11, refers to the Great Schism, but particularly to October, 1378, when messengers of the pope and apostate cardinals met at Gloucester. The "Belling of the Cat" episode might, as Huppé noted, refer to John of Gaunt. The B-text was not completed before 1378.

91. _____. "A New Collation of a *Piers Plowman* Manuscript (HM 137)." *Medium Aevum*, 17 (1948), 21-31.

Chambers noted many errors in Skeat's transcription of HM 137 but he stopped collation at the end of Passus IX (See 98). Bennett reviews Chambers's work and notes that he overlooked one third of the errors. Bennett collates the remainder of the MS, finding that the proportion of error rises in the remaining passus. Includes a list of corrigenda in the Skeat text.

92. Blackman, Elsie. "Notes on the B-text MSS of *Piers Plowman*." *JEGP*, 17 (1918), 489-545.

Skeat's selection of the Laud MS as the basis for his edition of the B-text is incorrect. Chambers had pointed

out that some errors in B MSS are corruptions, and hypothe-
sized that the occurrence of certain errors in even good B
MSS indicates a lost archetypal MS from which they are
descended (102). Blackman collates all the known B-text
MSS and concludes that Chambers was correct. All MSS share
common mistakes and are based on a single bad copy. The
C-reviser used a much better B-version MS which has been
lost. Includes some provisional drafts of a revised B-
text. Summarizes the conclusions of 104.

93. B[randl], A. "Zu W. Langland." *Archiv*, 100 (1898), 334.
    [Notes a mention of a *PP* MS in 1396].

94. Brooks, E. St. John. "The *Piers Plowman* Manuscripts in
    Trinity College, Dublin." *Library*, (1951), 141-53.

    An examination of two Trinity College MSS--D.4.1
    (C-text), which contains the memorandum concerning WL's
    parentage, and D.4.12 (A-text). The memorandum is dated
    as late fourteenth or early fifteenth century. The scribe
    had access to some monastic records, perhaps from the
    Abergavenny Priory, and he copied these into the last
    folio of the text. It is possible that this MS originally
    belonged to the Priory.

95. Cargill, Oscar. "The Date of the A-text of *Piers Plough-
    man*." *PMLA*, 47 (1932), 354-62.

    PP is aimed specifically at the theological teaching
    of Thomas Bradwardine who believed that salvation comes
    not through merit but by the free grace of God. The first
    vision of the poem was written during the 1376 Parliament
    with the aim of returning William Wykeham and the Church
    Party to power. Passus II-IV are a political allegory
    based on an historical situation: Wrong is John of
    Gaunt, False is Lord Latimer, Flattery is Richard Lyons,
    Lady Meed is Alice Perrers, Guile is Adam de Bury.
    Criticized by Bennett, 89.

96. Carnegy, F. A. R. *An Attempt to Approach the C-text of
    Piers Plowman*. London: University of London Press,
    1934.

    Part of Carnegy's University of London thesis (97),
    based on Allen's findings (87). Includes an edition of
    Passus II, III, and IV of the C-text (Passus III, IV, and
    V in Skeat's edition).

97. _____. "Problems Connected with the Three Texts of
    Piers Plowman." University of London M.A. Thesis,
    1923 [Published in part as 96].

98. Chambers, R. W. "The Manuscripts of *Piers Plowman* in the Huntington Library, and their Value for Fixing the Text of the Poem." *Huntington Library Bulletin*, 8 (1935), 1-27. Includes "A Note on the Inscription in HM 128," by R. B. Haselden and H. C. Schultz, pp. 26-27.

Chambers discusses the two B-text MSS in the Library-- HM 128 (formerly Ashburnham CXXX) and HM 114 (formerly Phillipps 8252) as well as two C-text MSS--HM 137 (formerly Phillipps 8231) and HM 143. Chambers believes that HM 143 is the best basic text for a critical edition of C. Corrections of Skeat's readings of HM 137 as far as Passus IX are given in a footnote on p. 24. The note on the MS inscription "Robert or William langland made pers plough-man": this MS must have been in the possession of either John Bale or William Sparke.

99. _____. "A *Piers Plowman* Manuscript." *Cylchgrarvn Llfrgell Genedlaethal* [*National Library of Wales Journal*], 2 (1942), 42-43. [Plate of the MS, p. 41.]

National Library of Wales MS 733 is a composite MS, in which the C-continuation has been added to an A-text MS.

100. _____. "The Three Texts of *Piers Plowman* and Their Grammatical Forms." *MLR*, 14 (1919), 129-51.

Chambers answers Manly's contention that the three versions demonstrate differences in scholastic interest, noting a number of habitual errors in the versions which indicate the work of a single mind. Manly also believed that the dialect variations suggested multiple authorship; Chambers demonstrates that these differences represent the language of the scribes, not the author.

101. _____ and J. H. G. Grattan. "The Text of *Piers Plowman*." *MLR*, 4 (1908-1909), 357-89.

Manly believed that since the B-reviser used a scribally corrupt copy of the A-text, it is unlikely that he was the author of the original version of the poem. Chambers and Grattan feel that Manly was misled by using Skeat's edition of the Vernon MS. The B-reviser used a better MS than the Vernon. MSS of the TU group are much closer to the original A-text. Includes a critical text of A. V, 43-106.

102. _____ and J. H. G. Grattan. "The Text of *Piers Plowman*." *MLR*, 26 (1931), 1-51. Rptd. by the Folcroft Press, 1969.

The B-reviser used a better MS than any now extant. Occasionally, A and C are superior to the B-text. Errors

are found in all extant B MSS but the C-reviser's copy was
free of them. Chambers and Grattan review Mabel Day's
arguments for multiple authorship (23) and oppose her belief that C collated A with B: rather, C used a B MS and
probably did not use an A-text MS. The four cases where
Day believed that B had misunderstood A are shown to be
unlikely. Furthermore, Day's arguments concerning the
alliteration of the versions are not viable.

103. _____ and J. H. G. Grattan. "The Text of *Piers*
        Plowman: Critical Methods." *MLR*, 11 (1916), 257-75.

        Chambers and Grattan disagree with Knott's method of
determining the descent of *PP* MSS by means of a genealogy
(75 and 127). Genealogies are not helpful when there is
extensive cross-copying.

104. Chick, E. "A Preliminary Investigation of the Pedigree of
        the B-text MSS of *Piers Plowman*." Unpublished Uni-
        versity of London thesis, 1914 [Results summarized in
        92].

105. Coffman, G. R. "The Present State of a Critical Edition
        of *Piers Plowman*." *Speculum*, 20 (1945), 482-3 [A
        progress report on the projected EETS critical text
        under the direction of Chambers and Grattan].

106. Cowper, J.M., ed. *The Select Works of Robert Crowley*.
        EETS, extra series, 15, 1872.

107. Crawford, William R. "Robert Crowley's Editions of
        Piers Plowman: A Bibliographical and Textual
        Study." Unpublished Yale University Dissertation,
        1957.

108. Day, Mabel and Robert Steele, eds. *Mum and the Sothsegger*.
        EETS, o.s. 199, 1936.

109. Donaldson, E. Talbot. "Manuscripts R and F in the B-
        Tradition of *Piers Plowman*." *Transactions of the
        Connecticut Academy of Arts and Sciences*, 39 (1955),
        177-212.

110. _____. "The Texts of *Piers Plowman*: Scribes and
        Poets." *MP*, 50 (1952-1953), 269-73.

        Donaldson disagrees with Fowler's argument (114) that
the B and C poets made revisions from MSS that had already
suffered from scribal corruption and that they sometimes
allowed inferior readings to stand--thus, the B and C
poet could not be the same person as the A-poet. The
logic is faulty because Fowler assumes that the "scribal"
errors could not have been part of a conscious revision by
a single author. Fowler's claim that certain B readings

34

are inferior to A readings is not well-founded: it is very difficult to determine the difference between a poetic revision and a scribal error or corruption.

111.   Dwyer, Richard A. "The Appreciation of Handmade Literature." *Chaucer Review*, 8 (1974), 221-40.

        The transmission of *PP* texts is discussed pp. 224-5. Discusses the scribal variations in MS Lincoln Inn 150: the scribe freely amended the alliteration of the poem, attempting to make it conform to alliterative tradition.

112.   Fowler, David C. "Contamination in Manuscripts of the A-text of *Piers the Plowman*." *PMLA*, 66 (1951), 495-504.

        Fowler examines the process of determining whether a given MS demonstrates original readings or scribal errors. The UI group of A MSS contains contamination in variants. MS D is also contaminated and its readings should not be highly regarded.

113.   _____. "*Piers Plowman*." *TLS*, 47 (March 13, 1948), 149 [Request for information concerning the location of an A-text MS].

114.   _____. "The Relationship of the Three Texts of *Piers the Plowman*." *MP*, 50 (1952-1953), 5-22.

        The B- and C-texts derive from an original A-text MS which was already corrupt when it came to the B-poet. There was not a "pure original": *i.e.*, an authorial copy, free from scribal corruption. Fowler supports multiple authorship. Answered by Donaldson (110).

115.   Grattan, J. H. G. "The Text of *Piers Plowman*: A Newly Discovered Manuscript and its Affinities." *MLR*, 42 (1947), 1-8.

        Grattan examines the Chaderton MS, now in the University of Liverpool Library. It is a composite MS, in which part of the C-text has been appended to an A-text MS. This MS may help to correct readings, since it is not highly contaminated. Includes a transcription of the MS endnotes which ascribe the poem to Robert Langland.

116.   _____. "The Text of *Piers Plowman*: Critical Lucubrations with Special Reference to the Independent Substitution of Similars." *SP*, 44 (1947), 593-604.

        MSS contamination is frequently the result of a scribe's attempts to substitute similar readings in his text. Some substitution types which appear to indicate dissimilarities are found upon investigation to indicate harmony. Grattan also discusses spelling variants which are indicative of phonological differences, morphological variants of no semantic value, and synonym substitutions. One of the most valuable keys to inexplicable nonsense readings is the independent substitution of dissimilars.

117. Gwynn, A[ubrey]. "The Date of the B-text of *Piers Plowman*." *RES*, Original Series, 19 (1943), 1-24.

Gwynn argues for the early date of 1370-72 for the composition of Passus XIII-XX of the B-text. The A-text appears at a stage when quarrels between the clergy and the friars were particularly acute (1350-60). Curiously, the B-text is much stronger in its antifraternalism. The gluttonous friar in Passus XIII is identified as William Jordan, a contemporary Dominican controversialist. WL aligns himself with the Benedictine monk Uhtred de Boldon in his attack on Jordan. In his arguments concerning the salvation of the heathen, WL may be referring to a controversy that took place before 1370, when the Avignon popes were interested in missionary work in Persia and Armenia.

118. Haselden, R. B. and H. C. Schulz. "The Fragment of *Piers Plowman* in Ashburnham No. CXXX." *MP*, 29 (1932), 391-94.

This MS which contains the entire B-text and a B-text fragment is now Huntington MS 128. The fragment, which Skeat believed was a distinct piece, is really part of a completed text. Includes photostats of HM 128, Fol. 97R (Fragment) and HM 128, Fol. 122R of the whole text.

119. Hertzig, Marie J. "The Early English Recension and Continuity of Certain Middle English Texts in the Sixteenth Century." University of Pennsylvania dissertation, 1973. Abstracted, *DAI*, 34: 1913A-14A.

PP was available throughout the sixteenth century in two textual traditions--the A-text in manuscript and the B-text in printed editions. Discusses Skelton's and Spenser's familiarity with *PP*.

120. Huppé, Bernard F. "The A-text of *Piers Plowman* and the Norman Wars." *PMLA*, 54 (1939), 37-64.

On the basis of historical evidence, Huppé dates the A-text sometime after 1373. Lady Meed's speech (III, 182-201) includes a reference to Edward's battle in France on Black Monday. Lady Meed is a representation of Alice Perrers. By the time of the C-revision, the reference was no longer topical and was omitted. See 89.

121. _____. "The Date of the B-text of *Piers Plowman*." *SP*, 38 (1941), 34-44.

The *terminus ad quo* for the composition of the B-text
is in spring or summer of 1377, since Reason's sermon appears to refer to the death of Edward. The *terminus ad
quem* is sometime after the summer of 1378.

122. _____. *"Piers Plowman*: The Date of the B-text
Reconsidered." *SP*, 46 (1949), 6-13.

Huppé disagrees with Gwynn's early dating of the B-
text (117). B must have been composed between 1377 and
1379. Gwynn does not consider the mass of evidence for the
A-text being written after 1369.

123. Illston, Olga. "A Literary and Bibliographical Study of
the Work of Robert Crowley (1517-1588). Printer,
Puritan, and Poet." Unpublished University of London
M.A. Thesis, 1953.

124. Kane, George. *"Piers Plowman*: Problems and Methods of
Editing the B-text." *MLR*, 43 (1948), 1-25.

Kane reviews the textual studies of Chambers and
Grattan. Discusses the advantages of a critical text of
B: it will be superior to an archetypal B-version and
closer to the poet's autograph.

125. _____. "Textual Criticism of *Piers Plowman*." *TLS*
(March 17, 1950), p. 176.

Criticizes a review of Donaldson's *Piers Plowman:
The C-text and its Poet* (*TLS*, Feb. 10, 1950). The reviewer
contends that textual variations were probably the result
of oral transmission. Kane finds no evidence for this
assertion.

126. King, John N. "Robert Crowley's Editions of *Piers Plowman*:
A Tudor Apocalypse." *MP*, 73 (1975-1976), 342-52.

Although Crowley freely altered syntax and amended
difficult words for his readers, he generally respected
the text. Crowley went to extremes to connect the
Antichrist of *PP* with the Roman Catholic Church. An
educated seventeenth-century reader of Crowley's text,
Andrew Bostock, noted in the margins of his copy that the
editor had mistaken the poet's aim: Bostock commented that
PP is an orthodox appeal for reform within the Church.
Crowley, whose ideas descend largely from John Bale, used
the figure of the plowman as a radical spokesman for the
commons.

127. Knott, Thomas A. "An Essay toward the Critical Text of
the A-version of *Piers the Plowman*." *MP*, 12 (1914-
1915), 389-421.

A discussion of textual apparatus for a critical edition of the A-text. Extended in the introduction to the edition by Knott and Fowler (75). Includes a list and description of A-text MSS. Knott believes that Trinity College MS R.3.14 is the best copy text for A. Establishes MS genealogy.

128. Kron, Richard. *William Langleys Buch von Peter dem Pflüger*. Göttingen, 1885 [Classification of MSS].

129. Mitchell, A. G. "A Newly Discovered Manuscript of the C-text of *Piers Plowman*." *MLR*, 36 (1941), 243-4.

A brief description of C-text MS A, owned by Sir Louis Sterling. Related to Trinity College Dublin MS D.4.1.

130. _____. "Notes on the C-text of *Piers Plowman*." *London Mediaeval Studies*, 1 (1937-1939), 483-92.

Linguistic notes on problematic passages in the C-text. 1. C. II, 95: the adjectival nature of the genitive explains that "for no lordene love" means "for love of no lord." 2. C. III, 16-18: "hoes wyf a were . . ./ layn nought yf ye knowen" merges direct and indirect forms of speech. 3. C. IV, 140-42: one group of MSS differs from another by adding the words "as an ancre" in 1.141. Meed will be reformed by living as an anchorite.

131. _____ and G. H. Russell. "The Three Texts of *Piers the Plowman*." *JEGP*, 52 (1953), 445-56.

Fowler was incorrect to believe that the A-text used by C was corrupt. Mitchell and Russell contend that Fowler has been unable to prove that B and C commit errors inconsistent with unity of authorship. See 114.

132. Poole, Eric. "The Computer in Determining Stemmatic Relationships." *Computers and the Humanities*, 8 (1974), 207-16 [Tests a program with A. V, 105-88].

133. Russell, G. H. "The Evolution of a Poem: Some Reflections on the Textual Tradition of *Piers Plowman*." *Arts*, 2 (1962), 33-46.

134. _____. "Some Aspects of the Process of Revision in *Piers Plowman*." In *Piers Plowman: Critical Approaches*, ed. Hussey, 1969, pp. 27-49.

The C-reviser used a B-text MS, but it was not a fair copy. Because of corruptions in this MS, the C-revisions range from mere verbal corrections to extensive additions, extensions and deletions. The C-revision was designed not as a large scale rewriting of the whole poem, but as a limited operation to meet specific problems. Although this is the author's final reading of his theme, he did not revise the poem line by line. In the end, the poem was still evolving: judging from the last two passus, which are basically unchanged from the B-text, Russell concludes that the revision is incomplete.

135. _____ and Venetia Nathan. "A *Piers Plowman* Manuscript in the Huntington Library." *HLQ*, 26 (1963), 119-31.

> A description of HM 114, a unique composite MS, incorporating what an early editor believed to be the best of all three versions. Lists the incorporations from A, B, and C.

136. Samuels, M. L. "Some Applications of Middle English Dialectology." *ES*, 44 (1963), 81-94.

> *PP* MSS discussed p. 94. At least thirty-six *PP* MSS can be plotted and localized by means of dialect. Samuels concludes: 1. that C-text MSS circulated in WL's native Malvern; 2. B-text MSS circulated in cosmopolitan areas, especially Worcester and London; 3. A-text MSS are peripheral. There are no A MSS from the central areas in which the B and C MSS were circulated.

137. Seymour, M. C. "The Scribe of Huntington Library MS. HM 114." *Medium Aevum*, 43 (1974), 139-43.

138. Teichmann, Eduard. "Zum Texte von William Langland's Vision." *Anglia*, 15 (1893), 223-60.

> Teichmann calls for a new text to supersede Skeat's edition. Argues that choosing a single manuscript as a basis for a text is not a desirable editorial method: rather, all MSS must be collated. Evaluates the problems of scribal variation.

Selections or Complete Sections of the Poem

139. Bennett, J. A. W., ed. *Piers Plowman: The Prologue and Passus I-VII of the B Text as Found in Bodleian MS. Laud Misc. 581*. Clarendon Medieval and Tudor Studies, 1972 [Follows Skeat's edition as a basic text, correcting from MSS].

140. Brandl, A. and O. Zippel, eds. *Mittelenglische Sprach und Literaturproben*. Berlin, 1917, pp. 163-74 [Parts of B *Visio*].

141. Brook, Stella. *Piers Plowman: Selections from the B-text as found in Bodleian MS. Laud Misc. 581*. New

York: Barnes & Noble, 1975 [Four selections from the
B-text with parallel modernizations].

142. Cook, A. S., ed. *A Literary Middle English Reader*. Boston:
Houghton-Mifflin, 1915, pp. 334-52 [Parts of B *Visio*].

143. Davis, J. F., ed. *Langland: Piers Plowman, Prologue and
Passus I-VII, Text B*. London: University Tutorial
Press, 1896. Revised by E. S. Olszewska, 1928.

144. Drennan, C. M., ed. *Piers Plowman: Prologue and Passus
I, B Text*. London: Cassell, 1914.

145. Dunn, Charles W. and Edward T. Byrnes, eds. *Middle English
Literature*. New York: Harcourt Brace Jovanovich,
1973, pp. 277-338 [B-text Prologue, Passus I, V, VII,
parts of XVIII and XIX].

146. Fowler, David C., ed. "A Critical Text of *Piers the Plowman* A₂." Unpublished University of Chicago dissertation, 1949 [See 75].

147. Kluge, F., ed. *Mittelenglisches Lesebuch*. Halle, 1904,
pp. 110-15 [A-text Prologue and Passus I].

148. Mitchell, A. G., ed. "A Critical Edition of *Piers Plowman*,
C-Text, Prologue and Passus I-IV." Unpublished
University of London Thesis, 1939.

149. Morris, R., ed. *Specimens of Early English*. London:
Oxford University Press, 1867. Vol. II, pp. 249-90
[Parts of A *Visio*].

150. Mossé, Fernand. *Manuel de l'anglais du Moyen Age des
Origines au XIV siecle*. Paris, 1945. Part II trans.
by James A. Walker, *A Handbook of Middle English*.
Baltimore: Johns Hopkins Press, 1952, pp. 258-70
[Sections of A Prologue, B Prologue, C, Passus VI,
B, Passus V].

151. O'Kane, H. M., ed. and illus. *The Vision of William
concerning Piers the Plowman*. New Rochelle, New
York: Elston Press, 1901 [Skeat's B-text].

152. Onions, C. T., ed. *The Prologue to Piers Plowman*. London:
The Carmelite Classics, [1904].

153. Pamely, C. D., ed. *Piers Plowman: Prologue and Passus
V-VII, B-Text*. London: Sidgewick and Jackson, 1928.

154. Parish, E. L., ed. "A Critical Text of *Piers Plowman*, C-
Text, Passus IX and X." Unpublished University of
London Thesis, 1933.

155. Salter, Elizabeth and Derek Pearsall, eds. *Piers Plowman*.
York Medieval Texts. London: Northwestern University
Press, 1967 [Selections from the C-text. Based on HM
143 with corrections from British Museum Addit. MS
35157].

156. Sisam, K., ed. *Fourteenth-century Verse and Prose*. London:
Oxford University Press, 1921. Revised, 1937 [Part
of Passus VI].

157. Skeat, W. W., ed. *Parallel Extracts from Twenty-Nine
Manuscripts of Piers Plowman*. EETS, o.s. 17, 1866
[With a proposal for the EETS edition (76, 80, 84,
86)]. Revised as *Parallel Extracts from Forty-five
Manuscripts of Piers Plowman*. EETS, o.s. 17, second
ed., 1885.

158. _____., ed. *The Vision of William Concerning Piers
the Plowman, B Text: Prologue and Passus I-VII*.
Oxford: Clarendon Press, 1869. Rptd. 1923.

159. Wilcockson, Colin, ed. *Selections from Piers Plowman*.
London: Macmillan; New York: St. Martin's Press,
English Classics, new series, 1965.

Translations

160. Attwater, Donald and Rachel, trans. *The Book Concerning
Piers the Plowman*. New York: Everyman's Library,
1957 [Verse translation in alliterative half-lines.
Prologue and Passus I-VII trans. by Donald Attwater
in 1930 (167), remainder trans. by Rachel Attwater].

161. Burrell, A., trans. *Piers Plowman: The Vision of a
People's Christ*. New York: Everyman's Library,
1912. Rptd. 1931 [Verse translation. Conflation
of all three versions].

162. Goodridge, J. F., trans. *Piers the Ploughman*. Baltimore:
Penguin, 1959. Revised with a new preface, 1966
[Prose translation of the B-text. The Notes and
Commentary, p. 261 ff., includes a gloss on the text].

163. Klett, Werner, trans. *The Vision of William Concerning
Piers the Plowman*. Bonn: Anton Brand, 1935
[German translation of the B-text].

164. Wells, Henry W., trans. *The Vision of Piers Plowman*. New
York: Sheed and Ward Inc., 1945 [Translation of the
B-text with additions from the C-text].

165. Williams, Margaret R., trans. *Piers the Plowman by William
Langland*. New York: Random House, 1971 [Verse

translation in alliterative pattern. Introduction
includes a summary of the action and a table plotting
the structure of the poem].

Selections in Modern English

166. Abrams, N. H., *et al*, eds. *The Norton Anthology of English
Literature*. Revised edition. New York: Norton and
Company, 1968. Vol. I, pp. 273-82 [Parts of B-text
Prologue and Passus I].

167. Attwater, Donald, trans. *The Vision of William concerning
Piers the Plowman*. Woodcuts by Denis Tegetmeir. Lon-
don: Cassell, 1930 [Verse translation of the B
Visio].

168. Coghill, Nevill, trans. *Visions from Piers Plowman*.
London: Phoenix House, 1949 [B-text with some
omissions. In verse].

169. Hadow, G. E. and W. H., eds. *The Oxford Treasury of
English Literature*. Oxford: Clarendon Press, 1906,
p. 57.

170. Neilson, W. A. and G. K. T. Webster, eds. *Chief British
Poets of the Fourteenth and Fifteenth Centuries*.
Boston: Houghton Mifflin, 1916, pp. 48-78 [A-text
Prologue and Passus I-VII].

171. _____., trans. and eds. *Sir Gawain and the Green
Knight, Piers the Ploughman*. Boston: Houghton
Mifflin, 1917.

172. Skeat, W. W., trans. *The Vision of Piers the Plowman by
William Langland*. London: A. Moring, 1905
[B-text Prologue and Passus I-VII].

173. Spencer, Hazelton, *et al*, eds. *British Literature: Old
English to 1800*. Lexington, Mass.: D. C. Heath,
1952. Third edition, 1974, pp. 96-107 [A-text
Prologue and Part of B, XIII].

174. Warren, Kate M., trans. *Langland's Vision of Piers the
Plowman*. London: T. Fisher Unwin, 1895. Second
edition, 1899 [Prose translation of Skeat's B-text
with readings from Wright's B-text and Whitaker's
C-text. Prologue through Passus VII].

175. Weston, Jessie L. *Romance, Vision and Satire*. Boston:
Houghton Mifflin, 1912, pp. 239-328 [Verse translation
of the A-text with the Prologue of the B-text].

III. *Piers Plowman*: Critical Interpretation

Critical recognition of Langland's genuine poetic ability
is a relatively recent phenomenon. For more than three-hundred
years, his position in English literary history was determined
by a general misunderstanding of the purpose and design of *Piers
Plowman*. To most early commentators, the poem's narrative appeared chaotic, discontinuous, and incoherent; the allegory,
confused and shapeless. Langland was considered a careless
artist, less concerned with writing poetry than with espousing
popular causes and crying-out against the abuses of his day. The
image of Langland as a fervid Wycliffite preacher dominated the
criticism of *Piers Plowman* from the sixteenth through the nineteenth centuries.

Robert Crowley, the first editor of the poem, was largely
responsible for the long-lived belief that Langland was primarily
a social reformer and a forerunner of the Protestant Reformation--
a view that prevailed at least until the close of the nineteenth
century. In *Piers Plowman*, Crowley perceived a spirit well-suited
to his own age. Although he did not alter the poem in any significant way, he tended, in his preface and notes, to emphasize
Langland's criticism of the friars and of contemporary society as
a whole. In his preface, he states:

> We may justly coniect therfore [that] it [*Piers Plow-
> man*] was firste written about two hundred yeres paste,
> in the tyme of Kynge Edwarde the Thyrde. In whose
> tyme it pleased God to open the eyes of many to se
> hys truth, geuing them boldenes of herte, to open
> their mouthes and crye oute agaynste the workes of
> darckenes, as dyd John Wicklyfe, who also in those
> dayes translated the holye Byble into the Englishe
> tonge, and this writer [Langland] who in reportynge
> certayne visions and dreames, that he fayned hym selfe
> to haue dreamed, doth most christianlie enstructe the
> weak, and sharplye rebuke the obstynate blynde. There
> is no manner of vice, that reygneth in anye estate of

43

men, whyche thys wryter hath not godly, learnedlye, and
wittilye rebuked.[1]

For Crowley and his readers, the poet represented the first
spark of protest against the Roman Church. Langland's antifraternalism, his apparent distrust of all clerics, and his
hatred of simony and ecclesiastical corruption endeared his work
to the sixteenth century, apparently to the exclusion of the poem's
other merits.

Whitaker, the first modern editor of *Piers Plowman*, recognized the fallacy of considering Langland a disciple of Wyclif:

> These abuses Langland, with many other good men who
> could endure to remain in the communion of the church
> of Rome, saw and deplored; but though he finally con-
> ducted his pilgrim out of the particular communion of
> Rome into the universal church, he permitted him to
> carry along with him too many remnants of his old
> faith, such as satisfaction for sin to be made by the
> sinner, together with the merit of works, and especially
> of voluntary poverty; but, above all, the worship of
> the cross; incumbrances with which the Lollards of
> his own, or the Protestants of a later age, would
> not willingly have received him as a proselyte.[2]

In spite of Whitaker's judgement the view of Langland as a Lollard
spokesman persisted.

Although Langland shared many beliefs with Wyclif (*e.g.*, the
disapproval of the possession of *temporalia* by clerics), he never
questioned the basic truths of the Catholic Church. Furthermore,
Langland was essentially a political conservative: J. J. Jusserand
pointed out that Langland's views were generally in accord with
the opinions of the House of Commons.[3] While it is certainly
true that Langland often spoke out against abuses in both Church
and state, his point of view was not particularly radical.

Crowley portrayed Langland as a visionary, and emphasized
what he thought to be the poet's predictions of the dissolution
of the monasteries. But Langland was, first and foremost, a
satirist and a teacher of individual moral and social values:
"Loke not vpon this boke therefore, to talke of wonders paste or
to come but to emend thy own misse, whych thou shalt fynd here
most charitably rebuked."[4]

The name Piers Plowman quickly became associated with the hard-working, simple, and honest Englishman and it was used as a catchword in the proliferation of social protest pamphlets in the later years of the sixteenth century. Thomas Nashe, for example, in his *Piers Penniless His Supplication to the Devil* (1592), used Piers as his spokesman against the follies of his age.

In the Renaissance, Langland was known essentially as a satirist. George Puttenham, in his *Art of English Poesy* (1589), noted: "He that wrote the satire of *Piers Plowman* seemed to have been a malcontent of that time, and therefore bent himself wholly to tax the disorders of that age and specially the pride of the Roman clergy, of whose fall he seemeth to be a very true prophet."[5] The idea that *Piers Plowman* was wholly a satire prevailed well into the present century: J. E. Wells, in his *A Manual of the Writings in Middle English, 1050-1400*, classified the poem under the heading of "Satire and Complaint."[6] Most readers were familiar with the first eight passus only, where the concentration of satire is particularly strong (especially in the Prologue and the presentation of the Seven Deadly Sins). At the conclusion of the *Visio*, however, the poem turns away from satiric attacks on contemporary vices toward larger theological concerns. Today, *Piers* is no longer considered a "pure" satire. While it employs many of the techniques of satire and complaint, the poem partakes of other genres as well--*e.g.*, the consolation, the dream vision, and the debate.

Langland was frequently criticized for his inability to maintain a continuous, logically structured narrative. The allegory, his major narrative device, was often considered confused and uneven. Crowley observed that "The sence is somewhat darcke, but not so harde, but that it maye be vnderstande of such as wyll not sticke to breake the shell of the nutte for the kernelles sake."[7] Two hundred years later, Thomas Warton commented that Langland's manner was "extremely perplexed" and that he frequently tends to "disgust the reader with obscurities."[8] Even Whitaker, who generally admired Langland's poetic abilities, noted that "He often sinks into imbecility, and not unfrequently spins out his

thread of allegory into mere tenuity."[9] Whitaker also observed
that Langland "contrived to support and animate an allegory (the
most insipid for the most part and tedious of all vehicles of
instruction) through a bulky volume."[10]

The allegory of *Piers Plowman* is indeed problematic, primarily because the poem is not a consistent "personification allegory." Although most of the major characters are personifications,
Biblical, historical, and legendary figures, such as Moses and
Trajan, appear in the narrative as well. The Dreamer, Will, is
portrayed realistically but he also serves as an embodiment of the
human faculty. Piers functions as a complex symbol whose signifi-
cations shift rapidly throughout the poem, from the simple plowman
to his final identification with Christ. Furthermore, characters
mysteriously appear and disappear and scenes and landscapes change
rapidly, frequently without transition.

Recently, several critics have attempted to provide us with
the background necessary for an understanding of Langland's
complex use of allegory. Charles Muscatine, Morton W. Bloomfield,
Elizabeth Salter, Pamela Gradon, and Robert Worth Frank, for
example, have helped to clarify this complex mode of expression
which many nineteenth-century critics considered simplistic and
tedious. Only now are we beginning to perceive coherence and
unity in the mysterious workings of Langland's allegory. Muscatine,
for example, believes that the poem's action may best be described
as "surrealistic": the spatial inconsistencies of the narrative
operate in concert with such traits as the "periodic establishment
and collapse of the dream frame, the alteration of allegory and
literalism, the violent changes of tone and temper, the peculiar
equivalence of concrete and abstract terms, and the indistinctness
of the genre."[11]

Misconceptions about Langland's artistic capabilities were
frequently based on a more general misunderstanding of the
overall literary climate of the later Middle Ages. Early literary
historians generally divided late fourteenth-century English
poetry into two mutually exclusive categories, representing two
distinct poetic traditions--the courtly and the popular.[12] The

courtly tradition, best exemplified by Chaucer and Gower, represented the flowering of late medieval verse. This poetry had no direct antecedents in earlier English literature: it drew its inspiration, and frequently its subject matter as well, from the poetry of the continent. It was generally considered to be intelligent, urbane, and metrically refined. The popular tradition, represented by Langland, the author of *The Parlement of the Thre Ages*, and several other anonymous poets, was usually described as "native," crude, unpolished, and unlearned. While this division is in some ways helpful, it is also deceptively simple.

C. S. Lewis noted that *Piers Plowman* "is not even 'popular' in any very obvious sense. A poem every way unsuitable for recitation cannot have been addressed to those who could not read."[13] "Langland," Lewis continues, "is a learned poet. He writes for clerks and for clerkly minded gentlemen." By and large, recent scholarly opinion concurs with Lewis's observations. As we discover more about late medieval literature, we are able to see that the traditional dichotomy between courtly and popular verse is no longer wholly valid.

For centuries, Langland was compared to his contemporary, Chaucer, usually to Langland's disadvantage. Chaucer's descriptive powers, his ease and grace in narration, his comic effects, and subtle use of irony tended to obscure the very different poetic gifts of Langland. By comparison, Langland's verse was metrically imperfect, his comedy more blunt and brutal, and his fiction discontinuous and garbled. While Lewis is certainly correct that Langland "is not, indeed, the greatest poet of his century,"[14] we must recognize that his art is very different from Chaucer's and that it cannot be properly evaluated by Chaucerian standards. According to the traditional division between courtly and popular verse, these poets represent two poles of literary expression: together, however, they represent the full range and brilliance of fourteenth-century English poetry.

NOTES

[1]Quoted by A. H. Bright, *New Light on Piers Plowman* (London: Oxford University Press, 1928), Appendix C, p. 80.

[2]Quoted by Skeat, *CP*, II, xlii.

[3]J. J. Jusserand, *Piers Plowman, A Contribution to the History of English Mysticism*. Revised and enlarged. Trans. M. E. R. (New York: Russell, 1895), *passim*.

[4]Quoted by Bright, *New Light*, Appendix C, p. 81.

[5]*The Art of English Poesy* (1589). Book I, Chapter XXXI. In *The Renaissance in England*, ed. Hyder E. Rollins and Herschel Baker (Lexington, Mass: D. C. Heath and Company, 1954), p. 644.

[6]J. E. Wells, *A Manual of the Writings in Middle English 1050-1400*, supplements i-ix (New Haven: Yale University Press, 1916-51), pp. 244-268 (original volume).

[7]Quoted by Bright, *New Light*, Appendix C, p. 81.

[8]Thomas Warton, *The History of English Poetry From the Close of the Eleventh to the Commencement of the Eighteenth Century* (London: J. Dodsley, 1774), Vol. I, Section 8, pp. 266-67.

[9]Quoted by Skeat, *CP*, II, xliv.

[10]Quoted by Skeat, *CP*, II, xl.

[11]Charles Muscatine, "Locus of Action in Medieval Narrative," *Romance Philology*, 17 (1963), p. 121.

[12]This division may be traced as far back as the Renaissance. Francis Meres, for example, in his "Comparative Discourse of Our English Poets with the Greek, Latin, and Italian Poets," *Palladis Tamia* (1598), separates Langland from the courtly poets, Chaucer, Gower, and Lydgate. Langland is compared to Homer, but is subordinated to the poets of the court.

[13]C. S. Lewis, *The Allegory of Love* (London: Oxford University Press, 1936), p. 159.

[14]Lewis, *Allegory*, p. 161.

176. Ackerman, Robert W. *Backgrounds to Medieval English Literature*. New York: Random House, 1966.

177. Adams, Ira. "Narrative Techniques and the Apocalyptic Mode of Thought in *Piers Plowman*." University of Virginia dissertation, 1973. Abstracted *DAI*, 33: 3627A-28A.

Adams disagrees with the conclusions of M. W. Bloomfield (219), arguing that *PP* is not a product of monastic philosophy. The central concern of *PP* is not with social but with individual perfection. WL is a pessimist and can accept no merely human solutions to social problems--he is also a "proto-Protestant." *PP* has a circular structure--the end returns to the beginning just as the quest for salvation is never ending.

178. Adams, John Festus. "The Dreamer's Quest for Salvation in *Piers Plowman*." University of Washington dissertation, 1960. Abstracted *DA*, 21: 1553.

179. _____. "*Piers Plowman* and the Three Ages of Man." *JEGP*, 61 (1962), 23-41.

The Dreamer's life is the life of man: Dowel, Dobet, and Dobest provide "modes of meaning about which cluster a variety of elements significant to each stage of his progress": *i.e.*, youth, middle age, and old age. The *Visio* provides the Dreamer with a panoramic view of actual life and introduces the problem of salvation. The *Vita* offers a specific case study showing the Dreamer's progress through life on his quest for salvation. The ages of his life and the divisions of the poem center on the temptations, mental faculties and spiritual crises peculiar to each age.

180. Adams, Robert. "Langland and the Liturgy Revisited." *SP*, 73 (1976), 266-84.

Adams reviews scholarship on WL's use of the liturgy, finding that Greta Hort's tabulations indicating a high percentage of quotations from the Missal and Breviary are misleading (See 389). Hort based her conclusions on a sixteenth-century version of the Breviary which included many passages not found in the versions that WL would have used. WL was familiar with the Divine Office, "but was not much given to reading the Breviary" (p. 280). Sixty-seven of WL's scriptural quotations (25% of the total) can be found in gospels and epistles for Sundays and major feast days. Adams disagrees with DiPasquale's conclusions (307): there is no evidence that WL structured his poem explicitly or implicitly after the liturgical year.

181. Aers, David. *Piers Plowman and Christian Allegory*. London: Edward Arnold, 1975.

Biblical exegesis in the later Middle Ages degenerated into a "wholly mechanical" process and was seldom imaginative. WL never employs the simple four-fold method: he is concerned instead with the process and development of concepts. WL searches for what Aers terms a "disclosure model" through which he may reveal his meanings almost as they unfold to him. The artistic effort is itself a search for truth; the reader is called on to participate in this process "whose totality is the vision the writer has won back in the action of composition" (p. 63). In this kind of writing the poetic process and its imagistic organization is integral to the poet's exploration and vision. Aers discusses WL's conception of himself as "maker"--he is an experimenter, conscious of his role as "poet-vates." The character Piers functions as a "lens" or filter through which the Dreamer and the reader view experience. The qualities Piers embodies are linked to the knower's (Dreamer's and reader's) mode of perception at any given time or in any given context. Piers "appears and acts towards all men as the saving agent appropriate to their own perception" (p. 79).

182. Alden, R. M. *The Rise of Formal Satire in England under Classical Influence*. Philadelphia: University of Pennsylvania Press, 1899.

183. Alford, John A. "Haukyn's Coat: Some Observations on *Piers Plowman* B. XIV. 22-7." *Medium Aevum*, 43 (1974), 133-38.

The meaning of Haukyn's coat is "not constant." It is a "multifarious and shifting . . . image of man's spiritual history." Haukyn stains the coat, but through penance he will gain "the coat of salvation." The image allows WL to combine "the reciprocal themes of sin and redemption," and to compress "the various implications of one of St. Paul's favourite [sic] metaphors, 'For this corruptible must put on incorruption, and this mortal must put on immortality' (I Cor. xv. 53)."

184. _____. "Literature and Law in Medieval England." *PMLA*, 92 (1977), 941-51.

Discusses *PP* pp. 944-45. Provides a brief history of medieval literary debates between Christ and Satan, finding the most elaborate treatment of this motif in the Harrowing of Hell episode in *PP*. Lucifer is confident that he can maintain possession of his domain because his "seisin" is protected by a statute of limitations. He is defeated by the principle of *bona fides*.

185. _____. "A Note on *Piers Plowman* B.XVIII. 390: 'Til *Parce* It Hote.'" *MP*, 69 (1972), 323-25.

Alford explains the significance of the phrase "til parce it hote" in Christ's speech to Lucifer: "Thei shul be clensed clereliche and wasshen of her synnes/ In my prisoun purgatorie til parce it hote." The word "parce" begins the Office of the Dead. By WL's time, it was generally used in reference to purgatory, "probably as a common formula in penitential prayers." Alford reads the line, "they shall be cleansed thoroughly and washed of their sins in my prison purgatory, until mercy commands an end."

186. _____. "*Piers Plowman* and the Tradition of Biblical *Imitatio*." University of North Carolina, Chapel Hill dissertation, 1970. Abstracted *DAI*, 31: 3536A-37A.

WL is one of a number of medieval authors who consciously imitated the Bible instead of classical authors. The Biblical quotations of *PP* are not merely coincidental-- WL uses Biblical allusion, paraphrase, verbal reminiscences, and Biblical reasoning. The Bible gave WL not only its authority but also its language and the terms by which he ordered his own thinking.

187. _____. "Some Unidentified Quotations in *Piers Plowman*." *MP*, 72 (1975), 390-99.

Attempts to locate sources for several quotations. Uses Skeat as basic text with cross references to the Athlone Press editions of A and B: A.X, 92; A. XI, 238; A. XI, 303; B. Prol., 141-42; B.Prol., 144; B.I, 88-91; B.I, 139; B. II, 27; B. IV, 120; B.V, 448; B.V, 612; B.IX, 181; B.X, 253; B.X, 259-60; B.XII, 52; B.XII, 283; B.XIII, 427; B.XIV, 59; B. XIV, 144; B.XIV, 169; B.XIV, 180; B.XIV, 275; B.XV, 59-60; B.XV, 62; B.XVI, 223; B. XVIII, 237; B. XVIII, 390; B. XVIII, 407-8; B. XIX, 290; B.XX, 34; C. II, 84-87; C.II, 140; C. III, 27; C.V, 188; C.VII, 257; C.VIII, 87; C.X, 212; C.X, 265-66; C.X, 274; C.XI, 94; C.XI, 289; C.XII, 160; C.XII, 296; C.XII, 304; C.XIII, 39; C.XIII, 152; C.XV, 208; C.XVI, 263; C.XVII, 116; C.XVII, 221; C.XVII, 224; C. XIX, 242; C.XXI, 249; C. XXI, 453; C.XXII, 295.

188. Allen, Judson Boyce. *The Friar as Critic: Literary Attitudes in the Later Middle Ages*. Nashville, Tenn.: Vanderbilt University Press, 1971.

There are two kinds of allegory, the spiritual and the literal, which might also be termed "theological" and "poetic." Allen notes that "in *Piers Plowman* there is no simple, single, heroic action calling for isometric rela-

tionship with the central act of Christ; there are no
simple polarities; there is only the weltering variety
of layered dreams" (p. 149). The poem moves towards some
goal but we are never certain what the goal is.

189. Amassian, Margaret and James Sadowsky. "Mede and Mercede:
A Study of the Grammatical Metaphor in *Piers Plowman*,
C: IV: 335-409." *NM*, 72 (1971), 457-76.

WL is well within a medieval tradition in using
grammatical metaphor to distinguish the two types of mede.
God's mede and man's mede are symbolized by a direct
grammatical relationship (noun and adjective). The passage develops a sense of alternate connections between
antecedent and relative, substantive and adjective, God
and man, master and servant, king and commons, good and
bad rewards, order and chaos.

190. Ames, Ruth M. *The Fulfillment of the Scriptures: Abraham,
Moses, and Piers*. Evanston, Illinois: Northwestern
University Press, 1970.

PP is basically a survey of salvation history, and
Biblical typology is the key to its meaning. WL's theme
descends from the ancient doctrine of the fulfillment of
the Scriptures: the Old Testament prefigures the New
and the New clarifies and corroborates the Old. One of
the major concerns of *PP* is the history of Revelation--
the Dreamer only gradually understands the unfolding of
God's plan as he participates in the history of salvation.
The poem moves from the Old Law, where Piers enforces the
Ten Commandments, to the New Testament where he assumes
Christ's armor. Throughout the poem, God has an unchange-
able nature which is taught in both Testaments. In the
Pardon scene, there is no real conflict between the views
of Piers and the priest, but the priest recognizes only the
letter while Piers foresees the spirit. The priest symbolizes the Old Law, and Piers, the New. At the end of
the poem, the wicked are condemned by the Old and the New
Law. The Dreamer, enlightened by Abraham, Moses and
Christ, and strengthened by the sacraments of the Church,
must fulfill the Law in his own life in order to gain the
pardon granted to Piers.

191. Anderson, Judith H. "Aspects of Allegory in *Piers Plowman*
and *The Faerie Queene*." Yale University dissertation,
1965. Abstracted *DA*, 26: 4622.

192. _____. *The Growth of a Personal Voice: Piers
Plowman and the Faerie Queene*. New Haven and London:
Yale University Press, 1976.

52

Anderson is concerned with the evolution of narrative consciousness in *PP* and the *Faerie Queene*: "Together they illuminate the special problems of the evolving narrative consciousness in an allegorical poem, both the form it takes and the effects it has in narrative expression" (p. 4). The poet's role in both poems shifts with changes in the nature and location of truth. Within each we find an expansion of the personal voice of the poet and the development of characters more fully personal in themselves. Both poems grow more personal and experiential as theological and philosophical concerns lose their objective status and their truths become more relative to one person. Even allegory itself becomes more personal: in both poems there is a strong element of directly personal realization which distinguishes them from most allegories. Both are concerned with the workings of the mind and the search for unified meaning. The poet's posture, his relation to the poem, evolves throughout the narrative. "At the end of Spenser's poem, as at the end of Langland's, we see a final personalizing of the vision and see it come down to an individual realization of faith in one's God" (p. 203).

193. Ashton, J. W. "Rhymes of . . . Randolf, Erl of Chestre." *ELH*, 5 (1938), 195-206.

Ashton examines the line, "Ich can rymes of Robyn Hode and of Randolf, erl of chestre" (C. VIII, 11). The reference is probably to Ranulf de Blundeville, Earl of Chester. Ashton attempts to reconstruct a biography of Ranulf by examining references in Holinshed. The exciting events of Ranulf's life likely became the subject matter of popular ballads in WL's day and later entered into drama (*e.g.*, Anthony Munday's *John Kent and John Cumber*).

194. Baird, Joseph L. "Secte and Suit Again: Chaucer and Langland." *Chaucer Review*, 6 (1971), 117-19.

Baird extends the argument of his earlier article, "The 'Secte' of the Wyf of Bathe" (*Chaucer Review*, 2 (1968), 188-90), that "secte" means "suit of law." He examines *PP*, B.V, 495-98 where "secte" is used in a punning sense to refer both to a legal suit with Satan and a suit of clothing--*i.e.*, our flesh, in which Christ died.

195. Baker, Denise N. "Langland's Artistry: The Strategy and Structure of *Piers Plowman*." University of Virginia dissertation, 1976. Abstracted *DAI*, 36: 6109A.

The inconsistencies of *PP* result from WL's attempts to engage his reader in a dialectic rather than didactic fashion. His aim is not to convince the reader, but to convert him in the process of experiencing the poem. The winding, confusing structure of the poem is designed to

transform the psychology of the reader. WL is both testing
and teaching his readers and he frequently withholds or
distorts information to mislead us. The "converted"
reader understands the meaning of the never-ending pilgrimage of Conscience.

196. Baldwin, Charles Sears. "Moral Allegory, *Piers Plowman*."
     Three Medieval Centuries of Literature in England
     1100-1400. New York: Phaeton Press, 1968, pp.
     158-69.

     Argues that *PP* should be read as a sequence of ideas
     rather than a sequence of actions. The purification of
     society and of the individual and the salvation in the
     active life have counterparts later in theology and
     Church government, the special devotion of monastic life,
     and the mission of the Church to save society.

197. Barney, Stephen A. "The Plowshare of the Tongue: the
     Progress of a Symbol from the Bible to *Piers Plowman*."
     MS, 35 (1973), 261-93.

     In the Middle Ages, the Church applied images of
     cultivation to its offices of missionary preaching. WL
     employs similar images throughout *PP*. His immediate source
     may have been either the *Glossa Ordinaria* or the Sermons
     of Thomas Brinton. The plowshare is the preacher's tongue,
     the plow, a penitential act, the field, the human heart,
     and the plowman, the good priest. Piers rejects the
     pardon because it emphasizes physical labor and his duties
     are missionary and spiritual. Piers represents the true
     priesthood which supersedes the corrupt contemporary
     clergy. When Piers meets the priest in the Pardon scene,
     he is confronting his antithesis. The structure of *PP*
     arises from the Dreamer's inability to follow the shortest
     route to salvation--the Church.

198. Baugh, Albert C. "*Piers Plowman* and Other Alliterative
     Poems." *A Literary History of England*. New York:
     Appleton-Century-Crofts, 1948. Part II, Chapter XV,
     240-49.

     PP is the greatest of all alliterative poems of
     social protest. Baugh provides a hypothetical biography
     of WL based on the C-text and a summary of the poem's
     action. Manly's claim for multiple authorship cannot be
     easily dismissed.

199. Baum, Paul Franklin. "The Fable of the Belling of the
     Cat." *MLN*, 34 (1919), 462-70.

     Deals with the transmission of this originally oriental
     folk motif into the west either by oral or literary means.
     The fable of the belling of the cat was well known in the

thirteenth century in the West. It first occurs in Odo of Cheriton's *Fabulae* (c. 1220). Langland could have read it in Odo or it could have reached him by oral transmission. Baum provides a partial list of analogues to the fable in Oriental and Western literature.

200. Belleza, Paulo. "Di Alcune Notevoli Coincidenzie tra la *Divina Comedia* e la *Visione di Pietro l'Aratore*." *Rendicanti del Regio Instituto Lombardo di Scienze e Littere*, Serie II, 29. Milano, 1897.

201. _____. "Langland and Dante." *N&Q*, 8th series, 6 (1894), 81-83.

Although it is impossible to ascertain whether WL read Dante, there are many similarities between *PP* and the *Divine Comedy*. The B Prologue, for example, appears to be "a more extended version" of the eleventh canto of the *Paradiso* (3-9). Belleza also notes parallels in the two poets' use of symbolic figures, especially Sloth, Covetousness, and Meed.

202. _____. "Langlands Figure des 'Plowman' in der Neuesten Englischen Litteratur." *EStudien*, 21 (1895), 325-26.

WL's image of the plowman as a figure of social unrest and a herald of uprising is used later by Macaulay (*Speeches*) and Tennyson (*Locksley Hall Sixty Years After*).

203. Bennett, H. S. "The Author and His Public in the Fourteenth and Fifteenth Centuries." *E&S*, 23 (1937), 1-24.

204. _____. *Chaucer and the Fifteenth Century*. Oxford: Clarendon Press, 1947.

Bennett believes that WL was "careless of poetic art, and careful only to put into the most forceful of words the many ideas that a deep knowledge of the England of his day had impressed upon him. He is a satirist, critic, reformer, moralist, and many other things, but all are directed to the creating of a new state of affairs in the realm so that Righteousness and Truth shall prevail" (p. 15).

205. _____. "The Production and Dissemination of Vernacular Manuscripts in the Fifteenth Century." *Library*, fifth series, 1 (1946-1947), 167-78.

206. Bennett, J. A. W. "Chaucer's Contemporary." *Piers Plowman: Critical Approaches*, ed. Hussey, 1969, pp. 310-24.

The traditional view of WL as a poet of the common people in contrast to the courtly Chaucer is misleading. WL and Chaucer share a fundamental "Englishness," not only in their topographical descriptions but in their narrative methods as well. Similarities between the Prologue of *PP* and the General Prologue of the *Canterbury Tales* suggest that Chaucer may have read *PP*. Furthermore, several of Chaucer's characters may be based on Langland's characters. Bennett examines the similarities between Chaucer's Prioress and WL's Abbess, Chaucer's Clerk and WL's Study, Chaucer's Knight and WL's Christian Knight. Most of the trades, occupations, and characters of the Prologue of the *Canterbury Tales* have antecedents in *PP*. The *Parlement of Foules* echoes the opening of the *PP* Prologue.

207. _____. "Lombards' Letters (*Piers Plowman*, B. V, 251)." *MLR*, 40 (1945), 309-10.

The lines "And with Lumbardes lettres I ladde golde to Rome,/ And toke it by taille here and told hem there lasse" in the confession of Avarice refer to the papacy's use of Italian bankers as agents of papal dues. From these negotiations, the bankers received a portion of the profit. The "lettres" refer to bills of exchange used when money was received into papal court. Avarice received the amount due the papal treasury from the local collectors and gave them a receipt for it. But upon reaching Rome, he claimed to have collected less money, and received an extra profit.

208. _____. "Sum Rex, Sum Princeps, Etc. (*Piers Plowman* B. Prologue, 132-8)." *N&Q*, new series, 7 (1960), 364.

Skeat believed that the Angel's Latin address was WL's original composition. Bennett notes, however, that the speech appears earlier in MS Lambeth 61 (f. 147v), following a sermon preached in 1315.

209. _____. "William Langland's World of Visions." *Listener*, 43 (1950), 381-82.

210. Benson, C. David. "An Augustinian Irony in *Piers Plowman*." *N&Q*, 23 (1976), 51-54.

Benson examines Will's discussion of good works, salvation, and learning at the end of Passus X in the B-text (XI in A, XII in C), where the Dreamer uses Augustine as an authority to support his opinions. WL is clearly rebuking the Dreamer's anti-intellectualism by having him quote a learned authority in an attack on learning.

211. Biggar, Raymond George. "Langland's and Chaucer's Treatment of Monks, Friars, and Priests." University of

Wisconsin dissertation, 1961. Abstracted *DA*, 22: 1992.

212. Birnes, William J. "Christ as Advocate: The Legal Metaphor of *Piers Plowman*." *AnM*, 16 (1975), 71-93.

WL conceived of the law as "the most important stabilizing force in the community of man." Accordingly, he believed that strict adherence to the law would remedy most social ills. In *PP*, Christ becomes the embodiment of law and establishes law as the basis of all government. WL develops a legal-political framework for his theological discussions: in the Harrowing of Hell scene, earthly law and divine law are fused.

213. _____. "Patterns of Legality in *Piers Plowman*." New York University dissertation, 1974. Abstracted *DAI*, 35: 1040A.

Law is a governing concept in the theme of *PP*. WL recognized two distinct kinds of law--divine and temporal. A fusion of these laws occurs in the Harrowing of Hell scene when Christ subsumes all laws, becoming the personification of Law, stability and order.

214. Blamires, Alcuin G. "*Mum & the Sothsegger* and Langlandian Idiom." *NM*, 76 (1975), 583-604.

Discusses the narrative and rhetorical similarities of *PP* and *Mum*. Both poems demonstrate a curious discontinuity and structural dislocation and both employ "embryonic" allegories or short allegorical sketches. Most importantly, both use a number of medieval literary genres in combination, including sermon, debate, satire, quest, and dream vision. Suggests that Skeat's attribution of *Mum* to WL is more credible than most recent critics recognize although Blamires himself reaches no conclusion regarding this possibility.

215. Blanch, Robert J., ed. *Style and Symbolism in Piers Plowman*. Knoxville: University of Tennessee Press, 1969.

Contents: (See separate listings)
Morton W. Bloomfield. "The Present State of *Piers Plowman* Studies." (220)
A. H. Smith. "*Piers Plowman* and the Pursuit of Poetry." (557)
Nevill K. Coghill. "The Pardon of Piers Plowman." (274)
T. P. Dunning. "The Structure of the B-text of *Piers Plowman*." (317)
John Lawlor. "The Imaginative Unity of *Piers Plowman*." (440)
Zeeman, Elizabeth [Salter]. "*Piers Plowman* and the Pilgrimage to Truth." (623)

P. M. Kean. "Love, Law, and *Lewte* in *Piers Plowman*." (420)

Howard William Troyer. "Who is Piers Plowman?" (592)

A. G. Mitchell. "Lady Meed and the Art of *Piers Plowman*." (470)

Stella Maguire. "The Significance of Haukyn, *Activa Vita*, in *Piers Plowman*." (452)

John Burrow. "The Action of Langland's Second Vision." (24)

R. E. Kaske. "*Ex vi transicionis* and Its Passage in *Piers Plowman*." (408)

E. Talbot Donaldson. "The Grammar of Book's Speech in *Piers Plowman*." (309)

216. Bloomfield, Morton W. "The Pardons of Pamplona and the Pardoner of Rounceval: *Piers Plowman* B XVII 252 (C XX 218)." *PQ*, 35 (1956), 60-68.

Skeat's gloss on the line "And porchace al the pardoun of Paumpelon and of Rome" is inadequate. The term "Paumpelon" is an allusion to the Hospital of St. Mary Rounceval, Charing Cross. WL is yoking the pardons of the Bishop of Pamplona with those of the Pope in order to cast special obloquy on St. Mary Rounceval whose activities in "pardon mongering" made it worthy of WL's satire. Chaucer alludes to the same problem in his portrait of the Pardoner.

217. _____. "*Piers Plowman* and the Three Grades of Chastity." *Anglia*, 76 (1958), 227-53.

The subject of the grades of Christian perfection is presented in *PP* by means of a chastity metaphor. This concept appears in several triadic configurations: marriage, widowhood, virginity/chastity, continence, virginity/lay, priest, religious. Bloomfield examines two passages which employ this concept. First, Imaginitif's speech (B.XII, 31-52) where WL warns against lapses of virginity; Lucifer heads this list because he was guilty of lechery. Second, the Tree of Charity scene in B. XVI (C. XIX): this is actually the tree of chastity. Bloomfield argues that two graphic portrayals of the tree (one from MS Troyes, 252, the other, a Joachite tree) parallel WL's treatment of the subject. Expanded treatment of this concept is given in 219.

218. _____. "*Piers Plowman* as a Fourteenth-century Apocalypse." *Centennial Review of Arts and Sciences*, 5 (1961), 281-95.

219. _____. *Piers Plowman as a Fourteenth-century Apocalypse*. New Brunswick, N. J.: Rutgers University Press, [1962].

The main concern of *PP* is not salvation but Christian perfection on a social scale. In the *Visio*, the Dreamer is a passive observer but in the *Vita*, he becomes an active seeker after perfection. The *Vita* is composed of a discussion of the three grades of perfection: *Do-wel* concerns the ordering of self to the natural world--here, patient poverty is found to be the best way of life for most Christians; *Do-bet* concerns the ordering of self to Christ; *Do-best* returns to society and history and emphasizes the coming of the kingdom of God. The genre of *PP* is indistinct: it is primarily an apocalypse--an eschatological warning to contemporary society. But the poem also partakes of three other literary genres: the allegorical dream narrative, the *consolatio* (both horizontal and vertical), and the encyclopedic or Menippean satire. *PP* also employs three ideas or forms from religious literature--the contempt of the world theme, glosses or commentaries on Scripture, and the sermon. WL used all six of these forms in a unique combination but he could not solve the formal problems of his poem--the confusion of genre is a reflection of the quest for perfection. WL's thought is strongly influenced by monastic philosophy: the monks are the key to the establishment of a new society, while the friars represent the corruption of present society. WL's theories on the coming of a new world age appear to be influenced by Joachim of Flora (Fiore) (1132-1202). Joachim predicted a trinity of ages, and believed that human history will lead to divine fulfillment as human society grows more perfect. WL had an acute apocalyptic sense of history and was stimulated to write *PP* as a warning to his contemporaries.

220. _____. "The Present State of *Piers Plowman* Studies." *Speculum*, 14 (1939), 215-32. Rptd. in *Style and Symbolism in Piers Plowman*, ed. Blanch, 1969, pp. 3-25.

A general evaluation of the progress of *PP* criticism to 1939. Discusses the authorship controversy, the attempts to construct a biography from the text, the need for critical editions, and possible sources of the poem. Bloomfield suggests that future *PP* studies examine the meaning of WL's individual words and lines, and the general backgrounds of his age.

221. _____. *The Seven Deadly Sins: An Introduction to the History of a Religious Concept, with Special Reference to Medieval English Literature*. East Lansing: Michigan State College Press, 1952.

See Chapter VI, "The Cardinal Sins in the *Divine Comedy* and in English Literature of the Fourteenth Century," pp. 157-201. The confession of the Seven Deadly Sins in *PP* is the greatest confession scene in English Literature, rivalled only by Spenser. WL is extremely flexible in his portraits of the Sins and he is able to combine specific and abstract elements, giving his personifications a shifting and fluid character. The Seven Deadly Sins appear throughout *PP*: in the Confession Scene, the Haukyn episode, the Vision of the Tree of Charity, and the Barn of Unity scene. WL uses them in various configurations.

222. Blythe, Joan H. "Images of Wrath: Lydgate and Langland." University of North Carolina, Chapel Hill dissertation, 1971. Abstracted *DAI*, 32: 908A.

Examines the tradition of the personification of Wrath in English literature. WL's image of Wrath derives from vernacular presentations of the Sins rather than from formal Latin treatises. His purpose is social not catechical (as was Deguileville's in his *Pelerinage de la Vie Humaine*, trans. Lydgate). Both WL and Lydgate employ several images from iconographical handbooks.

223. Bond, Ronald B. "A Study of *Invidia* in Medieval and Renaissance English Literature." University of Toronto dissertation, 1974. Abstracted *DAI*, 35: 1087A.

224. Bonsdorff, Ingrid von. "Hankyn or Haukyn?" *MP*, 26 (1928-1929), 57-61.

MSS are divided in recording the name of the Active Man--Hankyn and Haukyn. Skeat chose Haukyn, although his copy-text, Laud Misc. 581, has Hankyn. Bonsdorff argues that Hankyn is the better choice since it was a popular name in WL's region and was a common name for merchants.

225. Bowers, A. Joan. "The Tree of Charity in *Piers Plowman*: Its Allegorical and Structural Significance." *Literary Monographs*, volume 6. Ed. Eric Rothstein and Joseph Anthony Wittreich, Jr. Madison: University of Wisconsin Press, 1975, pp. 1-34.

Bowers examines the imagistic unity of the B-text, focusing on the Tree of Charity image in Passus XVI. This *lignum vitae* image unifies *PP*. On one level, it represents a climactic moment in the narrative, but on another level, it serves as an allusive echo to lesser *lignum vitae* images throughout the poem, such as Adam and Eve's eating of the *lignum scientiae boni et male* as opposed to the *lignum vitae*, the description of Noah's Ark, and the construction of the Barn of Unity. This image has apocalyptic associations and is associated with the Plant of Peace in Passus I and XX: it emphasizes Christ's redemption of mankind' and his healing powers.

226. Bowers, R. H. "The Comic in Late Medieval Sensibility
      (*Piers Plowman* B. V)." *ABR*, 22 (1971), 353-63.

Bowers discusses the mixture of sacred and profane,
and grotesque and beautiful elements in medieval aesthe-
tics. Most modern readers are accustomed to thinking in
terms of "medieval pessimism" and have difficulty in
accepting the comic tendencies of medieval religious art.
There is a basic medieval optimism that is generally not
recognized. WL demonstrates this optimism, for example, in
the Confession of the Seven Deadly Sins: WL emphasizes
the positive role of Repentance whose function is not
merely to castigate the Sins but to save them. The focus
is both on the seriousness of the Sins and their comic
aspects, for the two are not mutually exclusive.

227. _____. "'Foleuyles Lawes' (*Piers Plowman*, C. XXII.
      247)." *N&Q*, new series, 8 (1961), 327-8.

The term "Foleuyles Lawes" apparently refers to a
harsh mode of redressing justice. Skeat believed that
"Foleuyle" was a proper name, but could not identify it.
The term may refer to the five notorious Folville brothers
of Ashby-Folville who were involved in a private war with
Sir Roger Belers, a baron under Edward III. Belers was
murdered by Eustace Folville. It is likely that the
murder was considered justifiable by the populace and in
alluding to it, WL is suggesting "justifiable redress."

228. _____. "*Piers Plowman* and the Literary Historians."
      CE, 21 (1960), 1-4.

Most critics of *PP* labor to make the poem more complex
than it actually is. *PP* is not a satire, but a consolation
and an education poem: Will is drawn in the tradition of
Boethius.

229. Bradley, Henry. "Some Cruces in *Piers Plowman*." *MLR*,
      5 (1910), 340-42.

First, in the line, "With half a laumpe lyne in
latyne *ex vi transicionis*" (B. XIII, 151), the Latin phrase
may refer to a grammatical metaphor indicating that a
particular interpretation of a proposition is necessitated
by the grammatical form (case, number and tense) of one
of the proposition's words. If the Latin word for "laumpe
lyne" (the cord by which a lamp is suspended) is cut in
two, one of the halves will carry the inflection which
conveys the meaning. The Latin word in this case may have
been *in corde*: thus, in the next line, "I bere there-inne
aboute fast ybounde Dowel," *in corde* should be substituted
for "there-inne." Second, in B. VI, 328-29, there is an
enigmatic allusion to the prognostics who are to herald
the disappearance of pestilence and the coming of famine.

In C. IX, 351-52 the prophecy is revised. Bradley finds evidence to suggest that there is an obscure allusion to the date 1388 in these lines.

230. _____ . "The Word 'Moillere' in *Piers the Plowman*." *MLR*, 2 (1906-1907), 163-64.

Skeat's readings of A. II, 87 and 101 are incorrect. He recorded the Vernon MS reading "Iuweler" and noted that the word referred to "woman" or "wife." The proper reading is "moillere," meaning legitimate child. (See, *e.g.*, C. III, 120).

231. Brett, Cyril. "Notes on Old and Middle English." *MLR*, 22 (1927), 260-62.

Includes two notes on *PP*. First, Skeat's note on the word "Aliri" does not adequately explain how this term pertains to the behavior of beggars (A. VII, 115/ B. VI, 124/ C. IX, 129). "Aliri" refers to a common trick of beggars who pretended to be maimed. Second, Brett disagrees with Owst's explanation of the Angel and "the Goliardeys" in B. Prol., 123 ff. See 496. The Angel stresses "pietas," or mercy. The "Goliardeys" is a word-master, who, by clinging to the letter of the law, stresses justice. The words of the "Goliardeys" are not a reinforcement of the Angel's speech but an argument against it. The king is forced to mediate between these positions.

232. Brian, Beverly D. "Satire in *Piers Plowman*." Duke University dissertation, 1970. Abstracted *DAI*, 30: 4936A.

233. Bright, Alan H. "Sources of *Piers Plowman*." *TLS*, 29 (April 24, 1930), 352.

WL may have used a book of proverbs now in the Rylands Library. The MS may be dated to c. 1362. B. I, 139; B. V, 448; B. XVII, 315 ff; B. V, 258, demonstrate WL's acquaintance with this text. WL probably had access to the MS between 1363 and 1377, since he did not use it in the composition of the A- and C-texts.

234. Brooke, Stopford A. *English Literature*. London: Macmillan, 1897.

See pp. 52-58. WL and Wyclif had much in common. Their work differs from all previous writing; it is distinguished by its popular power and by the depth of its religious feeling. WL's reformist poem is a popular work which was eagerly listened to by the free laborers and fugitive serfs. Includes a summary of the poem.

235. Brooke-Rose, Christine. "Ezra Pound: Piers Plowman in
the Modern Wasteland." *Review of English Literature*,
2 (1961), 74-88.

Brooke-Rose compares Pound's *Cantos* to PP. Both works
demonstrate anti-semitism and employ the techniques of
dreams and the pilgrimage of discovery.

236. Brosamer, James Joseph. "The Personae of *Piers Plowman*:
Narrator, Dreamer, and Will." University of Oregon
dissertation, 1976. Abstracted *DAI*, 37: 1559A.

237. Browne, Robert E. "World, Flesh, and Devil: The Imper-
sonal Style in English Religious and Moral Verse from the
Middle Ages to Donne." Case Western Reserve University
dissertation, 1974. Abstracted *DAI*, 34: 5158A-59A.

238. Bruneder, Hans. *Personifikation und Symbol in William
Langlands Piers Plowman*. Wein, 1963.

WL is able to give variety and fluidity to his poem
by the use of two separate kinds of characters: realistic,
concrete individuals who are drawn with naturalistic
detail, and personifications which display abstract qualities. In this mixture of character modes, WL foreshadows
Chaucer and Spenser.

239. Burdach, Konrad. "Antgaben über Weitere Hinweises auf
Langland." *Euphorion*, 26 (1925), 330.

240. _____. *Der Dichter des Ackerman aus Böhmen und
Seine Zeit in Vom Mittelalter zur Reformation*, III,
2, hälfte 1. Berlin, 1926.

See pp. 140 ff. Burdach discusses the overall design
of *PP*, finding that there is a fundamental unity between
the *Visio* and *Vita*. The Pardon scene serves to blend the
two together by signifying the poem's movement away from
the active life towards the contemplative life. Analyzes
the use of *PP* by John Ball and his followers. Burdach
also provides the first close examination of the C-text
and argues that the C-poet possessed great intellectual
and imaginative scope. The Epistle of James (2.2. ff.),
which stresses the importance of patient poverty, may be
the source of Langland's Banquet scene. Piers is never
identified with Christ; he is always wholly human, and is
meant to be a successor of Peter, the true Pope.

241. Burrow, J. A. "An Approach to the *Dream of the Rood*."
Neophilologus, 43 (1959), 123-33.

See especially pp. 132-33--a comparison of *PP* with
the *Dream of the Rood*. The Harrowing of Hell scene in the
Dream is very close to WL's treatment. In both, there is

a strong personal theme which is implicit from the first.
The principle of development in both poems lies in the
dreamer. At the beginning of Passus XVIII before the
vision of the Crucifixion, the Dreamer is weary, but when
it is over, he awakes with joy. In both poems there is a
general movement from fear and sorrow to hope.

242. _____. "The Action of Langland's Second Vision."
Essays in Criticism, 15 (1965), 247-68. Rptd. in
Style and Symbolism in Piers Plowman, ed. Blanch,
1969, pp. 209-27.

Burrow approaches the second vision as a thematic
unit (Passus V-VII, B-text). The action follows a basic
Sermon-Confession-Pilgrimage-Pardon sequence, and outlines
a plan for the salvation of society. The allegory goes
astray in the Pardon scene because WL does not sustain
the consistency of the literal level of the narrative: he
substitutes the pilgrimage to Truth for the pilgrimage to
Rome and then replaces this with a pilgrimage at the
plough. The pilgrimage, however, is not "shelved"--Dowel
is life on the half-acre. The Pardon is good but the
priest is a sophist who comprehends only the *litera* of the
document. Piers tears only the paper from Rome--the
meaning of the Pardon is not destroyed or abandoned.

243. _____. "The Audience of *Piers Plowman*." *Anglia*,
75 (1957), 373-84.

Unlike extant Chaucer MSS, *PP* MSS are not decorated
and appear to have not been read by the bibliophiles at
court. The Vernon MS was designed to be read by the
clergy--the A-text appears in this MS within a miscellany
of religious prose and verse. *PP* is not a "popular" poem.
In the fifteenth century, *PP* had a wide audience of
prosperous, literate laymen. Unlike most alliterative
poems, its appeal was not regional. In fact, it is distinguished from most poems of the Alliterative Revival
by its extreme economy, avoidance of "characteristically
alliterative" words, and "plain" style.

244. _____. *Ricardian Poetry: Chaucer, Gower, Langland,
and the Gawain Poet*. London: Routledge & K. Paul;
New Haven: Yale University Press, 1971.

A general discussion of style and narrative technique
in the four major poets of the fourteenth century. WL
developed a distinctive "plain" style based primarily on
the exclusion of traditional poetic expressions, particularly the special diction and formulaic expressions of the
Alliterative Revival. "Langland is the only one of our '
four poets capable of sustained grandeur and sublimity of
utterance: yet he is also the poet who, when he falls,
falls lowest. Perhaps if he had been in a position to

submit more to the traditional disciplines of the alliterative poet, he might have commanded a style richer and in its fashion more correct, without sacrificing the toughness and flexibility of the line which are among his special achievements" (p. 35).

245. _____. "Words, Works and Will: Theme and Structure in *Piers Plowman*." *Piers Plowman: Critical Approaches*, ed. Hussey, 1969, pp. 111-24.

As a satirist and moralist, WL was preoccupied with the problems of formalism (*i.e.*, reducing actions into mere words without real will or purpose). The concern with hypocrisy, which is the natural outgrowth of formalism, affects WL's view of the poem he is in the process of composing. He is aware of what is "bogus" in his own creation and this awareness manifests itself in the structural peculiarities of the poem. Piers's abandonment of the physical act of plowing symbolizes his rejection of what appears to be formalism. At this point, WL must change his entire narrative method: with Piers's tearing of the Pardon, WL forsakes his attempt to embody his conception of the good life in allegory. He then examines whether words or formulations can accomplish what "works" or allegorical actions failed to do. Hence, Imaginitif replaces the more concrete Piers. Will's dissatisfaction with his successive visions is the driving force of the poem.

246. Burton, Dorothy Jean. "The Compact with the Devil in the Middle English *Vision of Piers Plowman*, B.II." *California Folklore Quarterly*, 5 (1946), 179-84.

WL implements a common folk motif, "the compact with the devil," in his depiction of the betrothal of Meed and Falsehood. WL deliberately omits certain elements from the folktale and subordinates the story to his allegorical plan. The folk motif is not immediately recognizable because WL omits the summons for diabolical assistance and triangulates the compact. "The very casualness of the poet . . . in adopting or abandoning such a folktale reference at will, shows thus early a fusion of folk and formal elements which was to pay rich dividends in English Literature" (p. 184).

247. Busan, W. F. "The People of *Piers Plowman*." Unpublished Boston University dissertation, 1943.

248. Byrne, Sister Mary of the Incarnation. *The Tradition of the Nun in Mediaeval England*. Published dissertation, Catholic University of America, 1932.

A general history of the treatment of the nun in literature from the seventh to the sixteenth century. In

Chapter V (pp. 161-84), Byrne notes that WL, unlike
earlier satirists, directly attacks nuns: he places nuns
with monks, friars, and any ecclesiastics who have broken
their vows.

249.   Cali, Pietro. *Allegory and Vision in Dante and Langland
           (A Comparative Study)*. Cork: Cork University Press,
           1971.

        Both *PP* and the *Divine Comedy* have as their central
theme the problem of individual salvation. Both WL and
Dante employ a mixture of allegory and realism in their
explorations of the themes of sin, repentance, revelation,
and salvation. The openings of both poems introduce guides
who respond to the inquisitive minds of the dreamers--
both dreamers are about to be launched into the experience
of sin in order to conquer it. WL is more concerned than
Dante with the real problems of his age. He provides us
with a series of negative moments which alternate with
positive statements so that there is a continuous affirmation of divine truths against the ugly reality of actual
life. There is no structural equivalent for this in the
Divine Comedy where the presentation of evil (*Inferno*) is
clearly separated from the presentation of divine truth
(*Paradiso*). The *Vita* corresponds to the *Purgatorio* insofar
as it shows man trying to climb to a knowledge of God. The
unity of both *PP* and the *Divine Comedy* lies in the dreamer
who moves from bewilderment and despair, to hope.

250.   Cantarow, Ellen. "A Wilderness of Opinions Confounded:
           Allegory and Ideology." *CE*, 34 (1972-1973), 215-52.

        Allegory emerges from a particular class and social
order. Its formal characteristics are well-suited to
convey conservative notions: it is not a medium which
propagates ideas of change. The late fourteenth century
was essentially autocratic and conservative: WL tends to
justify what still existed in class relationships. He is
not a radical and his poem does not advocate rebellion.

251.   Carnegy, Francis A. R. "The Relations Between the Social
           and Divine Order in William Langland's *Vision of
           Piers Plowman*." *Sprache und Kultur der Germanischen
           und Romanischen Voker*, A, Anglistische Reihe. Breslau:
           Verlag Priebatschs Buchhandlung, 1934.

        Manual labor and its role in society is a dominant
theme in *PP*. Throughout the poem, WL stresses the relationship between the spiritual and temporal and the social
and divine orders. The *Visio* seeks reform in contemporary
England, whereas the *Vita* deals with theological concerns.
The ideal of the *Visio* is the honest plowman, Piers.
Piers's relationship with Truth is analogous to the proper
relationship between laborer and employer. WL believed

that the present social system should be maintained, but
felt that it should not operate by means of hate and
oppression. The order of the earthly kingdom should emulate
the order of heaven. Piers obeys the rules of Holy Church
necessary for salvation, but the people do not follow his
example. Their failure to till the soil properly symbolizes their failure at social harmony, and their inability to obey the rules necessary for salvation. When
Piers becomes identified with Christ, he represents the
final integration of the social and divine orders.

252. Carruthers, Mary Jean. "The Mind of Will: A Preface to
 Piers Plowman." Yale University dissertation, 1965.
 Abstracted *DA*, 26: 4625.

253. _____. *The Search for St. Truth: A Study of
 Meaning in Piers Plowman*. Evanston, Illinois: Northwestern University Press, 1973.

 The central concern of *PP* is with language as an instrument of thought. *PP* is not basically a moral, social,
or apocalyptic poem--it is an epistemological work concerned with the problems of knowing truly. For WL, allegory is a cognitive mode, a means of discovering truth via
the images and analogies of visible things. WL's desire
to achieve understanding is evident in his constant experi-
mentation with language. Throughout the poem, WL is
continually reexamining and remaking language. The fluid
structure of the poem reflects the poet's attempts to
apprehend the meaning of a world in the process of per-
petual change. Semantic chaos leads to narrative chaos.
By the end of the first five passus, human language has
been discredited--it has lost all meaningful reference: as
the relationship between sign and signification becomes
unstable and ambiguous, the whole foundation of knowledge,
including God's revelation of himself in signs, is
jeopardized. Will embarks on a long cognitive search in
an effort to "read rightly": eventually, he learns a
new epistemology--a figural logic whose key is Christ.
When Will awakes from his vision of the Harrowing of Hell,
he has a vision of the Cross which is not a sign--it is
"extralinguistic, even extrasignatory." This underscores
the complete inadequacy of language as a medium of knowing
and expressing truth. The ending of *PP* is highly pessi-
mistic but after the destruction of this world, a new
language may be born. *PP* is deliberately unfinished--it
rejects every possible informing structure.

254. Case, Anne M. "Pursuit of Wisdom: A Study of the Knowledge
 of Good and Evil in *Piers Plowman*." Yale University
 dissertation, 1968. Abstracted *DA*, 29: 562A-63A.

 The search for Dowel is both the Dreamer's spiritual
quest and the poet's own "pursuit of wisdom," as he tries

to formulate a concept of goodness which will reconcile man to God without denying the power of evil in human life. The search for Dowel is a search for a means to reconcile various ways to salvation which appear to oppose one another. Dowel is the penitential ideal of patient poverty. As WL develops this idea, the poem reflects his growing conviction that man's suffering of evil is part of a glorious plan.

255. Cassidy, Frederic G. "The Merit of Malkyn." *MLN*, 63 (1948), 52-53.

Cassidy disagrees with Skeat's note to B.I, 182 that Malkyn "was a proverbial name for an unchaste slattern." On the contrary, Malkyn is not a wanton. She is desired by no man and is therefore possessed of maidenhood. Her virtue, however, is negative: she is chaste because she has not been tempted. Negative virtue has no real merit.

256. Cazamian, Louis. *The Development of English Humor*, I. New York: Macmillan, 1930. See pp. 85-88.

257. _____. *Études de Psychologie Litteraire*. Paris: Librairie Payout, 1913.

See pp. 197-224. Concerned with the aspects of fourteenth-century culture portrayed in the works of Chaucer and WL. *PP* "est le fruit âpre sauvage de la pure séve germanique. Il est plain de l'energie inculte de la profondeur morale, de l'aspiration mystique au l'Angleterre reconnait l'autre aspect d´elle même, et l'element le plus national peut-être de son genie."

258. Cejp, Ladislav. "An Interpretation of *Piers the Plowman*." *Philologica*, supplement to *Casopis pro Moderni Filologii*, 7 (1955), 17-29.

A preliminary study of the allegory of *PP*--completed 259, 260, 261. *PP* possesses three kinds of meaning-- literal, symbolical, and allegorical. The literal level is confused and inconsistent and the symbolical level offers no solution to the unity of the poem's meaning. The allegorical level which is composed of a system of allusions to real events, persons, and social situations provides the chief meaning of the narrative and governs the literal and allegorical levels.

259. _____. *An Introduction to the Study of Langland's Piers Plowman: B Text*. *Acta Universitatis Palackianae Olomucensis*, 9. Palackiko Universita V Olomusi, 1956.

In English with summary in Czech. The medieval author
worked with a conceptual system which allowed allegorical
meaning to function not only on the narrative level, but
on the lexical and semantic levels as well. Cejp discusses
the units of the poem's composition: great visions, partial
visions, passus, groups of paragraphs, paragraphs, and
alliterative lines. The poem has a clear formal unity which
is provided by topical allegory. This allegory is expressed
on the semantic level by means of direct and indirect
syllabic anagrams, as well as accoustic and visual allusions.
Cejp lists various examples of anagrams, allusive homonyms,
allusive synonyms, and symbols: for example, B.V, 542-45
contains an allusion to Wat Tyler (Tiller). Wyclif, John
Ball (John Schep), and Chaucer are alluded to in *PP*. Chaucer
is referred to as a "pecoke" (C.XV, 159-185). Imaginitif
appears, at certain points, to be identified as the Pearl-
Poet. John of Gaunt appears, heavily disguised, in Piers's
meeting with Hunger (Wat Tyler and Gaunt).

260. _____. *The Methods of Medieval Allegory and Langland's
Piers the Plowman. Statni Pedagogicke Nakladatelstvi*
(Prague), 5 (1961).

   In Czech with English summary. Repeats the argument of
259 but includes some additional information. WL is more
"radical" than is generally assumed. He and Wyclif are very
much alike: both disapprove of priests in lay occupations
and view the pope as an instigator of corruption. Cejp feels
that Piers is an allegorical representation of Wat Tyler--like
Tyler, Piers was a peasant, a heretic, and an outlaw.

261. _____. "Some General Meanings of Langland's Fundamental Concepts." *Philologica Pragensia*, 2 (1959),
2-22.

   A supplement to Cejp's earlier listings of allegorical
references and allusions in *PP*. Here he lists some definitions of problematic terms in the poem: *e.g.*, according to
Alanus de Insulis, *Petrus, id est, Christus* (B.XV, 206) has
two important meanings. First, "Petrus Ecclesiam figurat:
sicut enim a petra Christo, Petrus dicitur, sic Ecclesia ab
angular lapide Christo nomen interius matuatur, etc." Second,
"Tu es Petrus et super hanc petram aedificabo, etc." Thus,
Christus = petra (angularis)/Petrus = petra.

262. Chadwick, Dorothy. *Social Life in the Days of Piers Plowman*.
Cambridge: Cambridge University Press, 1922.

   Like Wyclif, WL believed that the worldly spirit of the
clergy was a direct result of the Church's massive wealth.
Although WL criticized papal policy, he preserved a fundamental faith in the pope's power to pardon--his attacks are
generally directed against papal agents rather than the pope
himself. WL believed that a reformed clergy might save the

entire nation. The Dreamer serves as the "mouthpiece of a reformer who combined an enquiring spirit with a prudent regard for time-honoured institutions and who dared to record what most men attempted to suppress" (p. 5). WL hearkens back to an earlier time when society and religion were stable. He seems to have drawn a great deal of his material from the drama: his vision of the Harrowing of Hell, for example, owes more to the drama than to the *Gospel of Nicodemus*. He adopted two important themes from miracle and morality plays-- the portrayal of life as a pilgrimage, and as a struggle between the forces of good and evil.

263. Chambers, R. W. "Long Will, Dante, and the Righteous Heathen." *Essays and Studies by Members of the English Association*, 9. Collected by W. P. Ker. Oxford University Press, 1924, pp. 50-69.

WL urgently needed some kind of assurance that the good heathen would be saved. Chambers compares WL to Dante, who, in his discussion of Trajan and Ripheus (*Paradiso* XIX, 19-25, 70-78), attempted to reach a conclusion concerning the salvation of the virtuous pagans. WL struggles with this idea in the B-text and concludes that the virtuous heathen will be saved through the infinite mercy of God. There are three major problems in the search for Dowel: predestination, the salvation of the learned and righteous heathen, and the problem of learning versus simple piety. Both Dante and WL rely on mystical interpretations of baptism.

264. _____. "*Piers Plowman*: A Comparative Study." *Man's Unconquerable Mind: Studies of English Writers from Bede to A. E. Housman and W. P. Ker*. London and Toronto: Jonathan Cape, 1939, pp. 88-171.

PP is the inheritor of not only the Anglo-Saxon poetic meter, but of the ancient Anglo-Saxon heroic traditions, as well. WL is not a proletarian scorning the classes above him: he dislikes the new poor as well as the new rich. He favors the traditional feudal structure and despises the new-moneyed capitalist economy. In the Pardon scene, Piers undergoes a dramatic change in character and becomes an angry preacher of Biblical learning. He is dissatisfied with himself and decides that he must find the way to Dobest. Dowel, Dobet, and Dobest correspond to the active, clerkly, and episcopal lives. They also signify honest labor, contemplative charity, and the righteous rule of the United Church.

265. _____. "Poets and Their Critics: Langland and Milton." *Proceedings of the British Academy*, 27 (1941), 109-44.

Chambers is primarily concerned with the problems of biographical or pseudo-biographical criticism of poetry.

Evaluates the place of WL in literary history: "It is with
William Langland's *Piers Plowman*, not with Chaucer, that the
great revival of English poetry begins" (p. 118). WL and
Milton have some general thematic similarities, although it
is unlikely that Milton read *PP*. WL and Milton share a
"fortitude of patience": both believe that although the
present state of affairs will change, God's goodness remains
constant.

266. Chaytor, H. J. *From Script to Print*. Cambridge: Cambridge
       University Press, 1945.

267. Chessell, Paul. "The Word Made Flesh: The Poetry of Lang-
       land." *Critical Review* (Melbourne, Sidney), 14 (1971),
       109-24.

WL's vivid, "plastic" language is a flexible idiom
which allows him both to state truths and to discover them.
WL's language might best be described as "incarnational"
since it constantly fuses the physical and the spiritual.
In the image of the Plant of Peace, for example, the physical
qualities of the image become spiritual. WL's poetry re-
joices in the Incarnation, while recreating the truth of it
anew. WL's imagery is not merely emblematic: in the Confession of the Seven Deadly Sins, for example, the portraits
are vital and "alive."

268. Chester, Frances Alice. *Piers Plowman's Pilgrimage: A
       Morality Play (from Will Langland's great epic of a
       May morning in the Malvern Hills)*. Music arranged
       and composed by Bridget Muller. London: S. French,
       1925.

269. Clutterbuck, Charlotte. "Hope and Good Works: *Leaute* in the
       C-Text of *Piers Plowman*." *RES*, new series, 28 (1977),
       129-40.

Agrees with P. M. Kean's argument that the primary
meaning of *leaute* is justice (418, 420), but adds that
it also implies the virtue of hope, which, with faith and
charity, connects man to God. The most important aspect of
hope is the good works or *leaute* which spring from it.

270. Coghill, Nevill K. "The Character of Piers Plowman Considered
       from the B-Text." *Medium Aevum*, 2 (1933), 108-35.
       Rptd. *Interpretations of Piers Plowman*, ed. Vasta, 1968,
       pp. 54-86.

Piers was designed to be an emblem or personification of
Dowel, Dobet, and Dobest, successively. Piers's entrances
and the transformations he undergoes are related to the
divisions of the poem. The qualities ascribed to Dowel,
Dobet, and Dobest correspond to Piers's moral qualities.
Piers appears as Dowel in the Pardon scene: he tears the

Pardon because the priest tells him that it is worthless.
Piers does not appear in *Dowel* because the *Visio* exhibits
Dowel allegorically, whereas the *Vita de Dowel* exhibits it
morally. Since he has already demonstrated how to handle
the active world, Piers does not need to appear again. Piers
becomes Dobet (VII, 117-20) and in Passus XIX he becomes
Dobest. Piers and Christ are parallel exemplars of the same
sets of ideas. Includes a diagram plotting the principal
comments on the meaning of the triad from Passus VIII to XIX.

271. _____. "God's Wenches and the Light that Spoke: Some
notes on Langland's kind of Poetry." *English and
Medieval Studies Presented to J. R. R. Tolkien on the
Occasion of his Seventieth Birthday*. Ed. Norman Davis
and C. L. Wrenn. London: George Allen and Unwin, 1962,
pp. 200-18.

WL is not a "tidy allegorist." He habitually fuses
allegory, symbolism, and realism. WL may have known *The
Castle of Love* which contains a parable of a king whose
thrall did amiss, the allegory of the castle with four
crenellated turrets, a narrative of the Redemption, the
Harrowing of Hell, the Resurrection, and the Ascension. He
did not, however, partake of its tedious allegorical detail.
WL's image of the four daughters of God may derive from the
Castle: by transforming the daughters into "wenches," the
poet vitalizes an allegorical image with a "homely natural-
ism." WL frequently concretizes metaphysical concepts. Con-
versely, WL lends transcendence to his image of Christ by
conceiving of him as a voice that speaks in darkness. This
is the "magic" of WL's poetry--the fusion of the divine with
the earthly.

272. _____. "Langland, the 'Naket,' the 'Nauȝty,' and the
Dole." *RES*, original series, 8 (1932), 303-9.

Coghill examines differences in WL's treatment of "poor
relief" in the A- and B-versions. The A-text has: "That
neodi ben, or naket and nouȝt haue to spend" (VII, 212).
The B-text has "That nedy ben, and nauȝty helpe hem with
thi godis" (VI, 226). This change does not indicate that
the poor should not be given the "dole." Rather, B sees these
poor as being "worthless and vile." His attitude represents
a mixture of kindness and reprobation.

273. _____. *Langland: Piers Plowman*. New York: Longmans
Green and Co., 1964.

A brief summary of the poem's argument and a review of
the authorship debate. Coghill recapitulates his earlier
conclusions. Compares WL with Samuel Beckett, noting similarities between *PP* and *Waiting for Godot*.

274.   . "The Pardon of Piers Plowman." Gollancz
             Memorial Lecture. *Proceedings of the British Academy*,
             30 (1944), 303-57. Rptd. *Style and Symbolism in Piers
             Plowman*, ed. Blanch, 1969, pp. 40-86 (Abridged).

     The A- and B-texts belong to different species of poetry.
The narrative of the A-text is fairly clear and straight-
forward until the Pardon scene when the allegory collapses.
The A-text raises questions which the B-text attempts to
answer: in B, WL makes several kinds of additions: those
which elaborate or enforce some aspect of Christian morality;
"foretastes" or insertions into the early part of the poem
which are elaborated later; those which depict the supernatural things of eternal glory. The theme of the B-text
is salvation, and its allegorical emphasis is anagogical
not tropological. Coghill also discusses the four senses
of allegory and illustrates the significance of Piers
according to this method.

275.   . "The Sexcentary of Langland." *London Mercury*,
             26 (May 1932), 40-51.

     A general discussion of the place of *PP* in literary
history, commemorating WL's sixth-hundredth birthday. Discusses the unity of the poem, and argues that it is well-
constructed. See 274.

276.   . "Two Notes on *Piers Plowman*: I. The Abbot of
             Abingdon and the date of the C-text and II. Chaucer's
             Debt to Langland." *Medium Aevum*, 4 (1935), 83-94.

     The first note concerns a mention of the Abbot of
Abingdon in B.X, 317-330 which may corroborate Skeat's dating
of the C-text to c. 1393-1394. The Abbot is not a specific
individual; rather, WL used the Abbot of Abingdon to signify any ill-governing abbot. When trouble broke out in
1394, WL, not wishing to become involved in a controversy,
omitted the reference from the C-text. The second note
concerns the similarity between WL's and Chaucer's descriptions of monks (B.X, 291-299, and General Prologue, *Canterbury
Tales*, 178-179: and B.X, 306-309 and General Prologue, 166,
190, 207). Chaucer pretends to describe a real person who
is actually compounded from allegorical elements, whereas WL
is more openly allegorical.

277. Coleman, Janet. "Sublimes et Litterati: The Audience for the
             Themes of Grace, Justification, and Predestination,
             Traced From the Disputes of 14th century *Moderni* to the
             Vernacular *Piers Plowman*." Yale University dissertation,
             1971. Abstracted *DAI*, 32: 382A.

278. College, Eric. "Aliri." *Medium Aevum*, 27 (1958), 111-13.

The word "aliri" refers to a beggar's trick of pretending to have a crippled or amputated leg. College notes that this deception is also depicted in Hieronymous Bosch's "The Temptation of St. Anthony." "Aliri" may survive today in a child's game. See 231, 327, 398.

279. _____ and W. O. Evans. *"Piers Plowman."* *Month*, 32 (1964), 304-13.

A general essay discussing WL's life, the authorship controversy, and the action of the poem. The primary concern of *PP* is the salvation of all mankind. The three lives are degrees of love and charity. Learning charity is the Dreamer's major aim.

280. Connolly, Terence L. *An Introduction to Chaucer and Langland: A Corrective to Long's History of English Literature*. New York: [?], 1925.

A general examination of fourteenth-century society, designed to correct "unsubstantiated" statements made by William J. Long (*English Literature: Its History and Its Significance for the Life of the English-Speaking World*. Boston: Ginn and Company, 1909. pp. 81-83 deal with WL). Chapter V, pp. 83-93 treats WL. WL was not a Wycliffite and precursor of the Protestant Reformation: his faith in the fundamental beliefs of the Catholic Church are never in question.

281. Cornelius, Roberta D. "The Figurative Castle: A Study in the Medieval Allegory of the Edifice with Especial Reference to Religious Writings." Unpublished Bryn Mawr College dissertation, 1930.

282. _____. *"Piers Plowman* and the *Roman de Fauvel."* *PMLA*, 47 (1932), 363-67.

Cornelius examines the similarities between *PP* and Gervais de Bus's *Le Roman de Fauvel* (Part I--c. 1310, Part II--c. 1314). Part II of *Fauvel* closely parallels the Lady Meed scene of *PP*. In both, an unworthy character attempts to wed a woman who is much above him, a long journey is made by the hero and his followers for the sake of the prospective wedding, and the wedding does not occur. *PP*'s Meed and *Fauvel*'s Fortune possess a similar dual nature.

283. Coulton, G. G. *Chaucer and His England*. London: Methuen, 1908. See pp. 10-11.

284. _____. "The Peasant Saint." *Medieval Panorama: The English Scene from Conquest to Reformation*. Cambridge: Cambridge University Press, 1939. Chapter XLI, pp. 534-54.

Coulton compares WL to Chaucer. For Chaucer, "the world was Vanity Fair in Thackeray's sense . . . to Langland, it was Vanity Fair in Bunyan's sense--a place of continual struggle and real danger" (p. 539). Coulton disagrees with Christopher Dawson's belief that PP ends in despair (294). WL refuses to feel defeat: he has a profound faith and his vision is ultimately hopeful. WL is not a "Roman Catholic poet": he represents the Englishman who was slowly disconnecting himself from Rome. WL is a "peasant saint," a common man asking the most important of all questions--what must man do to save his soul? He has very little in common with the schoolmen.

285. Courthope, W. J. "Langland." *A History of English Poetry*. New York: Macmillan, 1895. Vol. I, Chapter VI, pp. 200-46.

PP is the most vigorous projection of the conscience of the English people. WL respected the feudal system and saw simony and corruption in ecclesiastical orders as the major cause of social problems. PP is compared to the *Divine Comedy* in terms of theme and scope: Dante was "metaphysical" whereas WL was "ethical and practical." There is no poetical unity in the design of the poem beyond the unifying character of the Dreamer. The structure and theme of the poem were derived from the sermon arts.

286. Crewe, J. V. "Langland's Vision of Society in *Piers Ploughman*." *Theoria*, 39 (1973), 1-16.

Crewe believes that the central theme of PP is the use of money and the distribution of worldly goods. WL focuses on the problems of the temporal order coexisting with the eternal order--a paradox established in the Incarnation. Holy Church is the source of all good, while Meed is the source of all evil. Crewe also notes that in PP "representative scenes from medieval life pass almost pictorially by, but in each case, it is not the surface that concerns Langland, but the underlying mechanism" (p. 10).

287. Curran, Sonia T. "The Dreamer and his Visions: Rhetorical Determinants of Structure in *Piers Plowman*, B." University of Wisconsin, Madison, dissertation, 1973. Abstracted *DAI*, 34: 3339A.

WL did not have a simple, "tidy" narrative structure in mind, but rather two successive structures, corresponding to two stages of development within the Dreamer. WL uses two groups of rhetorical devices in order to allow the reader to participate in the evolution of the Dreamer's consciousness. In the first five visions, the Dreamer is a passive observer: in the second five, he becomes a participant in the action.

288. Curtius, Ernst Robert. *European Literature and the Latin Middle Ages*. Trans. Willard R. Trask. Bollingen Series, 36. New York: Pantheon, 1953.

289. D'Ardenne, S. T. R. O. "Me bi-fel a ferly, A Feyrie me þoughte. (PPL. A. Prol. 6)." *English Studies Presented to R. W. Zandvoort on the Occasion of his Seventieth Birthday*. Supplement to *English Studies*, 45 (1964). Amsterdam: Swets and Zeitlinger, 1964, pp. 143-45.

Skeat's Vernon MS reading of A. Prologue, 6 is incorrect. The proper reading is "Me bifel aferly, of fairie me þoughte." The word "fairie" means enchantment, not "due to fairy contrivance." D'Ardenne translates the line: "A marvel befell me, from Faerie it seemed to me."

290. Davlin, Sister Mary Clemente. "*Kynde Knowyng* as a Major Theme in *Piers Plowman* B." *RES*, new series, 22 (1971), 1-19.

Davlin contends that Will's quest for "kynde knowing" does not end with Anima's suggestion that he needs to learn to love--the quest continues in a different form. Will has exhausted his search for wisdom through theory--he recovers his initial desire to know God as love and begins to search for Him through love and suffering. Before the end of the poem, Will and the reader come to understand that each man's salvation is part of the process of "kynde knowing" which is the goal of life: *i.e.*, the quest for meaning and knowledge. In the *Visio*, "kynde knowing" is presented as a divine reality congruent with natural creation. It is more than knowledge--it is also love. *PP* is, in a sense, a *Bildungsroman*. Its major aim is the education of the hero. Its structure is experiential, not logical. Langland planned the false starts, ironic mistakes, and narrative incongruities so that we experience the acquisition of knowledge along with Will.

291. _____. "*Petrus, id est, Christus*: Piers the Plowman as 'The Whole Christ.'" *Chaucer Review*, 6 (1972), 280-92.

WL does not equate Piers with Christ: Piers represents the Christ-like element in human nature. WL's central purpose was to provide Will with experiential knowledge of the most profound Christian beliefs (the Trinity, the Incarnation, and the Whole Christ) and he manages this through symbolism. Piers functions as a fluid and variable symbol for the Whole Christ. Within this designation, Piers can signify the individual soul, the Christian Church, Peter the Apostle, and the later popes. In the last few passus, Piers clearly exhibits the qualities of the Whole Christ' but he remains a man--for men have been incorporated into Christ as a result of the Incarnation.

292. _____. "'Treuthe' in *Piers Plowman*: A Study in
Style and Sensibility." University of California,
Berkeley, dissertation, 1964. Abstracted *DA*, 25:
1905.

WL's approach to God is "affirmative": he emphasizes
God's goodness and nearness. He renders this in an objective,
romantic tone, using a style which might be termed "incarnational." Knowledge is an important theme in *PP*: *i.e.*,
"Kynde knowing" which represents the acquisition of experiential knowledge "in herte."

293. Dawson, Christopher. *Medieval Essays*. London: Sheed and
Ward, 1953. See Chapter XII, "*The Vision of Piers
Plowman*," pp. 239-71.

294. _____. "*The Vision of Piers Plowman*," *Medieval
Religion (The Forwood Lectures for 1934)*. London:
Sheed and Ward, 1934, pp. 155-95.

Fourteenth-century England experienced a breakdown of
the universal theocratic order of Christendom and an increase
of political nationalism and religious division: simul-
taneously, the old agrarian feudal society gave way to
capitalism and urban industrialism. Chaucer's work represents England's incorporation of continental culture, but
PP is a voice from another world--the "submerged world of
the common English." WL owes nothing to the courtly tradition. He is the inheritor of the grave Christian poetry
of the Anglo-Saxons, and his is the voice of the common poor.
PP concludes on a note of defeat and despair.

295. Day, Mabel. "'Din' and 'Doom' and *Piers Plowman*, A, II,
183." *MLR*, 26 (1931), 336-38.

Day had earlier suggested a change in the line "Dreede
at the dore stood and the dune herde" (A.II, 183). See 23.
Here she substantiates her view. The reading "dune," referring to the punitive expedition consequent to the king's
orders, is inadequate. Day believes that "doom" provides
a better picture of Dread skulking at the door, waiting to
hear of the doom without being noticed.

296. _____. "Duns Scotus and *Piers Plowman*." *RES*,
original series, 3 (1927), 333-34.

The Vision of the Tree of Charity in B.XVI is an
imitation of the famous simile of the tree in Duns Scotus's
De Rerum Principio, Art. IV, 3. Piers's use of the three
piles recalls the teaching of Duns Scotus who disagreed
with Aquinas in maintaining the primacy of the will above
the intellect.

77

297. _____. "'Mele Tyme of Seintes,' *Piers Plowman*, B,V,
     500." *MLR*, 27 (1932), 317-18.

     Day examines the lines: "Aboute mydday whan most liȝte
is, and mele tyme of seintes;/ Feddest with thi fresche blode
owre forfadres in derknesse." The souls referred to have
passed through purgatory and while awaiting their call to
heaven are fed once a day by a light which comes from
heaven. The time should be the ninth hour: the poet has
"mydday" because in the Middle Ages, the meaning of "noon"
changed from "ninth hour" to mid-day generally. This passage may have its source in the *Gospel of Nicodemus*.

298. _____. "*Piers Plowman* and Poor Relief." *RES*,
     original series, 8 (1932), 445-46.

     Day examines the changes in the poet's attitude towards
the economic subsidy of the poor in the B and C texts, concluding that although C appears to disapprove more strongly
of indiscriminate charity, this alone does not constitute
proof of multiple authorship.

299. Deanesley, Margaret. *The Lollard Bible and Other Medieval
     Biblical Versions*. Cambridge: Cambridge University
     Press, 1920.

300. _____. "Vernacular Books in England in the Fourteenth
     and Fifteenth Centuries." *MLR*, 15 (1920), 349-58.

301. Delany, Sheila. "Substructure and Superstructure: The
     Politics of Allegory in the Fourteenth Century."
     Science and Society, 38 (1974), 257-80.

     The transition from feudalism to capitalism in the
late Middle Ages accounts for dramatic changes in the nature
of allegory. In the late fourteenth century, there is a
general movement away from traditional allegorical forms.
Chaucer, Dante, and Langland, for example, move towards
realism. The older allegorical forms and the anagogical
patterns of thought served as "an important ideological
weapon in the arsenal of the feudal ruling class" (p. 268).
The new literary modes express a new social reality.

302. Demedis, Pandelis. "*Piers Plowman*, Prologue B, 196."
     Explicator, 33, iii (1974), Item 27.

     The usual reading of the lines "For better is a litel
losse þan a longe sorwe/þe mase amonge us all, þouȝ we mysse
a schrewe" in the fable of the belling of the cat does not
take into consideration the proper meaning of "mase." This
term probably refers to a group of personal bodyguards who
carried maces. By WL's time, the word came to symbolize
authority. Demedis reads the lines, "For better is a little

loss than a long sorrow/ Better the mace among us all, though
we miss a schrew mouse."

303. Devlin, Sister Mary Aquinas. "Bishop Thomas Brunton and his
Sermons." *Speculum*, 14 (1939), 324-44.

Devlin attempts to reconstruct the career of Thomas
Brunton (Brinton), Bishop of Rochester. One of Brunton's
sermons is almost certainly the immediate source of WL's
episode of the rat-parliament. Brunton (d. 1389) par-
ticipated in the 1382 Council at Blackfriars where Wyclif's
conclusions were officially condemned. Devlin notes that
"many of the evils satirized in *Piers Plowman* Bishop Brunton
has attacked in his sermons, which might be called a
homiletic commentary on this great medieval poem" (p. 341).

304. _____. "The Chronology of Bishop Brunton's Sermons."
PMLA, 51 (1936), 300-302.

Devlin provides a list of emendations to Eleanor
Kellogg's chronology of the sermons of Bishop Brunton (425).
Devlin bases her conclusions on allusions to contemporary
events in the sermons.

305. _____, ed. *The Sermons of Thomas Brinton, Bishop of
Rochester (1373-1389)*. Camden, Third Series, vols.
85 and 86. London: Royal Historical Society, 1954.

306. D'Israeli, Isaac. *Amenities of Literature*. Vol. I, New
York: J. & H. G. Langley, 1841.

307. Di Pasquale, Pasquale, Jr. "The Form of *Piers Plowman* and
the Liturgy." University of Pittsburgh dissertation,
1965. Abstracted *DA*, 26: 4626.

The cycle of the ecclesiastical year as found in the
Sarum Missal forms the central structure of *PP*. *PP* is a
satire: even Will is satirized for his falling asleep on
Easter day. Will is a symbol of the Christian in error,
whereas Piers represents the ideal Christian. *PP* has nothing
in common with mystical writings.

308. Dobson, R. B. and J. Taylor. *Rymes of Robyn Hood: An
Introduction to the English Outlaw*. Pittsburgh, Pa.:
University of Pittsburgh Press, 1976.

WL's reference to the "Rymes" in Sloth's confession is
the first mention of Robin Hood. Dobson and Taylor provide
background information on the possible identity of the "erle
of Chestre."

309. Donaldson, E. Talbot. "The Grammar of Book's Speech in
Piers Plowman." *Studies in Language and Literature
in Honour of Margaret Schlauch*. Ed. Mieczyslaw

Brahmer *et al.* Warszawa: Panstowe Wydawnictwo Naukowe, 1966, pp. 103-109. Rptd. *Style and Symbolism in Piers Plowman*, ed. Blanch, 1969, pp. 264-70.

Disagrees with the readings of R. E. Kaske (416) and Richard Hoffman (386) of the problematic speech of Book (B.XVIII, 252-257). Donaldson reviews the major syntactical problems which have given rise to misinterpretations. Once the negative conclusion "unless Jesus rise" has been stated, the rest of Jesus's actions become, in Book's mind, inevitable. He expresses this by recourse to the infinitive.

310. _____. "Patristic Exegesis in the Criticism of Medieval Literature: The Opposition." *Critical Approaches to Medieval Literature: Selected Papers From the English Institute, 1958-1959*, ed. Dorothy Bethurum. New York: Columbia University Press, 1960, pp. 1-26.

Donaldson generally opposes the use of patristic exegesis in literary criticism: "The patristic influence on Middle English poetry seems to me to consist in providing occasional symbols which, by their rich tradition, enhance the poetic contexts they appear in; but which are called into use naturally by those contexts and are given fresh meaning by them" (p. 2). Donaldson criticizes B. F. Huppé's and D. W. Robertson's *Piers Plowman and Scriptural Tradition* (528), maintaining that the symbols discussed therein are frequently the critics', not the poet's. Donaldson admits to the spiritual affiliations of the plowman image in *PP*, but denies that the equation of plowman with prelate is valid. Huppé and Robertson disregard the *littera* of the poem.

311. _____. *Piers Plowman. The C-Text and Its Poet*. New Haven and London: Yale University Press, 1949. Rptd. with a new preface, 1966.

Donaldson argues in behalf of single authorship and contends that the C-poet did not spoil the B-text. The C-poet performed four major types of revisions: 1. line by line revisions--a close reworking of B material, as in Passus I-V, IX-X; 2. new material and transpositions of B material, as in Passus VI-VIII; 3. plain omissions, such as the Pardon scene; 4. extensions and additions which do not alter the framework of the poem. The C-Reviser is generally more concerned with idea than with form, and he emphasizes the moral and theological implications of his narrative. He is thus more universal and less topical in his considerations. The C-poet's interest in the active life virtually ends with the *Visio*. The *Vita* takes up various stages of the contemplative life, centering on patience (Dowel) and charity (Dobet). C did not pervert the B-text, but rather developed lines of thought latent in

B.   Includes a summary of C-text studies, pp. 1-17; Appendix
A provides a listing of all *PP* MSS.

312.   Donna, Sister Rose Bernard. *Despair and Hope: A Study of
          Langland and Augustine*. Published Catholic University
          of America dissertation. Washington: Catholic Univer-
          sity of America Press, 1948.

          WL's subject matter coincides with Augustine's teaching,
particularly regarding the possibility of salvation. WL's
conception of the two opposing passions, hope and despair,
is theological and depends upon the concept of free will.
Wanhope must be consciously avoided: men may find hope in
the goodness of God, His grace, and His sacraments. Both
WL and Augustine employ the Platonic analogy of the body
and soul to rider and horse. *PP* does not end in despair:
it warns against despair and demonstrates that salvation
is possible.

313.   Döring, G. *Die Personennamen in Langlands Piers the Plough-
          man*. Published University of Leipzig dissertation,
          1922.

314.   Dunning, T. P. "Action and Contemplation in *Piers Plowman*."
          Piers Plowman: Critical Approaches, ed. Hussey,
          1969, pp. 213-25.

          Dunning examines the meaning of Dowel, Dobet, and Dobest
in the context of late fourteenth- and early fifteenth-century writings on Christian perfection. In an earlier article
(317), Dunning contended that the progress of the soul is
mirrored in the triad, while the *Visio* is mainly concerned
with the "animalis homo." According to contemporary theological thought, the active life, which consists in doing
good, and the contemplative life, which is essentially
meditative, must be combined in the individual Christian:
doing well, better, and best are not related to states or
ways. "By the exercise of Faith, Hope, and Charity, by
meditation of the life of Christ, especially on his passion . . . we do well and are on the way to doing better.
By making use of the means of holiness, of union with Him,
Christ has provided in the Church, we can even do best"
(p. 224).

315.   _____. "Langland and the Salvation of the Heathen."
          Medium Aevum, 12 (1943), 45-54.

          Dunning disagrees with critics who believe that WL's
attitude concerning the salvation of the heathen opposed
the teachings of the Church (see, for example, 263). WL's
treatment of this issue in Passus XI and XII of the B-text
is actually quite orthodox. These passus may have been
written to clarify the treatment of the salvation of the
heathen in the A-text. Although the Church feels that

baptism is the *sine qua non* of salvation, the Fathers believed that God wills the salvation of all men and that no adult is damned except through a fault of his own. Medieval theologians attempted to systematically explain the process of the salvation of the heathen by the existence of immediate divine inspiration in favor of the infidel of good will. Dunning discusses the positions of St. Basil, St. John Chrysostom, Dionysius the Areopagite, St. Thomas, and Duns Scotus. WL's source for the Trajan episode is probably the *Legenda Aurea*.

316. _____. *Piers Plowman: An Interpretation of the A-Text*. Dublin: Talbot Press, 1937.

The *Visio* and *Vita* of the A-text are complete and separate poems. The basic theme of the *Visio* is cupidity and the use of worldly goods. It is divided into four well-defined sections: the statement of the theme (Prologue and Passus I), the story of Lady Meed (Passus II-IV), the Vision of Repentance and Piers (Passus V-VII), and an Epilogue (Passus VIII). WL is not primarily a satirist. His subject is not the sanctification of the individual but the salvation of society. Most of the *Visio* is composed of allegorical expositions of the major ideas set forth in the Prologue and Passus I. In Passus I, cupidity is discussed in the abstract--in Passus II, she appears in the flesh. The third division of the *Visio*, the vision of Repentance and Piers, is an allegorical exposition of part two of Passus I where Holy Church gives prescriptions for the good and truthful man. Passus VI and VII elaborate on Holy Church's emphasis on fraternal charity. In the Pardon scene, Piers realizes that he has forgotten his true duties--all his labor is vanity if he does not look to the good of his soul. The *Vita* is not a continuation of the *Visio*. The *Visio*'s conclusions are not developed further, but are rather reiterated under a different aspect. The definitions of Dowel mean little in themselves. They serve as aids in the Dreamer's efforts to understand. Will finally realizes that to do well is to be a humble and patient laborer for God.

317. _____. "The Structure of the B-text of *Piers Plowman*." *RES*, new series, 7 (1956), 225-37. Rptd. *Style and Symbolism in Piers Plowman*, ed. Blanch, 1969, pp. 87-100.

The organizing factors of the B-text are the concepts of the Active, Contemplative, and Mixed lives. After examining contemporary religious thought (in the *Compendium Theological Veritatis*, the *Summa Confessorum*, and the *Occulus Sacerdotis*), Dunning discusses the way in which the concept of the three lives unifies the poem. The progress of the soul is mirrored in *Dowel*, *Dobet*, and *Dobest*, while the *Visio* focuses on the "animalis homo." The *Visio* stops short of the pilgrimage because man cannot be reformed on a social or corporate basis.

At the conclusion of the poem, the poet goes out into the
world to seek the true pope who will initiate genuine reform
--*i.e.*, the Piers of *Dobest*.

318. Durkin, J. T. "Kingship in the Vision of *Piers Plowman*."
         Thought, 14 (1939), 413-21.

      The proper role of the king is an important theme in the
Visio, particularly in the Meed scene. As Christ's representative in temporal affairs, the king must rule with love,
according to reason. The greatest problems of government
are moral. The king must exercise justice and mercy and
the people must obey the laws of the state. Durkin notes
the similarity between WL's point of view and that of the
mouse in the fable of the belling of the cat.

319. Eberhard, Oscar. *Der Baumaufstand vom Jahre 1381, in der
         englischen Poesie. Anglistische Forschungen*, 51 (1917).

      Eberhard evaluates WL's social criticism and the objects
of his satire in terms of late medieval social history. Discusses WL's relationship to peasant movements and the
Peasants' Revolt. Compares WL with Gower.

320. Eliason, Mary. "The Peasant and the Lawyer." *SP*, 48 (1951),
         506-26.

      An examination of the treatment of the peasant and the
lawyer in *PP* and the *Canterbury Tales*. WL and Chaucer are
contemporaries living on the verge of prosperous enterprise
and greater social equality. In *PP*, the peasants view the
lawyer as a symbol of a future equality which they might
attain. Chaucer's Man of Laws has risen above his peasant
background, but in his tale hearkens back to it.

321. Elliott, R. W. V. "The Langland Country." *Piers Plowman:
         Critical Approaches*, ed. Hussey, 1969, pp. 226-44.

      Elliott examines the terrain of *PP*, comparing it to the
terrains of other medieval dream visions. In *PP*, there is
no attempt to integrate landscapes into the texture of the
poem as there is in *Sir Gawain and the Green Knight*. The
Dreamer's journey and the terrain which he traverses,
however, express some of the bewilderment and confusion that
he experiences. The dreams in *PP* are highly realistic,
closer to the theories of Freud and Jung than to those of
Macrobius. WL's descriptive language is firmly rooted in
English topography. His topographical vocabulary may be
divided into two groups: first, common, simple, topographical terms, and second, specific words denoting fields,
forests, and woodlands. WL's diction is plain because his
intention is to depict a universal terrain rather than any
particular locale.

322. Elliot, Thomas L. "Complaint as a Middle English Genre:
     A Survey of the Tradition Culminating in the School
     of *Piers Plowman*." University of Michigan dissertation,
     1971. Abstracted *DAI*, 31: 4116A.

323. _____. "Middle English Complaints Against the Times:
     To Contemn the World or to Reform It?" *AnM*, 14
     (1973), 22-34.

     Satire and complaint are not identical. The complaint
     is a distinct literary type which appears in ME in two
     peculiar manifestations: the "short" songs and the larger
     narrative poems such as *PP*. Complaint was the primary mode
     of satiric expression in late Medieval England, especially
     in the North and West Midlands. *PP* is too complex to be
     called a complaint, but it has much in common with the
     shorter social complaint poems such as *Wynnere and Wastour*
     (c. 1353), *Parlement of the Thre Ages* (c. 1375-1400), *Pierce
     the Ploughman's Crede* (c. 1395), *Mum and the Sothsegger*
     (c. 1399-1405). These poems deal with certain recurrent
     themes such as kingship, the economy, and the church. Near
     the end of the fourteenth century there is a tendency away
     from the condemnation of society and a greater emphasis is
     placed on active reform.

324. Erzgräber, Willi. *William Langlands Piers Plowman (Eine
     Interpretation des C-Textes)*. Frankfürter Arbeiten
     aus dem Gebiete der Anglistik und der Amerika-Studien,
     Heft 3, Heidelberg, 1957.

     Erzgräber relates the ideas of the C-text to the theo-
     logical movements of the thirteenth and fourteenth centuries.
     He notes an apparent connection between WL's discussion of
     Liberum Arbitrium and the pseudo-Augustinian treatise,
     Spiritu et Anima, and discusses the similarities of WL's
     thought with Aquinas, Duns Scotus, and Augustine. The
     character of Conscience combines the two scholastic terms
     conscientia and *synderesis*. In the Meed scene, we have the
     king (practical intellect) under the influence of Reason
     (practical reason) and Conscience (synderesis and con-
     science). Includes a general appraisal of WL's relation
     to the main intellectual currents of the Middle Ages.

325. _____. "William Langlands *Piers Plowman* in Lichte
     der mittelalterlichen Philosophie und Theologie."
     Anglia, 73 (1955), 127-48.

326. Evans, W. O. "Charity in *Piers Plowman*." *Piers Plowman:
     Critical Approaches*, ed. Hussey, 1969, pp. 245-78.

     Dowel, Dobet, and Dobest represent degrees of excellence
     in the individual's ability to love God and man. Dowel is
     associated with passiveness: *i.e.* loving God by avoiding
     sin. Dobet implies concern for other men and Dobest is

concerned with active militancy in saving other men's souls.
Dowel and Dobet are stages on the road to Dobest, but they
can only be achieved by aiming at Dobest. WL had little
interest in formal religion—it is of secondary importance
as compared with the practice of charity. WL believed
strongly in universal brotherhood and felt that men who
do not love one another are unnatural. He also believed
that the pattern of life in heaven is reflected in life on
earth: "cortayse," for example, is analogous to grace.
WL recognized God as the source of love and charity, but
was troubled by the possibility that a charitable God might
torture some souls in eternal damnation.

327. Fairchild, Hoxie Neale. "'Leyde Here Legges Aliri.'" *MLN*,
     41 (1926), 378-81.

      "Aliri" refers to the practice of feigning an amputated
or crippled leg by taping or strapping it back against the
thigh. This deception was a common trick of beggars. See
Brett (231) and College (278).

328. Faris, David E. "Symbolic Geography in Middle English
     Literature: *Pearl, Piers Plowman, Yvain and Gawain*."
     Yale University dissertation, 1974. Abstracted *DAI*,
     34: 7228A.

      Faris evaluates the interaction between the hero and
the landscape in ME narrative. Usually, the landscape of
personification allegory presents overtly symbolic images:
WL, however, seems to have distrusted this use of metaphor
since allegorical landscape is especially sparse in *PP*.

329. Fisher, A. W. "A Note on *Piers the Plowman*." *MLN*, 23
     (1908), 231.

      Examines B.V, 28-9: "Thomme Stowue he tauȝte to take
two staues,/ And fecche Felice home fro the wyuen pyne."
Tom went to fetch his wife Felice, knowing that this venture
was bound to fail. He also knew that he could rely on her
disposition to aid in her rescue. Accordingly, he went with
two staves.

330. Fisher, John. "Wyclif, Langland, Gower, and the 'Pearl'
     Poet on the Subject of the Aristocracy." *Studies in
     Medieval Literature in Honor of Professor A. C. Baugh*,
     ed. MacEdward Leach. Philadelphia: University of
     Pennsylvania Press, 1961, pp. 139-57.

      Wyclif used the aristocracy to support his political
argument that the clergy must render obedience to temporal
lords. WL used the aristocracy to introduce an economic
discussion on the proper distribution of wealth. WL always
places the king above the entire society and he envisions
the knights as part of the "commune," whereas Wyclif places

the king and the knights together as part of a governing political system. WL does not appear very interested in legal reform and is more concerned with *spiritus iustice*.

331. Flom, George T. "A Note on *Piers Plowman*." *MLN*, 23 (1908), 156-67.

Examines the problematic line: "For hadde ȝe ratones ȝoure reed ȝe couthe not ruelie ȝow-selue" (C.I, 215). C. T. Onions had suggested (489) that *reik* was a better reading than *reed*. Flom believes that *reed* provides the only acceptable sense.

332. Flood, David. "Poverty in the Middle Ages." *Collectanea Franciscana*, 43 (1973), 409-15.

333. Fowler, David C. "The 'Forgotten' Pilgrimage in *Piers the Plowman*." *MLN*, 67 (1952), 524-26.

WL did not forget the pilgrimage to Truth proposed in Passus VII of the A-text. In the opening lines of Passus VIII we are told that Truth heard of the impending famine and sent the Pardon so that Piers could remain and plow for the common good.

334. _____. "*Piers Plowman*." *Recent Middle English Scholarship and Criticism: Survey and Desiderata*. Ed. J. Burke Severs. Pittsburgh, Pa.: Duquesne University Press, 1971, pp. 9-27.

A brief survey of major trends in *PP* scholarship since 1940, especially the recent emphasis on patristic exegesis. Fowler recapitulates his theory that the A-text was not composed by the poet of B and C (See 27). Suggests that future studies examine the poem "in its immediate historical context."

335. _____. *Piers the Plowman: Literary Relations of the A and B Texts*. Seattle: University of Washington Press, 1961.

The B-poet softens A's condemnation of the rich, distinguishes between poverty as an economic condition and patient poverty as a spiritual condition, affirms the value of learning, and condemns ignorant and covetous priests. In Passus XII, the B-poet reexamines the A-*Vita*, correcting what he considered misleading or erroneous statements: for example, Imaginitif convinces the Dreamer that learning does have value. In both A and B, Piers serves as the ideal representative of the humble poor, but in B he becomes "patient poverty personified." In the B-continuation, charity, rather than truth, is the object of Will's quest. In Passus XVI to XVIII the B-poet presents a Biblical-Historical pageant similar to those of the cycle plays. The

pageant culminates in the Harrowing of Hell scene in Passus
XVIII when Truth and Love and Righteousness and Peace come
together, representing the resolution of the paradox of
justice and mercy through the Redemption. In *Dobest*, Piers
becomes Peter, the priesthood of Holy Church. At the conclusion of the poem, the Dreamer is ready to enter the Barn
of Unity, and is prepared to trust in the wisdom of God.
The B-poet may have been a ranking member of the secular
clergy: unlike A, B has a genuine respect for the clergy
and a desire to see them assume their proper role in society.
It is apparent that the A-text and the B-text were not composed by the same poet. The B-poet may have been John of
Trevisa (See 27).

336. Frank, Robert Worth, Jr. "The Art of Reading Medieval Personification Allegory." *ELH*, 20 (1953), 237-50. Rptd.
Interpretations of Piers Plowman, ed. Vasta, 1968,
pp. 217-31.

There are basically two kinds of allegory: Dante's
type, "symbolic allegory," in which characters and details
are presented in concrete form and thus have both literal
and figurative value, and Langland's type, "personification
allegory," which uses abstractions as though they were concrete substances. This second type is closer to the literal
level than is symbolic allegory. Frank emphasizes our
failure to read personification allegory properly when we
treat the characters as symbols. Symbolic allegory involves
two interpretations--first, what the symbols mean, and
second, what are their relationships to one another, whereas
in personification allegory, the first interpretation is
unnecessary. Disagreeing with C. S. Lewis (445), Frank
contends that characters in personification allegory need
not be abstractions, nor are they necessarily personifications
of the inner life.

337. _____. "The Conclusion of *Piers Plowman*." *JEGP*, 49
(1950), 309-16.

Frank contends that the conclusion of *PP* is not apocalyptic, and that the coming of Antichrist does not signify the
arrival of Judgement Day. Antichrist represents the Pope,
and the friars are the instrument of his wicked purpose. By
depriving men of the true sacraments, they eliminate the
means to salvation. The end of the poem portrays an actual
ecclesiastical crisis with the friars threatening to destroy
the unity of Holy Church.

338. _____. "The Number of Visions in *Piers Plowman*."
MLN, 66 (1951), 309-12.

Skeat miscalculated the number of visions in the three
versions of *PP* by counting some inner dreams twice and by

missing others. There are three visions in the A-text,
ten in the B-text, and nine in the C-text.

339. _____. "The Pardon Scene in *Piers Plowman*." *Speculum*,
26 (1951), 317-31.

The pardon must be valid or the whole vision is a
tasteless joke. Since the pardon comes from Truth (God),
its truth is indisputable. But the fact that it was omitted
from the C-text suggests that it was not crucial to the
meaning of the poem or that WL realized that it was enigmatic. WL intended the tearing of the pardon to signify Piers's
rejection of indulgences and his acceptance of the command
to do well. The *Vita* is not another attempt to find truth
(for this has been found in the pardon). The *Vita* deals
with the problem of salvation. Piers does not reject the
Active Life for the Contemplative Life.

340. _____. *Piers Plowman and the Scheme of Salvation: An
Interpretation of Dowel, Dobet, and Dobest*. New Haven:
Yale University Press, 1957.

Dowel, Dobet, and Dobest do not represent the Active,
Contemplative, and Mixed lives but describe a single way of
life for all men. The entire poem is a reply to the question
the Dreamer asks Holy Church in the first vision. The answer
has two parts--the *Visio* and the *Vita*. The *Visio* examines
doing well from various perspectives, while the *Vita* characterizes the difficulties of doing well. WL believed that
the reform of society will come through a human agent, but
also recognized that God has a plan for man's salvation.
Each person of the Trinity makes a specific contribution in
the scheme of salvation, and these are epitomized in the
Dowel triad. God the Father is represented by Dowel, God
the Son, by Dobet, and the Holy Ghost, by Dobest. In the
Vita, Will learns how salvation will occur. In *Dowel*, Will
is shown the role of wit and learning in the scheme of salvation. In *Dobest*, WL depicts the age of Christ. The
assistance of Christ gives man greater ability to put into
action what was discussed in *Dowel*. *Dobet* is a vision of
what has already occurred in the redemption. *Dobest* depicts
the state of the contemporary world. This section is based
doctrinally on the gifts of the Holy Ghost by which the
scheme of salvation was completed and made available to man.
This is the world of the *Visio* again, but the dreamer has
learned, and he now sees it with different eyes. The fair
field is a battleground for souls, and the society is not
living by the all-important law of *redde quo debbes*. The
conclusion of the poem is not apocalyptic: the drama of
salvation continues as long as mankind exists and as long
as there is a Piers Plowman--the divine goodness inherent
in man.

341. Fries, Maureen. "Images of Women in Middle English Literature." *CE*, 35 (1974), 851-52.

Notes that Lady Meed is an archetype of the darker side of femininity, related to the Whore of Babylon. Discusses various aspects of the stereotyping of women in Middle English literature.

342. Fuller, Anne Havens. "Scripture in *Piers Plowman* B." *MS*, 23 (1961), 352-62.

A revision and completion of "Quotations from the [Vulgate] Bible" in Skeat's edition (EETS o.s. 67, pp. 503-508). Fuller first lists all scriptural quotations in the B-text, then notes specific errors in Skeat's tabulations.

343. Gaffney, Wilbur. "The Allegory of the Christ Knight in *Piers Plowman*." *PMLA*, 46 (1931), 155-68.

Gaffney attempts to determine the source of WL's description of Christ jousting in a tournament (B. XVI, XVIII, XIX). The motif was too common and widespread to allow for an exact determination of WL's source. It appears in homiletic literature, the *Gesta Romanorum*, the *Ancrene Riwle*, assorted lyrics, and cycle plays. A poem ascribed to Nicholas Bozon (found in MS Phillips 8336 and MS Cotton Junius AV), however, has more specific affinities to WL's rendition than any other version. Although WL shifts the tone from the romantic to the heroic, he retains Bozon's fundamental structure.

344. Gallemore, Melvin A. "The Sermons of Bishop Thomas Brinton and the B-Text of *Piers Plowman*." University of Washington dissertation, 1967. Abstracted *DA*, 27: 3008A.

345. Gasquet, Francis Aidan. *English Monastic Life*. London: Methuen, 1904.

346. _____. *Monastic Life in the Middle Ages*. London: G. Bell and Sons, 1922.

347. Gebhard, H. *Langlands und Gowers Kritik der Kirchlichen Verhaltnisse ihrer Zeit*. Published University of Strassbourg dissertation, 1911.

348. Gerould, Gordon H. "The Structural Integrity of *Piers Plowman* B." *SP*, 45 (1948), 60-75.

Gerould believes that there is a steady plot progression through the nine visions of the B-text. The allegory is elaborate but not digressive. Will is the central figure. Through those cumulative experiences WL communicated his views regarding man's unending struggle for righteousness. In one sense, the poem is Will's spiritual biography but it has a wider significance. Piers is not a shapeshifter but a constant symbol. He is not transformed from a simple laborer to a mediator between God and man, but represents a summation of these attributes. The terms Dowel, Dobet, and Dobest are simply different aspects of one way of life to which any Christian may aspire.

349. Globe, Alexander V. "Apocalyptic Themes in the *Sibylline Oracles*, the Revelation, Langland, Spenser, and Marvell." University of Toronto dissertation, 1971. Abstracted *DAI*, 32: 918A-19A.

Throughout the Middle Ages, there was a widespread body of information purporting to reveal God's plan for the end of the world. This apocalyptic tradition stems from the Sibylline oracles which were composed mostly in Alexandria between 160 B.C. and 200 A.D. WL uses this material in his portrayal of Holy Church as the Bride of Christ and Lady Meed as Babylon. He also refers to the Sibylline tradition concerning the Emperor of the Last Days (B. III, 282-327), and models Passus XVII-XX on the medieval exegesis of Revelation 20.

350. Gluntz, H. H. *Die Literarästhetik de europäischen Mittelalters*. Vol. II, *Das Abendland Forschungen zur Geschichte Europäischen Geisteslebens*. Ed. Herbert Schöffer. Bochum-Langerdreer, 1937. See pp. 533-35.

Gluntz believes that the conclusion of *PP* is apocalyptic and that the poem ends in despair. In the *Visio*, Piers appears as a godly king who regulates the worldly concerns of his people. He then appears as Christ in the Crucifixion and Harrowing of Hell, and finally becomes the God of Judgement Day. In the Pardon scene, Piers is the perfect man who symbolizes both the commonweal and individual good. He tears the pardon when his first goal of the well-working commonweal is attained. He then hears another command--to prove his individual worth. The tearing of the pardon signifies the end of one era and the beginning of another.

351. Gradon, Pamela. *Form and Style in Early English Literature*. London: Methuen, 1971.

See pp. 60-77, 99-113. The term "personification allegory" is simplistic and misleading. Allegory is a complex literary form influenced by biblical typology, literary fictions, and classical rhetoric. It is also influenced by a rich mythographic tradition that has nothing to do with scriptural exegesis. An abstraction is not, in itself, allegorical. When WL speaks of Reason or Conscience, he is not referring to another entity but to these abstractions. In *PP* we see a growing tendency towards realism. WL tends to mix the metaphorical and the realistic. His dramatic liveliness of speech and action derives from this exploitation of the literal level--he treats his abstractions dramatically rather than allegorically. Piers is a figura. Through Piers, WL emphasizes certain aspects of his central concept, human nature. Piers represents Christ's human nature as well as man's nature as perfectable by grace.

352. Guest, Edwin. *The History of English Rhythms*. London: W. Pickering, 1838. Revised edition by W. W. Skeat. London: G. Bell and Sons, 1882.

353. Gunther, E. *Englische Leben im 14 Jahrhundert nach The Vision*. Published University of Leipzig dissertation, 1889.

354. Gwatkin, H. M. and J. P. Whitney, eds. *The Cambridge Medieval History*. 6 vols. New York: Cambridge University Press, 1911-1929.

355. Gwynn, Aubrey. *The English Austin Friars in the Time of Wyclif*. Oxford: Oxford University Press, 1940.

See pp. 221-24. WL intensifies his criticism of friars in the B-text. In A, he accused them of personal misconduct, but in B he states that they are guilty of interfering with the clergy in general. In B.X. 317-20, 323-27, the friars are specifically attacked for desiring worldly wealth. WL's beliefs are similar to those of the Austin Friars who contended that the Church had no right to possess temporal goods. WL, however, was also suspicious of the Austin Friars. He believed that the clergy should be compelled to live from the alms of the faithful.

356. Hall, Bernard G. "Sources of *Piers Plowman*." *TLS*, 29 (May 1, 1930), 370.

Addendum to Bright's note (233) on the proverbs in the Rylands MS as a possible source for passages in *PP*. There is stronger evidence to suggest WL's familiarity with the MS--two marginal notes from the Rylands MS are used in the B-text: "Qui parcit" and "Hui michi."

357. Hall, G. D. G. "The Abbot of Abingdon and the Tenants of Winkfield." *Medium Aevum*, 28 (1959), 91-95.

Hall agrees with Coghill's theory that the reference to the Abbot of Abingdon was omitted from the C-text because WL wanted to avoid involvement in a controversy (276). Hall notes that there were, in fact, tenants holding to the king and others to the Abbot of Abingdon. The latter may have felt themselves too heavily drawn on. When the inspection of Domesday indicated that they need not pay fees to the Abbot, since his holdings came *ex dono regis*, the tenants hoped for some relief.

358. Hamilton, A. C. "Spenser and Langland." *SP*, 55 (1958), 533-48.

Hamilton speculates that Spenser read *PP*, since *PP* was the "single continued allegory or darke conceit" written in England before his time. *PP* and Book I of the *Faerie Queene* are parallel in structure and theme. Passus I-V correspond to Cantos I-V. Holy Church and Mede are analogous to Una and Duessa. The heroes, Will and Redcrosse, are both on a quest for a vision of Truth. The use of personification allegory in the House of Pride suggests WL's Confession of the Seven Deadly Sins. Passus VI-VII correspond to Cantos VI-VII. The Pardon Scene in *PP* is analogous to Redcrosse's struggle with Orgolio. Arthur corresponds to Piers, Ignaro, to the literal-minded priest. Hamilton compares the tearing of the Pardon to the tearing of the veil of Arthur's shield. After the tearing of the Pardon, the plots of both poems fall into three clear subdivisions. In *PP*, these subdivisions are *Dowel, Dobet,* and *Dobest*. In the *Faerie Queene*, they are the episode at the House of Penance, the slaying of the dragon, and the wedding of Una and Redcrosse.

359. _____. "The Visions of *Piers Plowman* and *The Faerie Queene*." *Form and Convention in the Poetry of Edmund Spenser*. Ed. William Nelson. New York: Columbia University Press, 1961, pp. 1-34.

Develops his earlier thesis (358). *The Faerie Queene* and *PP* relate as analogues, but are quite different structurally. *PP*'s structure is cumulative, growing as if being shaped while written, whereas the structure of the *Faerie Queene* is rhetorical. The allegory of both poems must be read on the literal level: we should not attempt to "translate" the allegories, but rather retain them as metaphor.

360. Hammond, Donald F. "The Narrative Art of *Piers Plowman*." University of Florida dissertation, 1968. Abstracted *DA*, 29: 870A-71A.

Will is both the fictive persona and the narrator of the poem: both a model for, and the guide to, salvation. He has examined the relationship between God and man and he has found salvation. He presents his verses to us for our profit, and becomes our guide to the mysteries of salvation.

361. Hanford, J. H. "Dame Nature and Lady Life." *MP*, 15 (1918), 313-16.

Hanford denies the similarity noticed by Skeat between Lady Liffe in *Death and Liffe* and WL's Anima. The source for Lady Liffe is probably the description of Dame Nature in Alanus de Insulis's *De Planctu Naturae*.

362. Hanscom, Elizabeth Deering. "The Argument of the *Vision of Piers Plowman*." *PMLA*, 9 (1894), 403-50.

Hanscom notes that there is some sort of basic structure in *PP*, but feels that it is obtuse and frequently mishandled. All three versions are incomplete due to WL's inability or unwillingness to reach conclusions. "Lacking all the qualities which made Chaucer a great poet, Langland produced a work worthy in kind if not in degree, to rank with the *Canterbury Tales* as a picturebook of English men and manners in the fourteenth century" (p. 411).

363. Harper, James F. "Style in Medieval Art and Literature: Three Essays in Criticism." S.U.N.Y., Stony Brook dissertation, 1974. Abstracted *DAI*, 35: 3682A.

Chapter I compares WL's narrative techniques in the *Visio* with the visual techniques of Bosch's "Hay Wain": both depict the nature of avarice and cupidity as it destroys the social framework and prepares the way to Hell. Both Bosch and WL are satirists who share a grim view of man's inhumanity.

364. Harrington, David Van. "Techniques of Characterization in *Piers Plowman*." University of Washington dissertation, 1960. Abstracted *DA*, 21: 1554.

Harrington examines changes in WL's use of allegorical personifications in the three versions of *PP*. From the A- to the C-versions, there is a general movement away from abstract concepts toward clearer, more fully developed personifications. Unlike most medieval allegorists, WL prefers to indicate the nature of a personification by means of action and speech rather than by outward appearance. His personifications function in two ways: 1. they cause others to be affected by the concepts they represent (*e.g.*, Hunger), or 2. they reveal their own names by means of action (*e.g.*, Meed).

365. Harwood, Britton J. "'Clergye' and the Action of the Third Vision in *Piers Plowman*." *MP*, 70 (1973), 279-90.

In the third vision of the B-text, Will probes various ways of knowing--Thought, Wit, Study, and Imaginitif--in order to find the proper way to know Christ. Clergy personifies an object of knowledge: by failing to yield the belief sought by the Dreamer, he becomes an important motive for the Dreamer's puzzling behavior. He fails to give the Dreamer a vision of God because his mode of knowledge is

essentially one of "trinitarian dogmatics." There is something unreal in this mode of knowing and Will realizes that
his is not the proper answer.

366. _____. "Imaginitive in *Piers Plowman*." *Medium
Aevum*, 44 (1975), 249-63.

Imaginitif's failure to provide Will with a "kynde
knowing" is consistent with the medieval theory of the
imagination. Imaginitif is neither memory nor a prophetic
faculty which provides revelatory images. Rather he is
the power of recognizing similarities. He is the only
character who tries to prove his points by means of
serious and exact analogy. The Dreamer's desire to believe
"kyndeli on criste" is not satisfied by Imaginitif.

367. _____. "Langland's *Kynde Wit*." *JEGP*, 75 (1976),
330-36.

Discusses and modifies Randolph Quirk's contention
that kynde wit and wit represent the *vis cognativa* and the
ratio particularis (see 516). Kynde wit is not instinctual
knowledge: its substance is the knowledge of material
benefit. The benefit perceived by this idea lies sometimes
in the transformability of the physical world for the benefit of man. It is by kynde wit that Piers knows Truth:
"By leading the *bona temporalia* out of physical nature,
kynde wit confers a 'hyre' of its own at nightfall."

368. _____. "*Liberum-Arbitrium* in the C-text of *Piers
Plowman*." *PQ*, 52 (1973), 680-95.

Liberum-Arbitrium is a separate faculty constituted of
reason and will, the act of which is choice. He describes
himself as the result of conversion, specifically recognizing and choosing Christ as the source of all value.
The three props of the Tree of Charity represent the
mental powers--volition, knowledge, and choice--which
Liberum Arbitrium deploys in making a loving choice. He
is useless, however, to unregenerate man. This is demonstrated when the fruit of charity cannot abide the test of
death. The poem moves from the frustrated stewardship of
Liberum-Arbitrium to the supposition for the liberty of
Liberum-Arbitrium--the knowledge of the suffering of Christ.

369. _____. "*Piers Plowman*: Fourteenth Century Skepti-
cism and the Theology of Suffering." *Bucknell Review*,
19, iii (1971), 119-36.

The action of *PP* is "epistemological." The shifts in
perspective and material reflect the testing of various
modes of knowing. The modes of knowing presiding over the
successive parts of the poem are often personified and
sometimes debate with the Dreamer. They hypostatize powers

of his own mind and yet he separates himself from them because they give answers to questions other than the one he has asked. Will's desire to believe in Christ will not be satisfied with moral prescription. He seeks a belief about the nature of the world as it conditions any human activity. His search for salvation is metaphysical as distinct from moral. The epistemological movement of the poem begins with Reason (*Visio*). *Dowel* explores the modes of wit leading up to Conscience. Conscience is man's knowledge of God's suffering and human suffering. Because of his love, God chose to suffer as a means of knowing man's sins. Man suffers in order to know the immediacy of God's love. This constitutes a kind of hypostatic union.

370. _____. "*Piers Plowman* and the Ways of Knowing." S.U.N.Y., Buffalo dissertation, 1971. Abstracted *DAI*, 31: 4772A.

371. _____, and Ruth F. Smith. "Inwit and the Castle of *Caro* in *Piers Plowman*." *NM*, 71 (1970), 648-54.

Examines the allegorical figures of the Castle of Caro (B. IX, 1-70). Inwit is not "intellect" or "reason." Rather, it derives from the Dominican concept of synderesis which is a kind of intuitive but not deliberative mental faculty. It is a quality which adds the "phenomenon of certainty to a mental process otherwise dependent upon extrinsic authority and the relativity of changing concepts" (p. 648).

372. Hazelton, Richard Marquand. "Two Texts of the 'Disticha Catonis' and its Commentary with Special Reference to Chaucer, Langland, and Gower." Rutgers University dissertation, 1956. Abstracted *DAI*, 16: 1899.

An edition of a medieval school textbook with full gloss by thirteenth- and fourteenth-century commentators. Editor's introduction discusses the possible influence of the "Disticha Catonis" on WL.

373. Hemingway, Samuel B. "The Two St. Pauls." *MLN*, 32 (1917), 57-58.

The allusions to St. Paul the Apostle in *PP* (B. XV, 235 ff.) and Chaucer's Pardoner's *Prologue*, 443´ ff., may relate to the tradition of St. Paul the Hermit who was frequently confused with Paul the Apostle. Paul the Hermit generally appears in medieval art clad only in a woven mat. In both WL and Chaucer, he is referred to as a weaver.

374. Heyworth, P. L. "*Jack Upland's Rejoinder*, A Lollard Interpolator and *Piers Plowman* B. X. 245f." *Medium Aevum*, 36 (1967), 242-48.

Heyworth demonstrates the popularity of *PP* in the later Middle Ages and the similarities early readers saw between the poem and the Lollard cause. In MS Digby 41 there is a rejoinder to the Lollard piece *Jack Upland* and a Lollard reply to the rejoinder. The Lollard interpolator of this reply evidently knew *PP* very well because he employs WL's arguments against the censures of friars who do not censure their own behavior.

375. Hieatt, Constance. *The Realism of Dream Visions: The Poetic Exploitation of the Dream-Experience in Chaucer and his Contemporaries.* De Proprietibus Litterarum, series practica 2. Paris: The Hague, 1967.

See pp. 89-97. Hieatt examines the way in which medieval literary dream visions imitate the genuine dream experience. Compares WL's use of dreams with Chaucer's: "The waking sequences . . . provide a personal motivation for the visions which follow, and are therefore, while differently expressed, not essentially different from the waking prologues to Chaucer's dream visions" (p. 94). The realism of WL's dreams begins on the verbal level--the ambiguous use of words and illogical sentence structures appear to imitate actual dreams. Unlike *Pearl* and Chaucer's dream visions, *PP* reflects the actual texture of a dream. Structurally, the technique of starting and stopping dreams allows WL to easily abandon an idea when he has exhausted it and to change to another topic.

376. Higgs, Elton D. "The Path to Involvement: The Centrality of the Dreamer in *Piers Plowman*." *Tulane Studies in English*, 21 (1974), 1-34.

The Dreamer serves to unify the poem. The central action of *PP* takes place in his mind, and his dreams govern the poem's structure. Each dream marks a major step in Will's progress by answering crucial questions he has raised. By the end of the poem, we, like Will, discover "a terrifying inability to pay what we owe."

377. _____. "The Dream as a Literary Framework in the Works of Chaucer, Langland, and the Pearl Poet." University of Pittsburgh dissertation, 1965. Abstracted *DA*, 27 (1966): 1030A.

378. Hill, Thomas D. "Davidic Typology and the Characterization of Christ: *Piers Plowman* B. XIX, 95-103." *N&Q*, new series, 23 (1976), 291-94.

In Conscience's description of Christ's battle with sin and death, the allusions to "guerilla tactics" do not refer to Robert Bruce, as Skeat supposed, but to David (Samuel 1 and 2). In medieval biblical exegesis, David and Christ are linked through their historic roles. David's tactics are "in some sense an adumbration of Christ's preaching."

379. _____. "A Liturgical Allusion in *Piers Plowman* B. XVI. 88: '*Filius*, bi the Fader will and frenesse of *Spiritus Sancti*.'" *N&Q*, new series, 22 (1975), 531-32.

Translates ll. 86-89: "and Piers, out of pure anger, seized that one stave and hit after him [*i.e.*, the devil] recklessly, [with the stave] Filius by the Father's will and free generosity of the Holy Spirit." Piers's action, which has its source in a prayer from the *Ordo Missal*, is emblematic of the Incarnation. Also notes that the word "Iouke" in l. 92 is a hawking term: WL uses it as an exegetical allusion to Christ being "perched" in Mary's womb.

380. _____. "Two Notes on Exegetical Allusion in Langland: *Piers Plowman* XI, 161-167, and B, I, 115-124." *NM*, 75 (1974), 92-97.

1. Discusses Holy Church's description of the fall of the angels (B. I, 115-124), arguing that "alle that hoped it mi3te be so" (1.118) refers to the "neutral angels." The "numberlessness" of Satan and his followers is an attribute which bears moral and cosmological significance. 2. God is described as writing the Mosaic tablets "with his on fynger" (B. XI, 161-167). This alludes to the widespread exegetical figure of the Holy Spirit as the "finger" of God.

381. Hilton, Rodney. *Bond Men Made Free: Medieval Peasant Movements and the English Uprising of 1381*. New York: Viking, 1973.

382. _____. *The Decline of Serfdom in Medieval England*. London: Melbourne, 1969.

383. Hirsch-Reich, B. "Eine neue 'oeuvre de synthese' uber Joachim von Fiora." *Recherches de Theologie Ancienne et Médiévale*, 26 (1959), 128-37.

384. Hittmair, Rudolf. "Der Begriff der Arbeit bei Langland." *Festschrift für Karl Luick*. Marburg, 1925, pp. 204-18.

Examines the meaning of the plowing of the half-acre. Salvation is to be attained only through work, and each individual must perform the task assigned to him.

385. Hobsbaum, Philip. "*Piers Plowman* Through Modern Eyes." *Poetry Review*, 61 (1970-1971), 335-62.

Attacks scholars who, in refusing to accept modernized texts of *PP*, encourage modern readers to view the poem as

archaic and difficult. The *Visio* is superior in every way
to the more dense and obtuse *Vita*.

386. Hoffman, Richard L. "The Burning of the 'Boke' in *Piers
    Plowman*." *MLQ*, 25 (1964), 57-65.

    Hoffman disagrees with R. E. Kaske's explanation of the
grammar of Book's speech (416). B. XVIII, 255 is a conditional statement which emphasizes Book's certainty that
what he preaches will come to pass. The purpose of his
speech is to bear witness to the divinity of Christ. A
second conditional statement, B. XVIII, 256-257, emphasizes
Book's conviction "that even those who lived under the Old
law will ultimately believe his enduring testimony and
acknowledge the divine nature of Christ." He does not
prophesize his own future destruction but is completely
assured of his immortality. Criticized by Donaldson (309).

387. Holleran, J. V. "The Role of the Dreamer in *Piers Plowman*."
    AnM, 7 (1966), 33-50.

    The Dreamer supplies the dramatic framework of the
narrative of *PP*. The poem is divided into three parts,
corresponding to three different quests of the Dreamer.
In the first (Passus I-VII), he seeks adventure, but he is
frightened by a vision of damnation and decides to seek
salvation. The second quest traces his pursuit of truth
until he despairs (Passus VIII-XI). In the third quest, he
resumes his search for truth and does what he must do to
be saved. The dreams represent progressive stages in the
Dreamer's growing spiritual awareness. By the end of the
poem, his impetuosity and intellectual pride have been
replaced by patient Christian humility.

388. Hollowway, Julia B. "The Figure of the Pilgrim in Medieval
    Poetry." University of California, Berkeley disser-
    tation, 1974. Abstracted *DAI*, 35: 225A-26A.

389. Hort, Greta. *Piers Plowman and Contemporary Religious
    Thought*. New York: Macmillan, 1938.

    Of 301 Biblical quotations in *PP*, 216 are found in the
Breviary. WL may not have read *De Causa Dei*, but he was
certainly familiar with Bradwardine's theories concerning
predestination. Although not especially learned, WL had
a wide acquaintance with medieval theologians including
Augustine, Aquinas, and Lombard. WL's concept of "kynde
knowing" is related to the *lex naturalis* of Aquinas and to
the concept of synderesis. The answer to the *salus animarum*
is "Et qui bona egerunt & c" which is an essentially Pelagian
faith in the power of an individual to earn his own salvation.
WL does not use precise scholastic reasoning in his arguments
on predestination, although his method is scholastic. WL's
doctrines are not frankly heretical but are certainly the

product of a free-thinking mind. He keeps well within orthodoxy but subtly undermines a great deal of traditional
Church teaching.

390. Howard, Donald R. "The Body Politic and the Lust of the
        Eyes: *Piers Plowman*." *The Three Temptations*:
        Medieval Man in Search of the World. Princeton, N.J.:
        Princeton University Press, 1966, pp. 163-214.

   WL's central concern is the use of worldly goods and
the role they play in damaging salvation. The king's decision
to dwell with Reason and Conscience represents the ideal of
the poem--the remainder of the narrative explores why this
ideal is not followed in real life. Present society is
corrupt primarily because of the unjust distribution of
goods. WL envisions a harmonious Christian *mundus* where
the order of earthly society mirrors the order of heaven.
From an idealist's point of view, the Pardon is perfect;
but for a realist, like the priest, it is too otherworldly.
Piers accepts the Pardon angrily because it ignores human
limitations. The Pardon scene illustrates the dichotomy
that while men ought to strive for perfection, they are by
nature, flawed. In the *Vita*, WL explores the inner world
of the individual to explain why men do not do as they
should. The *Vita* examines the Christian *mundus* in two
opposing perspectives: "it examines the qualities in the
life of the individual necessary to the success of the
proposed social system, and it examines the limitations of
this system when seen against the scheme of things eternal"
(p. 195).

391. Hudson, Anne. "A Lollard Sermon Cycle and its Implications."
        Medium Aevum, 40 (1971), 142-56.

392. Huizinga, J. *The Waning of the Middle Ages*. London:
        Edward Arnold, 1924. Rptd. St. Martin's Press, 1949.

393. Hussey, S. S. "Langland, Hilton, and the Three Lives."
        RES, new series, 7 (1956), 132-50. Rptd. *Interpretations
        of Piers Plowman*, ed. Vasta, 1968, pp. 232-58.

   Dowel, Dobet, and Dobest cannot be equated with the
Active, Contemplative, and Mixed lives. WL's concept of the
three lives relates in some ways to the ideas of Walter
Hilton, but there are important differences. For Hilton,
the Mixed life is clearly not superior to the other two
lives, whereas Dobest is superior to Dowel and Dobet.
Hilton conceived of the Contemplative as the most important
way of life, whereas WL considered the Mixed life (which
mediates between Active and Contemplative) most important.
The members of WL's triad are not separate states--Dobet
includes Dowel, and Dobest subsumes both. They represent
degrees of the single good life leading to salvation.

394. _____, ed. *Piers Plowman: Critical Approaches*. London: Methuen, 1969.

Contents: (See separate listings)
S. S. Hussey. "Introduction."
G. H. Russell. "Some Aspects of the Process of Revision in *Piers Plowman*." (134)
Rosemary Woolf. "The Tearing of the Pardon." (620)
P. M. Kean. "Justice, Kingship and the Good Life in the Second Part of *Piers Plowman*." (418)
J. A. Burrow. "Words, Works, and Will: Theme and Structure in *Piers Plowman*." (245)
Priscilla Jenkins. "Conscience: The Frustration of Allegory." (397)
Barbara Raw. "Piers and the Image of God in Man." (520)
David Mills. "The Rôle of the Dreamer in *Piers Plowman*." (468)
T. P. Dunning. "Action and Contemplation in *Piers Plowman*." (314)
R. W. V. Elliott. "The Langland Country." (321)
W. O. Evans. "Charity in *Piers Plowman*." (326)
S. T. Knight. "Satire in *Piers Plowman*." (433)
J. A. W. Bennett. "Chaucer's Contemporary." (206)
Review Article: John Lawlor. "*Piers Plowman: Critical Approaches*." *Yearbook of English Studies*, 2 (1972), 237-41.

395. Iijima, Ikuzo. *Langland and Chaucer: A Study of the Two Types of Genius in English Poetry*. Boston: Four Seas, 1925.

396. Isaacson, Melanie Kell. "The Unachieved Quest for Social Perfection from the 'Roman de Carité' to *Piers Plowman*." Stanford University dissertation, 1976. Abstracted *DAI*, 36: 6076A.

Examines the motif of the quest to reform society into an ideal Christian community (the reformed temporal city) in the *Roman de la Rose, Roman de Fauvel*, and *La Voie de Paradis*. In both "Roman de Carité" and *PP*, the society remains imperfect within time. Social virtue is not exiled by vice, but is self-exiled after a vision of Christian perfection.

397. Jenkins, Priscilla. "Conscience: The Frustration of Allegory." *Piers Plowman: Critical Approaches*, ed. Hussey, 1969, pp. 125-42.

There are two distinct narrative modes in *PP*--the allegorical and the literal. Together they express a range of experience central to the poem's meaning. The allegorical mode suggests idealization and simplification, while the literal mode presents a world of compromise, confusion, and frequent indifference to moral issues. Conscience is designed to frustrate allegorical "tidiness." The wedding of Conscience and Meed could occur only in the ideal world constructed by Reason. But in the real world, man is sinful, and his economic behavior is corrupt. The marriage would have denied the reality. Hence, Conscience must be inconsistent (in refusing the marriage) in order to faithfully represent genuine human behavior.

398.   Jeremy, Sister Mary. "'Leggis a-lery,' *Piers Plowman* A., VII, 115." *ELN*, 1 (1964), 250-51.

Sister Jeremy suggests that the word "aliri" has survived in the child's rhyme, "One, two, three O'leary." The word lost its original meaning and became associated with a proper name. See 278.

399.   Jochums, Milford C. "The Legend of the Voice from Heaven." *N&Q*, new series, 11 (1964), 44-47.

Jochums traces this motif as it appears in Giraldus, the *Polychronicon*, Reginald Pecock, *PP* (C. XVIII, 220-224) and Milton. The legend refers to the excessive holdings of lands and goods by the Church. A voice from heaven indicated that the day Constantine gave goods to the pope, the temporal entered into the spiritual realm and poisoned it.

400.   Johnston, G. K. W. "*Piers Plowman*, B-Text, Prologue, 78-79." *N&Q*, new series, 6 (1959), 243-44.

Agrees with Mitchell's gloss on the line "worth bothe his eres" (472). If the bishop were "worth both his ears" (*i.e.*, worthy to have them because he made proper use of them), he would soon learn of the abuses practiced by pardoners. This serves to warn him to be more vigilant. Disagrees with Spencer (566).

401.   _____. "A Reading in *Piers Plowman*." *American Notes and Queries*, 1 (1962), 35-36.

In "Law is so lordeliche and loth to make end,/With-oute present₃ or pans she pleseth wel fewe" (B. III, 160-161), the pronoun "she" is a scribal error. As a result of this error, commentators believe that the lines refer to Lady Meed. The pronoun should be "he," referring to Law.

402.   Jones, F. "Dickens and Langland in Adjudication upon Meed." *Victorian Newsletter*, no. 33 (1968), 53-56.

Jones compares the economic background of Dickens's *Hard Times* with the society of the *Visio*. Both Dickens and WL view greed as the major cause of social troubles, and advocate the use of property for the good of all society. The profit motive violates the collective responsibility of men in society. Presents a rendition of the *Visio* as it might have been written by Dickens.

403. Jones, H. S. V. "Imaginitif in *Piers Plowman*." *JEGP*, 13 (1914), 583-88.

   Imaginitif does not represent the imagination or fancy. In Richard of St. Victor's *Benjamin Major*, Imagination conducts man from worldly concerns to the higher service of God: without imagination, reason cannot know. WL uses Imaginitif in the same sense. Imaginitif takes Will in charge after he attempted to know by reason alone. In medieval psychology, imagination is not a faculty of lower grade than reason but rather a mediator between the world of sense and the intellectual world.

404. Jones, W. R. "Lollards and Images: The Defense of Religious Art in Later Medieval England." *Journal of the History of Ideas*, 34 (1972), 27-50. [Discusses Lollard views of graphic and literary art in the fourteenth and fifteenth centuries].

405. Jusserand, J. J. *Piers Plowman, A Contribution to the History of English Mysticism*. Revised and enlarged, trans. M. E. R. London: Russell and Russell, 1894. Reissued, 1965. Originally published as *L'Epopée mystique de Langland*. Paris: Librairie Hachette, 1893.

   Discusses the Meed scene in terms of historical allegory. The king is Edward III who was an old and incapable administrator during the crisis of 1376-1377. His mistress, Alice Perrers (Meed), allowed corruption to reign. In the fable of the belling of the cat, Edward is the old cat, Richard II is the new cat, Peter de la Mare is the rat (spokesman for the commons) and WL is represented by the mouse. Jusserand constructs a detailed biography of the poet based primarily on the character of Will: *e.g.*, when Holy Church tells Will that she made him free (C-Text), this indicates that WL was born of peasants but entered minor orders and was thereby made legally free. WL is politically conservative and "shares the opinions of the Commons of England with whom, in fact, he rarely disagrees; so much so that his work has, at times, the appearance of a poetical commentary on the Parliament Rolls." Compares WL with Dante, Joachim of Flora, Deguilleville, and fourteenth-century German mystics such as Rulman Merswin. WL was the victim, not the master of his thought. His work is not finely crafted and he obtains artistic effects without conscious effort.

406. K., A. R. "Parked." *American Speech*, 2 (1927), 215.

407. Kane, George. *"The Vision of Piers Plowman." Middle English Literature: A Critical Study of the Romances, the*

Religious Lyrics, Piers Plowman. London: Methuen, 1951, pp. 182-248.

PP is a "paradox of total greatness and local failures." It is a unique poem, standing apart from all stylistic groupings of surviving alliterative poetry. WL uses three kinds of poetic irony: 1. the irony of implied contrasts; 2. ironic learned allusions for a very knowledgeable audience; 3. stylistic irony which is based on the use of indecorous poetic figures. "The loftiest poetry in *Piers Plowman* results when the emotional, intellectual, and moral impulses of his [WL's] religion make themselves felt and find expression either in close proximity or together" (p. 217). At times, however, WL mistook his religious fervor for a "furor poeticus" and wrote "diffuse and prosy verse."

408. Kaske, R. E. "'Ex vi transicionis' and Its Passage in *Piers Plowman*." *JEGP*, 62 (1963), 32-60.

Discusses Patience's riddle (B. XIII, 135-156). Basing his explication on Scriptural passages and glosses, and Peter Elias's commentary on Priscian's *Institutiones*, Kaske argues that "ex vi transicionis" is a term from medieval grammar. He paraphrases 11.151-156: "By means of the fundamental Christian injunction to charity . . . and through a relationship comparable to that by which a transitive verb 'rules' *ex vi transicionis*, its direct object in the accusative case, I, Patience, contain and guard as if in a protective box the other virtues . . . which are themselves interrelated and maintained, as if tightly bound, by charity, with the support of prudence/wisdom/knowledge . . . both of which virtues receive their power ultimately through the Redemption, conclusively manifested by Christ's resurrection on Easter Morning; and I, Patience, am esteemed along with this complex of virtues, in the arts where I enter bringing it with me."

409. _____. "Holy Church's Speech and the Structure of *Piers Plowman*." *Chaucer and Middle English Studies in Honour of Rossell Hope Robbins*. Ed. Beryl Rowland. London: Allen and Unwin, 1974 pp. 320-27.

The structure of *PP* is related to the liturgical year beginning at the start of Advent and ending with the last Sunday before Advent. Holy Church's speech governs the general thematic movement of the poem. *PP* has two large sections--the first treats the use of natural goods and artificial wealth (*Visio*) while the second treats truth and love (*Vita*). The pilgrimage to truth cannot occur until the problems of natural goods are solved. Passus VII is transitional: after the failure of the reform of the appetites, the poem moves to a consideration of specifically Christian man.

410. _____. "Langland and the 'Paradisus Claustralis.'"
MLN, 72 (1957), 481-83.

    Discusses B. X, 300-305. Kaske discovers that the first
two lines coincide "virtually word for word" with Benvenuto
da Imola's commentary on *Paradiso*, XI, 12, which he, in turn,
took from Petrus Ravennas. A sermon attributed to Petrus
pictures the cloister as paradise. These lines are commonplace and should not be interpreted autobiographically.
See 64.

411. _____. "Langland's Walnut-Simile." *JEGP*, 58 (1959),
650-54.

    The walnut simile in B. XI, 248-310 is of exegetical
origin. The division of the walnut into hull, shell, and
kernel derives from Pliny's *Natural History*. The reference
to the bitter shell and sweet kernel appears in Canticles
6:10 and Numbers 17:8 as well as in the commentary of
Rabanus Maurus and the *Glossa Ordinaria*--these relate the
nut and kernel to various aspects of Christ.

412. _____. "*Gigas* the Giant in *Piers Plowman*." *JEGP*,
56 (1957), 177-85.

    Discusses B. XVIII, 249-251. "Gigas" occurs in a
medieval commentary on part of Psalm 18:6 where it is
metonymical for Christ. "Geaunt" occurs in a gloss on the
Latin commentary--"Gygas, that is to say for those who have
no Latin, the giant." In a gloss by St. Ambrose, the giants
of Genesis were depicted as "double" in nature. Christ was
considered to be "double" as well, and was aptly signified
the "geaunt." Kaske reads the passage: "For *Gygas* the
giant [*i.e.*, the double-natured one] contrived by means of a
trick [*i.e.*, the Incarnation by which he became double-
natured], to break, etc."

413. _____. "A Note on *Bras* in *Piers Plowman*, A, III,
189; B, III, 195." *PQ*, 31 (1952), 427-30.

    "Bras" is usually defined as "money" or "plunder."
Kaske suggests that the word actually refers to household
utensils--it signifies that everything has been taken from
the poor.

414. _____. "Patristic Exegesis in the Criticism of
Medieval Literature: The Defense." *Critical Interpretations of Medieval Literature: Selected Papers
from the English Institute, 1958-1959*. Ed. Dorothy
Bethurum. New York: Columbia University Press, 1960,
pp. 27-60.

    A general appraisal of the use of exegetical methods
to explore the meaning of medieval literature, particularly

to aid in the explication of problematic images. After defending this technique in theory, Kaske discusses some specific examples from WL and Chaucer. The problematic imagery of B. XI, 241-57 may be explained by the exegetical tradition which pictures Christ as the nut or almond. The Speech of Boke (B. XVIII, 228-57) may be traced to a homiletic gloss on Matthew, second chapter, and the "Gygas" allusion derives from Psalms 18:6. *Petrus, id est Christus* may be traced to the metaphor of Peter as Rock. The *Liberum Arbitrium* passage (C. XIX, 134-43) likens Piers to John the Baptist.

415.   _____. "*Piers Plowman* and Local Iconography." *Journal of the Warburg and Courtauld Institute*, 31 (1968), 159-69.

     Kaske examines the iconographical remains of churches surrounding the Malvern Hills and notes similarities between late medieval graphic art and WL's images. The twelfth century priory of St. Giles in Little Malvern contains a unique portrait of two pigs gorging themselves from a large pot which suggests WL's portrait of Gluttony. WL's Wrath states that monks beat him across his bare bottom--a similar portrait occurs in a church in Southrop, Glous: where *Ira* is depicted being beaten across the buttocks. The mirror of Middle Earth (B. XI) is related to a partially destroyed painting in the church of St. Mary at Kempley, Glous. The representation of Abraham bearing souls in his lap (B. XVI, 253-256) is pictured in the church of St. Mary's in Cleobury Mortimer.

416.   _____. "The Speech of 'Book' in *Piers Plowman*." *Anglia*, 77 (1959), 117-44.

     Book symbolizes the *litera* of the New Testament and bears individual witness to the coming of Christ--he unites the Old and the New Testaments in the Incarnation event. He also signifies both the Book of Nature and the Book of Scripture. Embracing past, present, and future, he parallels the way in which Scripture relates to physical time. The burning of Book presents a complex syntactical problem. Kaske reads this passage as: "I, Book, will be burned, but Jesus rise to life." This may relate to the Joachite prophecy that in the future age of the Holy Ghost, the letter of the Old and New Testaments will be consumed by fire, but the spirit will live. Book foresees the future conscription of the *litera* by the *Evangelium Aeternum*, the *intellectus spiritualis*. See 309, 386.

417. Kaulbach, Ernest N. "The Imagery and Theory of Synderesis in *Piers Plowman* B, Passus V, 544 ff. and Passus XIX." Cornell University dissertation, 1971. Abstracted *DAI*, 31: 4720A.

418. Kean, P. M. "Justice, Kingship and the Good Life in the
          Second Part of *Piers Plowman*." *Piers Plowman: Critical
          Approaches*, ed. Hussey, 1969, pp. 76-110.

          WL relates Christ's kingship to the acts of his earthly
      life--this constitutes the perfect good life which cannot
      be completely imitated by man. Each member of the Dowel
      triad, when seen in terms of Christ's life, takes on a
      significance which puts it out of the reach of the ordinary
      Christian. In B. XIX, WL relates the kingship of Christ
      to the terms Law, Lewte, and Love (See 420): then to Dowel,
      Dobet, and Dobest. The concepts of WL's triad do not relate
      exclusively to the inner life, or to society or history.
      Dowel, Dobet, and Dobest are designed to carry several
      meanings simultaneously.

419. _____. "Langland on the Incarnation." *RES*, new
          series, 16 (1965), 349-63.

          Kean examines the imagery of Holy Church's speech,
      focusing on lines 146-156 (B-text) where Holy Church defines
      the concept of truth or love. The image of the "plant of
      pees" is an incarnational image, deriving from exegetical
      tradition: Christ eats death (earth) by assuming flesh.
      This act gives man the power to rise above the earth just as a
      plant, drawing food from the earth, allows its flower to
      rise to heaven. WL mixes various exegetical images--the
      medicinal ointment and spice, the growing plant, the patriar-
      chal figure of Moses, and the philosophical concept of the
      pondus. The image of the piercing needle derives from the
      Book of Wisdom VII, 2ff. The paradoxical figure of the
      lightness of spirit and the heaviness of sin is derived
      from Aristotle.

420. _____. "Love, Law, and *Lewte* in *Piers Plowman*." *RES*,
          new series, 15 (1964), 241-61. Rptd. *Style and Symbolism
          in Piers Plowman*, ed. Blanch, 1969, pp. 132-55.

          The triad law, love, and *lewte* occurs as a leitmotif
      in the *Visio* (B). These terms are ultimately connected to
      the concept of kingship. WL's use of the terms relates to
      the formula of the *Secreta Secretorum* and the Coronation
      oath. Law is a significant power for WL: it arises out of
      natural reason and man's basic social nature. The Prologue
      and Passus I establish the theme of law and its association
      with love and mercy. *Lewte* is a general term for a virtuous
      way of life--it does not mean mere "loyalty" or "justice."
      For both WL and Dante, the ideal king and the ideal state
      are linked to the concept of the Messiah.

421. Keiler, Mabel M. "The Influence of *Piers Plowman* on the
          Macro Play of *Mankind*." *PMLA*, 26 (1911), 339-55.

The plowing of the half-acre and the characters Piers and Hunger in *PP* appear to be the direct source of the tilling of the field and the characters Hunger and Mercy in *Mankind*.

422. Kellogg, Alfred L. "Langland and Two Scriptural Texts." *Traditio*, 14 (1958), 385-98. Rptd. *Chaucer, Langland, Arthur: Essays in Middle English Literature*. New Brunswick, N.J.: Rutgers University Press, 1972, pp. 32-50.

Kellogg examines Holy Church's commentary on Lucifer (C. II, 108-111). This probably derives from Augustine's gloss on the old Latin Isaiah 14:13-14 in his *Enarrationes in Psalmos*. WL altered Augustine's "sedem" to "pedem," mixing the terms "pes" and "pondus" (foot and weight).

423. _____. "Langland's 'Canes Muti': The Paradox of Reform." *Essays in Literary History in Honor of J. Milton French*. Ed. Rudolf Kirk and C. F. Main. New Brunswick, N.J.: Rutgers University Press, 1960, pp. 25-35. Rptd. *Chaucer, Langland, Arthur: Essays in Middle English Literature*. New Brunswick, N.J.: Rutgers University Press, 1972, pp. 51-58.

Kellogg investigates Clergy's definition of Dobest, focusing on the meaning of B. X, 286-287. In commentaries on Isaiah 56:10, "canis" (watchdog) is interpreted as "priest." The priest was to act as the faithful watchdog of the people: the "dumb" priest fails in this vigilance, causing the people to be damned. In *PP*, the "borel clerkes" (friars) blame the priests for being dumb hounds. This passage is a rebuke to the secular clergy: WL is concerned that unchecked criticism might endanger the Church. The image is used in a similar way by John Bromyard in the *Summa Praedicantium*.

424. _____. "Satan, Langland, and the North." *Speculum*, 24 (1949), 413-14. Rptd. *Chaucer, Langland, Arthur: Essays in Middle English Literature*. New Brunswick, N.J.: Rutgers University Press, 1972, pp. 29-31.

Kellogg discusses the reason why Satan is said to prefer the North. This idea derives from Augustine's *Enarrationes in Psalmos*, XLVII, and *De Gratia Novi Testamenti Liber seu Epistola*, CXL. Satan is the founder of a northern city symbolizing the love of self.

425. Kellogg, Eleanor H. "Bishop Brunton and the Fable of the Rats." *PMLA*, 50 (1935), 57-67.

Kellogg attempts to determine the date of Brunton's sermon forty-four which is apparently the direct source of WL's fable of the belling of the cat. The sermon was probably delivered May 18, 1376, during the Good Parliament. Brunton urged that Edward III should be told of the wrongdoings exposed by the Parliament.

426. Kelly, Douglas. "Theory of Composition in Medieval Narrative Poetry and Geoffrey of Vinsauf's *Poetria Nova*." *MS*, 31 (1969), 117-48.

427. Kelly, Robert L. "Hugh Latimer as Piers Plowman." *Studies in English Literature, 1500-1900*, 17 (1977), 13-26.

Latimer places his "Sermon of the Plow" in the PP tradition, identifying himself with Piers--a figure who speaks with the authority of the Bible as interpreted by the orthodox medieval pulpit. Latimer as Piers "is the guise in which the sermonist addresses his countrymen as the prophet of the New Jerusalem to be achieved under King Edward."

428. Kent, Muriel. "A Fourteenth-Century English Poet Surveys the English Scene." *Hibbert Journal*, 40 (1942), 381-85.

A general examination of the relevance of PP for the modern age, emphasizing WL's reformist spirit. Notes that while WL was a harsh critic, he was never cynical.

429. Ker, W. P. *Medieval English Literature*. London: Williams and Norgate, 1912.

WL "uses too often a mechanical form of allegory which is little better than verbiage" (p. 196). The narrative line of the poem is frequently confused and discontinuous.

430. Kinney, Thomas L. "The Temper of Fourteenth-Century English Verse of Complaint." *AnM*, 7 (1966), 74-89.

The first seven passus of PP are related to the verse of complaint. But whereas complaint usually demonstrates despair, anger, resignation, bitterness, and frustration, WL is basically hopeful in his exhortations for reform.

431. Kirk, Elizabeth D. *The Dream Thought of Piers Plowman*. New Haven and London: Yale University Press, 1972.

The dramatic structure of PP is an enactment of the supervening of man's autonomy by God's omnipotence. This conflict can only be resolved by man's submission to the divine will. Piers is an ideal character but he is not the answer to the problems of mankind. His virtue is instinctive and simplistic and cannot cure corrupt human society. In the Pardon Scene, the status of the world as a self-contained entity is shattered by the truth of God. Piers has done his best in the world, but according to God's standards, it is not sufficient. By accepting the pardon, mankind accepts

God's awareness of man's finitude. In this scene, Piers is analogous to Job--he enacts a psychological sequence mirroring man's venting resentment at God's transcendent superiority. In the *Vita* the Dreamer learns more about a God who constantly overrides man's will. The conflict between God and man becomes internalized in the *Vita*. From Passus XV to the conclusion, the poem becomes apocalyptic--man can do nothing as Christian society moves "ineluctably toward disaster."

Review Articles: David C. Fowler. "A New Interpretation of the A and B Texts of *Piers Plowman*." *MP*, 71 (1974), 393-404; Katherine B. Trower. "Elizabeth D. Kirk's *The Dream Thought of Piers Plowman*." *Costerus*, n.s. 1 (1974), 151-64.

432. Kirk, Rudolf. "References to the Law in *Piers the Plowman*." *PMLA*, 48 (1933), 322-27.

References to the law increase substantially from the A-text to the B-Revision. In A, only thirteen legal terms are used and most of them are very common. In B, however, forty-five legal terms are used, and these are more specialized and professional. The B poet makes subtle distinctions between "canoun" and "decretals," for example. WL may have studied law between the composition of A and B.

433. Knight, S. T. "Satire in *Piers Plowman*." *Piers Plowman: Critical Approaches*, ed. Hussey, 1969, pp. 279-309.

PP is essentially a social satire, but a very ambitious one. Satire is frequent in the *Visio* but diminishes in the *Vita* when WL shifts to a more "intellectual" mode. But the poet's credibility as an investigator depends on the force with which he characterized ordinary life in the *Visio*. Satire provides the poem's opening and leads into a discussion of Christian duty. When the discussion moves to a more theoretical plane, satire anchors the discussion in reality. In the last few passus, the poem returns to a final satiric vision of the world.

434. Knowlton, E. C. "Nature in Middle English." *JEGP*, 20 (1921), 186-207.

PP discussed pp. 197-200. WL is outside the traditions concerning Nature which descend from Latin and Old French literature into Chaucer. *Kinde* in *PP* is not the feminine power subordinated to God as in the *Parlement of Foules*: rather, it is God himself. WL's image of Nature is relatively unaffected by classical imagery.

435. Kolbing, E. "Kleine beiträge zur erklärung und Textkritik englischer Dichter." *EStudien*, 5 (1882), 150-56.

436. Kratins, Ojars. *"Piers Plowman* and Arthurian Romance."
    Essays in Criticism, 13 (1963), 304.

    Piers's role is more symbolic than allegorical. "Similar
    to many places and persons of the Arthurian Romance, Piers
    is a symbolic figure that raises the atmosphere of the work
    to a mysterious significance and lends . . . a greater
    emotional intensity. As a symbol, Piers does not provide
    the key to the work, and any attempt to force him to yield
    a clear-cut allegorical significance only impoverishes the
    work as a whole."

437. Krochalis, Jeanne and Edward Peters, trans., and eds. *The
    World of Piers Plowman*. Philadelphia: University of
    Pennsylvania Press, 1975.

    Provides materials for the study of WL's cultural milieu
    as well as selections from works which appear to have directly
    influenced him. *Piers Plowman* "reflects a world in which
    spiritual discontentment and civil dissension often formed
    ephemeral, but persistent alliances. This book attempts to
    suggest some of the documentary evidence for the relationship
    of that poem to the world" (p. xiii). Includes Thomas
    Brinton's Sermon 44, selections from the *Legenda Aurea,
    Disticha Catonis*, Grossetête's *The Castle of Love*, and
    Deguilleville's *Pilgrimage of the Soul*.

438. Krumme, Riley Duane. "Wealth and Reform in *Piers Plowman*."
    Claremont Graduate School dissertation, 1975. Ab-
    stracted *DAI*, 36: 2848A.

439. Lattin, Linda. "Some Aspects of Medieval Number Symbolism
    in Langland's *Piers Plowman*, A-text." *Emporia State
    Research Studies*, 14 (1965), 5-13.

    The number of the passus often suggests the subject
    treated therein. Passus II, for example, treats the Wedding
    of Falsehood and Meed, signified by the number two (union).
    Passus VIII brings the pardon which provides immortality
    for mankind--the number eight signifies regeneration.
    Lattin provides a partial concordance to numbers in the
    A-text.

440. Lawlor, John. "The Imaginative Unity of *Piers Plowman*."
    RES, new series, 8 (1957), 113-26. Rptd. *Interpretations
    of Piers Plowman*, ed. Vasta, 1968, pp. 278-97.

    The focus of imaginative attention in *PP* is on our
    habitual incapacity to grasp that what we know as doctrine
    bears directly upon us. The poet's dominant faculty is
    his satiric intelligence. WL's poetry does not concern
    itself with the exposition of a single system of beliefs.
    It focuses on the individual reader's apprehension of truth--
    "his growing awareness, as the poem proceeds, of a path

inescapably opening before him." Dowel is not a variable term: it has a fixed meaning--right conduct.

441. _____. *Piers Plowman: An Essay in Criticism*. London: Edward Arnold, 1962.

In Part I, Lawlor provides a detailed reading of the argument of *PP*. In the Pardon Scene, Piers destroys only the paper, not the meaning of the document. The Pardon brings a new law: the society of the honest laborer has been superseded by a greater society in harmony with God's will. Piers now depends on, and trusts in, God. His resolve to do less is positive. With the Pardon Scene, the point of view of the poem changes. Up to this point, the good has been patiently sought--now it is examined in detail. In Part II, Lawlor discusses the poetic techniques of *PP*. The unsystematic nature of the argument mirrors the process of thought. The narrative digressions and confusion present an argument in which dialectics give way to revelation. WL exploits all the possibilities of language and his poetic speech is a direct expression of a wholeness of imagination. "The method of Langland's poem . . . is to present a Dreamer whose inexperience is matched only by his doctrinaire assurance, so that his coming to understanding constitutes at once the progressive argument of the poem and the lively demonstration of its central truth" (p. 285). WL is not given to complex allegorization. The Pardon Scene presents us with the truth and the remainder of the poem glosses its meaning.

442. _____. *"Piers Plowman*: The Pardon Reconsidered." *MLR*, 45 (1950), 449-58.

Piers is the only figure capable of saving the world, but when the Pardon arrives, even he is brought to correction. "The best man we have met stands in bitter self-reproach; no complacency is possible for the reader; he too must examine himself" (p. 450). Piers has been too busy about his livelihood and he must repent. The Pardon represents the highest universal moral law and it is given to those who have achieved the life of Dowel. Piers leaves the active life and enters into the contemplative life. He realizes that the law is so absolute that he cannot live up to it and he throws himself on the mercy of Christ. The act of tearing the Pardon is analogous to the tearing of the veil of the Temple. The old law has been replaced by the new law of love.

443. _____. "Two Scenes from *The Vision of Piers Plowman*." *To Nevill Coghill from Friends*. Ed. W. H. Auden and John Lawlor. London: Faber, 1966, pp. 43-63.

Two excerpts from an adaptation of *PP* for the modern theatre. The first scene depicts Will's conversation with

Holy Church. The second scene is the Dreamer's vision of
Christ crucified.

444. Lee, B. S. "Antichrist and the Allegory in Langland's Last
Passus." *University of Cape Town Studies in English*,
2 (1971), 1-12.

Antichrist in B. XX is not merely a schismatic pope. He
signifies a demonic power which inverts the normal order of
the world. In Augustine, WL found precedent for treating
Antichrist in terms of his followers (men of sin) rather than
as a single figure. WL translates the Antichrist into the
image of friars, thereby making the force of evil more vivid
and contemporary.

445. Lewis, C. S. *The Allegory of Love*. London: Oxford University Press, 1936.

See pp. 158-59. WL's satire is predictably directed
most strongly towards idle beggars, hypocritical churchmen,
and oppressors: ". . . even as a moralist he has no unique
'message' to deliver. As a cure for all our ills, he can
offer us only the old story--do-wel, do-bet, and do-best"
(p. 158). WL is a learned, not a "popular poet."

446. Lichstein, Diane P. "*Piers Plowman*: An Image of Neo-Platonic
Christendom." University of Pennsylvania dissertation,
1972. Abstracted *DAI*, 33: 1690A.

The meaning of the poem is largely carried by the
recurrence of the terms "truth," "kynde," and "treasure,"
rather than by a logical plan. WL was concerned with re-
building the Neo-platonic world view against the Neo-
Aristotelianism of William Ockham. Dowel, Dobet, and Dobest
are progressive stages of man in the image of God, with Piers
representing each in his successive appearances.

447. Lindemann, Erika. "Translation Techniques in William Langland's *Piers Plowman*." University of North Carolina,
Chapel Hill dissertation, 1973. Abstracted *DAI*, 34:
279A.

WL employed five basic techniques in translating and
versifying Latin quotations: 1. translating a continuous
string of words from one part of his source; 2. telescoping
his text, translating a discontinuous selection; 3. translating an entire quotation, adding a translation of material
he did not quote; 4. transposing clauses of Latin texts,
translating a new order of Latin words; 5. changing quotations
from one version to another. Lindemann also discusses WL's
metrics: by rewriting and reordering the words of the Latin
quotation, he often made passages conform to his alliterative
pattern.

448. Longo, Joseph A. *"Piers Plowman* and the Tropological Matrix:
Passus XI and XII." *Anglia*, 82 (1964), 291-308.

Longo examines a critical phase in Will's education--
the climax of the *Vita de Dowel*. By employing the characters
Scripture and Imaginitif, WL refutes Will's denunciation of
Christian principles (X). Passus XI and XII form an epi-
phany which resolves much of the previous action and points
the poem in a new direction. In this section, Will undergoes
a kind of "rites of passage": he is first separated from
conventional life, undergoes a symbolic death of the old
self, and is finally reborn. By the end of Passus XII, Will
has learned the importance of loyalty to duty, obedience, and
patient poverty.

449. Lunz, Elizabeth. "The Valley of Jehoshaphat in *Piers Plowman.*"
Tulane Studies in English, 20 (1972), 1-10.

Lunz argues that WL's use of the image of the Valley
of Jehoshaphat (C. XXI, 402-417) is independent of exegetical
tradition. WL rejects the exegetical tradition that depicts
the Valley as the place where the bloody Judgement Day will
occur. For WL, the Valley becomes an image of *caritas* where
there will be salvation for all.

450. Lupack, Allen C. *"Piers Plowman*, B. VII, 116." *Explicator*,
34, iv (1975), Item 31.

Lupack discusses the meaning of "pure tene." "Pure" is
not merely an intensifying adjective. It actually means
"morally untainted" or "righteous." Thus, it is righteous
indignation that Piers feels toward the Priest.

451. Machail, J. W. *"Piers Plowman* and English Life in the Fourteenth Century." *Cornhill Magazine*, n.s. 3 (1897),
42-58.

A general discussion of *PP* in relation to fourteenth-
century society. WL was a common man who wrote for the
common people--his poem provides a panorama of late medieval
life.

452. Maguire, Stella. "The Significance of Haukyn, *Activa Vita,*
in *Piers Plowman.*" *RES*, original series, 25 (1949),
97-109. Rptd. *Style and Symbolism in Piers Plowman*,
ed. Blanch, 1969, pp. 194-208.

The Dreamer's meeting with Haukyn (B. XIII-XIV) is of
crucial importance for the meaning of both the *Visio* and the
Vita. He is a symbol of the active life and has much in
common with the good members of the folk of the field. His
life is well-intentioned, but is based on temporal conceptions
of goodness, as opposed to Piers's life "lived in the light
of eternity." WL's introduction of the Seven Deadly Sins into

the account of Haukyn demonstrates the way in which Haukyn
draws together incidents of the *Visio*. The arguments of the
Visio are not to be discarded when we move to the *Vita*. The
Visio is concerned with various aspects of the Active life--
the proper use of temporal goods, the recognition of sin,
and the need for repentance. All these are synthesized
in the person of Haukyn.

453. Maisack, Helmut. *William Langlands Verhaltnis zum Zister-
      ziensischen Monchtum: Eine Untersuchung der vita in
      Piers Plowman*. Tübingen Inaugural dissertation,
      Bollingen, 1953.

         An interpretation of the B-text *Vita* against the back-
      ground of fourteenth-century Christian theology and earlier
      theological doctrines. Bernardine and Cistercian thought
      influenced WL's thinking. The image of the plowman and WL's
      emphasis on the plowing of the half-acre are indebted to
      the Cistercian emphasis on manual labor. Dowel may be
      identified as a Cistercian lay brother, and Dobet as a
      Cistercian monk. WL himself may have been a Cistercian lay
      brother.

454. Malard, Sandra G. "The Rhetorical Structure of *Piers Plow-
      man* C." University of Michigan dissertation, 1972.
      Abstracted *DAI*, 33: 2334A-35A.

         Malard investigates the way in which the audience relates
      to the movement of WL's fiction. *PP* is marked by fluctuations
      of aesthetic distance. The narrator sometimes addresses the
      audience directly. At times, he interprets the meaning of
      what he reports, and at other times, disclaims accurate
      knowledge. The Dreamer is alternately an individual with
      his own eccentricities, a personification of the human will,
      and an "Everyman" character.

455. Manning, Bernard Lord. *The People's Faith in the Time of
      Wyclif*. Cambridge: Cambridge University Press, 1919.

456. Marcett, M. E. *Uhtred de Boldon, Friar William Jordan, and
      Piers Plowman*. New York: The Author, 1938.

         Marcett discusses the influence of Uhtred de Boldon on
      WL's thought, focusing on the subjects of grace, predestina-
      tion, and the salvation of the heathen. WL was certainly
      acquainted with the controversy between Boldon and William
      Jordan, a Dominican Friar. Jordan considered Boldon a
      heretic because Boldon believed that original sin alone was
      not sufficient cause for damnation. Jordan is satirized
      as the Doctor of Divinity (B. XIII, 21-201). Includes a
      biography of Uhtred, a Latin text and examination of *Contra
      querelas fratrum*, and a biography of Jordan.

457. Martin, Jay. "Will as Fool and Wanderer in *Piers Plow-man*." *TSLL*, 3 (1961-1962), 535-48.

WL inherited several devices from classical Horatian and Juvenalian satire, such as the dialogue, the diatribe, memorabilia, and the chreia, but he superimposed the general forms of popular satire on to the classical framework. The confusion in *PP* is structural--WL could not find a solid artistic form to express his vision of life. The satiric mode of the fool conflicts with the allegorical mode of the wanderer. WL uses the fool as a structural device to link dreams and waking interludes, and as a commentator on the validity of the dreams. But Will is also a wanderer, and he questions whether the dreams can reach the truth at all.

458. Matlock, Charles M. "An Interpretation of *Piers Plowman* Based on the Medieval Dream Background." S.U.N.Y., Albany dissertation, 1972. Abstracted *DAI*, 33: 2940A-41A.

WL's use of the dream vision is unique and is closely related to the theories of Jung and Freud. WL supplements the traditional notions about dreams with his own experience of this phenomenon.

459. Matthew, Gervase. "Justice and Charity in the Vision of *Piers Plowman*." *Dominican Studies*, 1 (1948), 360-66.

At the basis of WL's social doctrine is a definition of justice popularized by St. Ambrose: justice is granting each man his due. Only charity is strong enough to preserve justice. Charity exists in three grades--"Caritas incipiens, proficiens, et perfecta." These correspond to Dowel, Dobet, and Dobest which are also represented by Piers the Plowman, the Teacher, and the Builder of the Barn of Unity.

460. McCully, John Raymond. "Conceptions of *Piers Plowman*: 1550's through 1970's." Rice University dissertation, 1976. Abstracted *DAI*, 37: 2164A.

A general review of critical reactions to *PP* since the sixteenth century. Focuses on modern scholarship, particularly the development of exegetical criticism.

461. McGinnis, Ethel. "*Piers Plowman* in English Literature to 1625." Unpublished Yale University dissertation, 1932.

462. McKisack, May. *The Fourteenth Century 1307-1399*. Oxford: Clarendon Press, 1959.

McKisack notes that "*Piers Plowman* offers us a congested canvas of late fourteenth-century society. The value of the poem as a source for social history has been widely recognized, more widely perhaps, than its poetic quality. Yet, in

contrast with *Troilus*, or the *Canterbury Tales*, or even with
the *Confessio Amantis*, the figures are two-dimensional, we
do not see them in the round . . ." (p. 527). *PP* is a
mysterious and archaic poem.

463. McNamara, J. F. "Responses of Ockhamist Theology in the
Poetry of the Pearl-Poet, Langland, and Chaucer."
Louisiana State University dissertation, 1968. Ab-
stracted *DAI*, 29: 3148A-49A.

The central doctrinal theme of *PP* is the relationship
between grace and merit. WL does not side with either the
Augustinians or the Ockhamists: the poem is an extended
dialectic in which various opinions on this issue oppose
one another.

464. Means, Michael H. "*Piers Plowman*: The Fragmented Consolatio." *The Consolatio Genre in Medieval English
Literature*. University of Florida Monographs, 36.
Gainesville: University of Florida Press, 1972,
pp. 66-90.

The subject of *PP* is the education or enlightenment of
the narrator concerning the nature of perfection and the
necessity of seeking it on both a social and individual level.
The narrator's instructors teach him what is appropriate to
their allegorical natures. Thought and Intellect, therefore,
say different things about perfection because they are projections of different faculties. Will resembles Boethius:
the desperate desire to know drives both to seek out every
source of knowledge. At the end of *Dobest*, Will applies his
knowledge to the spiritual depravity of the world.

465. Mensendieck, O. H. L. *Charakterentwicklung und ethischtheologische Anschauungen des Verfassers von Piers the
Plowman*. London: T. Wohlleben, 1900.

Dowel recounts the poet's belief in his early years in
the three ways of life--Active, Contemplative and Episcopal
(Dowel, Dobet, Dobest). WL later rejected this view and
came to believe that there was only one way of life for all
men--to follow Christ in both poverty and love. *Dobet* does
not preach a better way of life than that described in *Dowel*.
Rather, it provides examples of a life lived according to the
example of Christ. *Dobest* portrays the founding of the
Church and the Christian community. Dobest is the perfection
of good on earth according to the example of Christ (Dowel)
through the strength of Christ's work of salvation (Dobet).

466. _____. "Die Verfasserschaft der drei Texte des *Piers
the Plowman*." *Zeitschrift für Vergleichende Literatur*,
18 (1910), 10-31.

116

Mensendieck discusses WL's use of medieval psychology
in his personifications of mental faculties. His knowledge
appears to derive from encyclopedists, such as Bartholomaeus
Anglicus and Vincent de Beauvais.

467. Middleton, Anne. "Two Infinites: Grammatical Metaphor in
      Piers Plowman." *ELH*, 39 (1972), 169-88.

Middleton examines Clergy's definition of Dowel and
Dobet: "Dowel and Dobet aren two infinites/Whiche infinites,
with a feith fynden out Dobest" (B. XIII, 127-128). Clergy
demonstrates the way in which the terms have significance.
The terms do not denote the object of the search for perfection: rather, they order the progressive form of the
search. They are an attempt to make human knowledge
eschatologically adequate, "valid beyond the narrow base of
the world and experience upon which the terms of its
metaphors rest" (p. 172). The terms are infinities and
cannot be specifically defined. "Dowel and Dobet in themselves have no substance. They are only words whose grammatical form gives to the search for perfection the comforting
allusion that the quest is orderly and comprehensible. They
are the necessary fiction underlying any cognitive pilgrimage"
(p. 180).

468. Mills, David. "The Rôle of the Dreamer in *Piers Plowman*."
      Piers Plowman: Critical Approaches, ed. Hussey,
      1969, pp. 180-212.

The Dreamer represents the finite, in contrast to Piers,
who represents the infinite. He serves as the means of
asserting a sinful and worldly reality against the advice and
the claims of the characters of the *Vitae*. The Dreamer must
awake because there is always, within the dream, an assertion
of a reality which contradicts the ideal. He is contemporary
man, bound by time and space, and he cannot escape from
worldly understanding: hence, he makes no real progress.
When he first hears the term "Dowel" (used as a verb-adverb),
he misunderstands it as a noun and begins a search for
something which does not exist. He attempts to impose an
order on his vision by postulating a triad which has no
objective existence.

469. Milowicki, Edward J. "*Piers Plowman* and the Ways of
      Providence: A Study of Structure in Relation to Con-
      tent." University of Oregon dissertation, 1969.
      Abstracted *DAI*, 29: 3582A.

WL employed two theories concerning the operation of
Providence--one which conceived of Providence as operating
vertically and spatially (as in the Contemplative Life),
the other, operating horizontally through time.

470. Mitchell, A. G. *Lady Meed and the Art of Piers Plowman.*
     (Chambers Memorial Lecture) London: H. K. Lewis,
     1956. Rptd. *Style and Symbolism in Piers Plowman*,
     ed. Blanch, 1969, pp. 174-193.

    Mitchell disagrees with attempts to discuss the charac-
ter of Meed in terms of historical allegory. She is an
allegorical character who acts independent of historical
circumstances. Meed believes in her worth to all men and is
incapable of understanding criticism levelled at her: she
is not aware of her own wrongdoing and believes that she
is useful, even "indispensable," to men. She might be best
described as morally neutral.

471. _____. "The Text of *Piers Plowman*. C. Prologue 1.
     215." *Medium Aevum*, 8 (1939), 118-20.

    Comments on the dispute between Onions and Flom (331;
489) regarding the correct reading of C. I, 215. Mitchell
favors *reik*.

472. _____. "Worth Both his Ears." *MLN*, 59 (1944), 222.

    Mitchell examines B. Prol., 78-9. If the bishop were
truly a holy man, he would discover the wretched character
of the pardoner he has licensed. If he were "worth both
his ears"--*i.e.*, were he worthy to have them because he made
good use of them--he would learn of the pardoner's practices.

473. Moe, Henry Allen. "The Power of Poetic Vision." *PMLA*, 74
     (1959), 37-41.

    PP is perhaps the one poem that actually altered history.
WL's recommendation for the maintenance of tax-free religious
foundations was made law in the reign of Elizabeth (1601).
WL's ideas on the taxation of gifts for the general public
good (including funds for poor-relief and for educational
institutions) were followed to the letter.

474. _____. "*The Vision of Piers Plowman* and the Law of
     Foundations." *Proceedings of the American Philosophical
     Society*, 102 (1958), 371-75.

475. Morley, Henry. *English Writers.* London: Chapman and Hall,
     1866. Vol. I, Part II, pp. 757-67.

    The poet of *PP* employed a "language Saxon to the utmost,
as used by the common people round his home by the Welsh
border" (p. 757). Includes a brief summary of the poem.
The poet's name was probably William de Langland.

476. Mosher, J. A. *The Exemplum in the Early Religious and
     Didactic Literature in England.* New York: Columbia
     University Press, 1911.

477. Mroczkowski, Przemysław. "Piers and His Pardon: A Dynamic Analysis." *Studies in Language and Literature in Honour of Margaret Schlauch.* Ed. Mieczyslaw Brahmer, *et al.* Warsaw: Panstowe Wydawnictwo Naukowe, 1966, pp. 273-92.

In the Pardon scene, Piers is pulled both by a desire to see the proper arrangement of the material world and a fear of disturbing the proper union with God. His struggle possibly reflects the division of the poet's own soul.

478. _____. *"Piers Plowman:* The Allegory in Motion." *Prace historycznoliterackie,* 8 (1965), 7-45.

A running commentary on the first five passus of the B-text. *PP* is an allegory in composite motion. The dynamism of allegory in *PP* has a changeable rhythm and variable quality, different from the movement of a "plain" narrative in which the reader follows a succession of events. "In dramatic pictures or descriptive patches, in lyrical commiserations and hymnic sequences, it is the poet in the preacher that comes often to the fore" (p. 40).

479. Mullaney, Carol A. *"Piers Plowman*: A Study of Voice and Address Relationships in the Confessions of the Deadly Sins." Catholic University of America dissertation, 1971. Abstracted *DAI*, 32: 2063A.

Examines changes in voice-address relationships in the Confession scene in all three versions of *PP*. In A, speech is "corporate"; in B, it grows more private, with an emphasis on the act of confession; C retains the privacy but emphasizes moral principles. The three scenes operate on different artistic principles.

480. Murtaugh, Daniel M. "Piers Plowman and the Image of God." Yale University dissertation, 1968. Abstracted *DAI*, 29: 876A.

481. Muscatine, Charles. "Locus of Action in Medieval Narrative." *Romance Philology,* 17 (1963), 115-22.

Muscatine examines the relationship between late medieval graphic art and medieval narrative in terms of the delineation of space. There is a "Gothic" tension in late medieval art as it moves out of planimetric form to a rounding out or deepening of perspective, typical of the Renaissance. In narrative, spatial background is more than "setting"-- it is the organizing principle of the narrative. Allegory, though it deals with things that are generally non-spatial, generates its own kind of locus. By the time of *PP*, medieval narrative shows a strong geometry or geography of locus of action used structurally. WL's space seems surrealistic: while he uses flat, geometric, schematic, Romanesque, and naturalistic space, none of these becomes the controlling locus of his narrative. The locus of the characters and actions and their spatial environment is continually shifting. There is no constant spatially organized world as there is in Dante. WL is not clumsy in his narrative art, but he refuses to organize the poem by means of traditional structures. WL's treatment of the locus of action suggests the dissolution of the Gothic style.

482. _____. "*Piers Plowman*: The Poetry of Crisis." *Poetry and Crisis in the Age of Chaucer*. Notre Dame and London: University of Notre Dame Press, 1972, pp. 71-110.

For all its incongruity, PP has a strange integrity and coherence as a whole. The artistic character of the poem lies in its distinctive mingling of the spiritual and the concrete: the plan of the poem is obscure but the capricious interplay of literary forms produces a homogeneous effect which may be best described as "surrealistic." PP is a response to a cultural situation. The thought of the poem is hopeful and orthodox but its art suggests instability and the imminent collapse of orthodoxy. It carries the instability of the epoch in its structure, style, and argument.

483. Newstead, Helaine, ed. *Chaucer and his Contemporaries: Essays on Medieval Literature and Thought*. Greenwich, Conn.: Fawcett, 1968.

484. O'Grady, Gerald Lee. "*Piers Plowman* and the Medieval Tradition of Penance." University of Wisconsin dissertation, 1962. Abstracted *DA*, 23: 2117.

485. Oiji, Takeo. "Four Figures of Piers the Plowman." *Bulletin of the College of General Education. Tohoku U.* (Sendai, Japan), 12, ii (1971), 23-46.

486. _____. "Langland Kenkyu no Senku, Ikuzo Iijima." *Eigo Seinen [The Rising Generation]*, 120 (1975), 468-69. [Pioneer of Langland Studies, Ikuzo Iijima.] See 395.

487. _____. "Why did Piers rend his Pardon Assunder?" *Liberal Arts Review*, 5 (1960), [?].

488. Oliphant, R. "Langland's 'Sire Piers of Pridie.'" *N&Q*, new series, 7 (1960), 167-68.

The word "pridie" may be a Latin derivative. In John Myrc's *Instructions for Parish Priests*, "qui pridie" is suggested as a beginning phrase for a priest who has lost his place in the mass. This suggests that Sir Piers is a caricature of a careless priest.

489. Onions, C. T. "An Unrecorded Reading in *Piers Plowman*." *MLR*, 3 (1908), 170-71.

Onions suggests that in the line "for hadde ȝe ratones ȝoure reed ȝe couthe not ruelie ȝow-selue" (C. I, 215), the word "reed" is an inferior reading. The correct word is "reik." See Flom 331.

490. Orrick, Allan H. "'Declynede,' Passus IV, 1.133, *Piers the Plowman*, A-Text." *PQ*, 35 (1956), 213-15.

Orrick disputes the reading of "declynede" as a verb, arguing that it is used as an adjective. The line might be translated, "Clerks that were confessors grouped themselves together in order to interpret this quickly recited (narrated, presented) clause."

491. Orsten, Elizabeth M. "The Ambiguities in Langland's Rat Parliament." *MS*, 23 (1961), 216-39.

Most historical interpretations of the allegory are too restrictive and do not account for WL's subtle use of irony. WL is neither conservative nor revolutionary in his views on the Good and Bad Parliaments. The mouse represents Gaunt's point of view, not WL's. The mouse provides a 1377 view of the events of 1376. "He is a Gaunt-Figure out-Gaunting himself." Orsten also discusses analogues to the fable in Odo and Bozon.

492. _____. "Patientia in the B-Text of *Piers Plowman*." *MS*, 31 (1969), 317-33.

Patientia is not passive stoic virtue. WL's conception of *patientia* may derive from Augustine who saw patience as a branch of fortitude. This virtue is necessary for those who are economically poor because it eases the burden of earthly care: Patience is vital for Will's spiritual growth because it allows him to conquer despair.

493. _____. "The Treatment of Caritas, Iustitia and Related Theological Themes in the B-Text of *Piers Plowman*." University of Toronto dissertation, 1967. Abstracted *DAI*, 28: 2218A-19A.

494. Osgood, Charles G. *The Voice of England*. New York: Harper and Brothers, 1935. See pp. 87-93.

495. Owen, Dorothy L. *Piers Plowman, A Comparison with Some Earlier and Contemporary French Allegories*. Published M.A. Thesis, University of London, 1912. Rptd. by the Folcroft Library, 1971.

WL uses allegory to emphasize the main events of Christ's life, to state abstract and ethical truths, and to comment on contemporary society. Although these uses of allegory are also found in the *Voie de Paradis*, "Salut d' Enfer," and other French allegories, there can be no certainty as to whether WL read these works. It appears that he did know the *Roman de la Rose*: his portraits of Avarice and Envy are, for example, quite similar to those of the *Roman*. WL's use of allegory is quite original--most French allegories use allegory as a tool of intellect rather than imagination. WL is the first allegorist to use personifications as projections of his own mental faculties.

496. Owst, G. R. "The 'Angel' and the 'Goliardeys' of Langland's Prologue." *MLR*, 20 (1925), 270-79.

The Angel who addresses the king in the B Prologue represents Thomas Brunton. The Angel's warnings to the king echo Brunton's warnings to Edward III. The concurring voice of the "goliardeys" is Peter de la Mare--the spokesman of the commons. The "goliardeys" agrees with the Angel just as de la Mare agreed with Brunton. The lunatic represents the poet himself.

497. _____. *Literature and Pulpit in Medieval England: A Neglected Chapter in the History of English Letters and of the English People*. Cambridge: Cambridge University Press, 1933. Second ed., revised, Oxford: University Press, 1961.

Although *PP* belongs to the tradition of satire and complaint, its theme and structure are indebted to the *ars praedicandi*. Owst demonstrates, for example, that WL's portraits of the Seven Deadly Sins are similar to those found in medieval sermons. The character Piers Plowman descends from homiletic literature: the plowman can be found, for example, in the sermons of John Bromyard. The allegory of Lady Meed is from *Sermo Dom. Quinquag*. WL was probably familiar with the sermons of Bishop Thomas Brunton. The lunatic of the B Prologue is the poet himself and the Angel is Brunton. WL is a transitional figure--he is not totally free of the old, formal, didactic homily tradition and he is not quite in the realm of realism.

498. _____. *Preaching in Medieval England*. Cambridge: Cambridge University Press, 1926.

499. Palmer, Barbara Dallas. "The Guide and Leader: Studies in a Narrative Structural Motif." Michigan State University dissertation, 1969. Abstracted *DAI*, 31: 1236A-37A.

500. _____. "The Guide Convention in *Piers Plowman*." *Leeds Studies in English*, 5 (1971), 13-27.

The structure of *PP* is episodic, often without thematic or narrative connectives. The reader is never certain of the Dreamer's location, his state of consciousness, or the value of the figures he meets. WL could have unified the narrative by means of a guide figure. Both Holy Church and Piers act as guide figures but neither is successful. Holy Church fails because she is also part of the subject; Piers is an inadequate guide because his meaning is never fixed. For most of the poem, Will has no guide except several fragmentary ones. The result of this is "interpretive chaos" because the reader cannot determine what Will is understanding. The linear movement of the narrative breaks down and there is no progression from spiritual degeneracy to illumination. A consistent guide figure would have provided a means of understanding Will's progress.

501. Palmer, William Packard. "The Intellectual Background of *The Vision of Piers Plowman* with Particular Reference to the English and Latin Writings of John Wyclif." University of Kansas dissertation, 1957. Abstracted *DA*, 20 (1959): 1769.

Although Wyclif was a Neoplatonic realist and WL, an Aristotelian Thomist, their intellectual dispositions were similar. Both were sympathetic with mystical thought and were opposed to Neopelagianism. Both admired the monarchy and desired its continuation. They also shared "communistic tendencies" and a belief that the possession of *temporalia* was the root of all earthly evil.

502. Pantin, William A. *The English Church in the Fourteenth Century*. Cambridge: Cambridge University Press, 1955.

Pantin agrees with Owst's contention that *PP* is in the tradition of homiletic literature (p. 238). He also discusses WL's possible familiarity with Uhtred de Boldon, a Benedictine controversialist (pp. 170-72). A general history of the English Church in the later Middle Ages, focusing on Anglo-Papal relations and ecclesiastical controversy.

503. Patch, Gertrude Keiley. "The Allegorical Characters in *Piers Plowman*." Stanford University dissertation, 1957. Abstracted *DA*, 17: 2598.

Examines the meanings of WL's allegorical figures against the background of medieval Christian thought. Will is an allegorical character. He represents the will which must be trained to accept God as the supreme good. He first meets abstractions, such as Conscience and Reason, then begins to confront his own mental faculties. Piers symbolizes the Church, the mystical body of Christ.

504. Patch, H. R. "Characters in Medieval Literature." *MLN*, 40 (1925), 1-14.

See pp. 10-11. Patch compares Chaucer's methods of delineating character with WL's: Envy and Religion, in particular, demonstrate that WL, like Chaucer, imparts a dramatic quality to his characters. "It is only necessary to set them going with personal names and freer action in order to have something like the human comedy of the *Canterbury Tales*" (p. 11).

505. Paull, Michael R. "Mahomet and the Conversion of the Heathen in *Piers Plowman*." *ELN*, 10 (1972), 1-8.

Paull discusses the origin of the legend of Mahomet (B. XV, C. XVIII). Mahomet was considered responsible for inspiring the heathens to reject the Church. In *PP* he is a type of Antichrist because he inspires the clergy to turn away from the conversion of the heathen. Thematically, he looks back to Meed and ahead to Antichrist in the last passus. Examines the treatment of Mahomet by Wyclif and Jacques de Vitry.

506. Pearsall, Derek and Elizabeth Salter. *Landscapes and Seasons of the Medieval World*. Toronto: University of Toronto Press, 1973; London: Elek, 1973.

WL and the Gawain-Poet differ in their use of pictorial detail concerning nature. For WL, nature is generally used in analogy to man's condition. Therefore, he never visualizes natural scenes as vividly as the Gawain-Poet: *e.g.*, for WL, summer is symbolic of a spiritual state of ease, winter is an emblem of woe. See pp. 133-35, 148-49.

507. Pepler, Conrad. "The Beginning of the Way." *Life of the Spirit*, 1 (1946-1947), 101-5.

508. _____. "Conversion in Langland." *Life of the Spirit*, 1 (1946-1947), 136-41.

509. _____. *The English Religious Heritage*. St. Louis, Mo.: B. Herder and Co., 1958.

PP is a practical application of the traditional division of human life into *incipientes, proficientes, et perfecti*. The poem moves from sin to conversion, then enters into a consideration of the three lives or ways. Will is a divided personality with one set of practical notions in conflict with a set of divine notions. The first step towards conversion is the abandonment of the things of this world. Dowel, Dobet, and Dobest represent the persons of the Trinity, as well as the Active, Contemplative, and Mixed Lives. Pepler feels that WL's thought has much in common with the works of Walter Hilton. First published as 507, 508, 510, 511.

510. _____. "Langland's Way to Unity." *Life of the Spirit*, 1 (1946-1947), 198-204.

511. _____. "The Way Opens." *Life of the Spirit*, 1 (1946-1947), 169-72.

512. Peter, John D. *Complaint and Satire in Early English Literature*. Oxford: Clarendon Press, 1956.

> WL is a simpler and more direct poet than Chaucer--his attitudes are less ambivalent and his verse tends to be conceptual rather than concrete and particular. His portrait of Sloth, for example, is a kind of caricature, whereas Chaucer's portrait of the Monk is realistic. Chaucer is a satirist, WL is a writer of complaint. See Chapter III, "Complaint in Medieval England," pp. 40-59.

513. Polak, Lucie. "A Note on the Pilgrim in *Piers Plowman*." *N&Q*, new series, 17 (1970), 282-85.

> Discusses the travels of the pilgrim (A. VI, 8-16). The references to Babylon and Armenia appear in contemporary accounts of actual pilgrimages. The pilgrim may have been a "professional pilgrim" and he may have gone into Jerusalem by crossing Armenia.

514. Powell, C. L. "The Castle of the Body." *SP*, 16 (1919), 197-205.

> Powell examines the conceit of the body as a castle in Grossetête's *Castle of Love*, and the *Sawles Warde*. WL may be indebted to the latter work for his description of the body in A.X. Spenser's portrait of the House of Alma may derive from *PP*.

515. Prince, Helen M. "Long Will: The First-Person Narrator in *Piers Plowman*." Northwestern University dissertation, 1970. Abstracted *DAI*, 30: 4423A-24A.

> Examines the character of Will throughout the poem, tracing the extent of his control over the meaning and structure of the poem. Will does what he must, but he lacks the conviction to turn directly to Christ. We should read the poem as the portrait of the consciousness of one person, "closely related to an historical being, William Langland."

516. Quirk, Randolf. "Langland's Use of 'Kind Wit' and 'Inwit.'" *JEGP*, 52 (1953), 182-88.

> WL's use of the terms "Kind wit" and "Inwit" is unique in ME. The use of "kind" in conjunction with "wit" distinguished it from absolute or divine reason: it is a gift of God (Kind) and a teacher of Conscience. "Inwit" is related to *animus*--man's intellectual powers. In *PP*, Inwit and Conscience are not synonymous. WL's use of these terms is precise and technical--based on scholastic philosophy. Con-

science is one of Inwit's activities--his awareness of right
and wrong brought to bear on action.

517. _____. "Vis Imaginitiva." *JEGP*, 53 (1954), 81-83.

Quirk notes that the use of the term "Imaginitif" is
rare in ME. Generally, it refers to the common sense or
reproductive imagination, but WL uses it in a different sense.
"Imaginitif" in *PP* may derive from Aristotle's definition
of imagination as both a deliberative and sensitive faculty.
Most medieval writers, including Aquinas, Bacon, and Pecock,
use it only in the second sense. WL may have been influenced
by Victorine thought which saw the imagination as part of
the reasoning process. The only other medieval English
writer to give imagination a deliberative function is Lydgate.

518. Radigan, John D. "The Clouded Vision: Satire and the Way
to God in *Piers Plowman*." Syracuse University dissertation, 1976. Abstracted *DAI*, 36: 6712A.

WL's satire is not restricted to isolated outbursts
against society. Each vision of *PP* has a central target
which WL attacks by means of a *reductio ad absurdum* argument:
the first vision attacks wealth, the second, laziness, the
third, the Dreamer's rash thinking, and the fourth, hypocrisy.

519. Rauch, Rufus William. "Langland and Medieval Functionalism."
Annual Report of the American Historical Association,
3 (1942), 39-56.

WL believes that the universe is harmonized by all parts
of the heavenly and earthly hierarchy performing their individual functions. The key to social betterment is the
redemption of the individual. WL attacks individuals and
institutions only because they are neglecting their God-
ordained duties. Evil begins on a small scale by afflicting
the individual, but quickly spreads and infects the social
system.

520. Raw, Barbara. "Piers and the Image of God in Man."
Piers Plowman: Critical Approaches, ed. Hussey,
1969, pp. 143-79.

The theme of *PP* is the restoration of the divine image
in man. The imprint of the divine in man is permanent and
inalienable, although it has been obscured by original sin.
Historically, the *Visio* corresponds to the Old Testament
period, *Dobet* to the Gospels, and *Dobest* to the Age of the
Church from its foundation to the end of the world. The
restoration of the divine image in the individual also occurs
in three stages: first, man conforms his will to God's
(Dowel); second, he accepts the gift of the Son--redemption
(Dobet); third, he accepts the gift of the spirit (Dobest).
The evolution of Piers's character symbolizes the restoration

of mankind as a whole, while Will represents the restoration of the divine image in individual man.

521. Reidy, John. "Peris the Ploughman, whiche a Pardoun He Hadde." *Papers of the Michigan Academy of Science, Arts, and Letters*, 50 (1965), 535-44.

   The Pardon Scene is hopelessly enigmatic: Piers may be opting for the second stage of the Active life--meditation and penance. Piers achieves the full Active life which borders on the Contemplative Life.

522. Riach, Mary. "Langland's Dreamer and the Transformation of the Third Vision." *Essays in Criticism*, 19 (1969), 6-18.

   The third vision of the B-text is a crucial step in Will's education, and in the evolution of the three texts of *PP*. In this vision, Imaginitif attacks Will's opinions on learning and virtuous living and provides an authoritative resolution to his intellectual confusion. The Dreamer is now seen in a new, ironic light because Imaginitif turns much of the material of the A *Vita* against him and "subjects him to a searching, humiliating revelation of the unwarranted pride he had shown in his search for Dowel in the A-text" (p. 17).

523. Richardson, M. E. "Characters in *Piers Plowman*." *TLS*, 39 (January 13, 1940), 24.

   Identifies WL's portrait of Covetise with one William Hervey who is mentioned in the Patent Rolls for 1361-1364. Hervey, a money lender and wood trader, was connected with Geoffrey de la Rokayle.

524. _____. "The Characters in *Piers Plowman*: The Bishop of Bethlehem." *N&Q*, continuous series, 180 (1941), 116-17.

   Identifies the Bishop of C. XVIII, 277-280 with one William Bromfelde. "Surrye," usually glossed as "Syria," may instead refer to the bishop's patrons.

525. _____. "*Piers Plowman*." *TLS*, 38 (March 11, 1939), 149-50.

   Identifies Rose the Regratour (Avarice's wife) with one "Rose la Hokestere," mentioned in the 1350 Pleas and Memoranda Rolls of London.

526. Risse, Robert G., Jr. "The Augustinian Paraphrase of Isaiah 14:13-14 in *Piers Plowman* and the Commentary on the Fables of Avianus." *PQ*, 45 (1966), 712-17.

Reexamines Holy Church's commentary on Lucifer (C. II, 108-11) in light of Kellogg's discovery that WL altered "sedem" to "pedem." Kellogg believed that WL's source was Augustine's *Enarrationes in Psalmos* (422). Risse argues that the source was more probably the popular commentary on the Fables of Avianus. The passage in question occurs twenty-nine times in MSS of the *Fables*, but the reading "pedem" for "sedem" never occurs. WL's alteration of this word was deliberate and original.

527. Robertson, D. W., Jr. "The Doctrine of Charity in Medieval Literary Gardens: A Topical Approach Through Symbolism and Allegory." *Speculum*, 26 (1951), 24-49.

528. _____ and Bernard F. Huppé. *Piers Plowman and Scriptural Tradition*. Princeton, N.J.: Princeton University Press, 1951.

Piers represents God's ministry on earth in the *status praelatorum*: he is the ideal, actualized in Christ, of the priest of the people. The present-day Church is insufficient: it needs the true successors of Peter in the *status praelatorum*. The character Will is a representative of the faculty Will rather than any individual person. At the beginning of the poem he represents the will unguided by reason--like most of the folk of the field, he is in a state of spiritual slumber, and is blinded by an attachment to the world. In order for man to reach the Holy City, he must forsake *temporalia* and learn to love (*caritas*). The "kynde knowing" Will seeks is *Deus caritas*. Holy Church represents the anagogical Church--the ideal toward which the Church Militant should strive. By Passus XII, Will has learned humility and has overcome his heretical tendencies. He is now prepared to seek Dowel in the Church Militant. His request to eat the fruit of Charity demonstrates that he is becoming contemplative. In Passus XVII, after his meeting with the Samaritan, Will is no longer a hermit, a faculty in isolation. He has been united with memory and intellect in the image of God. Will is a device by means of which the poet may set off the actual against the ideal in the poem. The people who mislead him typify the misleading forces of the actual world. Although there are problems in the coherence of the literal level of *PP*, its sentence unfolds clearly and logically.

529. Robinson, Ian. *Chaucer and the English Tradition*. Cambridge: Cambridge University Press, 1972.

See pp. 201-18. Chaucer tells stories, WL exhorts. *PP* offers us a group of subjects, interests, and traditions missing in Chaucer's work. In terms of narrative art, however, WL is clearly inferior to Chaucer: he frequently merely preaches.

530. Roth, Francis. *The English Austin Friars 1249-1538*. Vol. I, *History*. New York: Augustinian Historical Institute, 1966.

A comprehensive history of the Austin Friars in late Medieval England. A note on p. 359 alludes to the long-standing popular tradition that WL was a member of the Austin Friar's community at Woodhouse, or that he received early training there.

531. Roush, George Jonathan. "The Political Plowman: The Expression of Political Ideals in *Piers Plowman* and Its Successors." University of California dissertation, 1966. Abstracted *DA*, 27: 752A.

Examines *PP* as a political poem. Its basic theory is orthodox and conservative. WL was well-versed in politics and law. Roush also traces the influence of *PP* in the sixteenth century.

532. Russell, G. H. "The Salvation of the Heathen: The Exploration of a Theme in *Piers Plowman*." *Journal of the Warburg and Courtauld Institute*, 29 (1966), 101-16.

Russell examines the salvation of the heathen theme in the three versions of *PP*, focusing on changes between the B- and C-texts. In the C-revision, B's explicit statements on the necessity of sacramental baptism are removed and in the last scene, WL offers Uhtred de Boldon's positive doctrine on the soul's attainment of the right of salvation at the moment of death without sacramental baptism.

533. Ryan, Thomas A. "The Poetry of Reform: Christian Socialism in the First Dream of *Dowel*." Brown University dissertation, 1972. Abstracted *DAI*, 32: 5750A.

534. Ryan, William M. "Modern Idioms in *Piers Plowman*." *American Speech*, 34 (1959), 67-69.

Examines five "modern idioms" that occur in *PP*: 1. "overdo it" (C. XIV, 189-191); 2. "the why's and wherefore's" (B. XII, 217-218); 3. "plenty and peace" (C. XVIII, 91-93); 4. "life and limb" (B. XIX, 100-101); 5. "First and foremost" (B. XIX, 115-117). The last two occurrences antedate *OED* citations.

535. _____. *William Langland*. New York: Twayne, 1968.

A general introduction to WL and *PP*. Ryan summarizes the authorship problems and provides a general review of criticism.

536. Saintsbury, George. *A History of Criticism and Literary Taste in Europe*. 3 Vols. New York: Dodd, Mead, and Co., 1900. Vol. I, *Classical and Medieval Criticism*.

537. _____. "Langland and Gower." *A Short History of English Literature*. New York: Macmillan, 1898. Book III, Chapter II, pp. 131-42.

Saintsbury warns critics against deriving hypothetical biographical material from the fiction of the poem. WL is not more "Saxon" in vocabulary than Chaucer. Summarizes the argument of the B-text. The traditional view of Chaucer as a court poet and WL as a poet of the people is a gross oversimplification.

538. St. Jacques, Raymond C. "Conscience's Final Pilgrimage in *Piers Plowman* and the Cyclical Structure of the Liturgy." *Revue de l'Université d'Ottawa*, 40 (1970), 210-23.

St. Jacques argues that the cyclical structure of the liturgical year provided WL with a model for the circular design of *PP*: the treatment of certain themes in *PP* corresponds to their seasonal positions in medieval sermon cycles. Pride as the enemy of the Church is a frequent theme in Pentecost sermons and the need to repulse pride by mortification is demonstrated in Lent. Ember days sermons frequently employ an imagery of farming analogous to Piers's tilling of the half-acre. Conscience's final pilgrimage is related to the liturgy of Advent which frequently focuses on the second coming.

539. Salter, Elizabeth. "Medieval Poetry and the Figural View of Reality." *Proceedings of the British Academy*, 54 (1968), 73-92. See Zeeman, Elizabeth.

The essential messages of *PP* are conveyed at their greatest intensity by figural or typological means. The Bible provided WL with a traditional system of correspondences as well as a creative view of history. *PP* is like no other extant literary allegory and discussing it in terms of personification allegory or four-fold allegorical meaning is not very helpful. The Dreamer possesses a figural reality: he functions as both a living historical individual and as a sign. Piers is also a *figura*: not only is he a type of Christ--he is also part of the process of the fulfillment of the divine promise. *PP* is not incoherent: its incremental repetitions are not a sign of confusion.

540. _____. *Piers Plowman: An Introduction*. Oxford: Basil Blackwell, 1962.

PP is clearly indebted to the *ars praedicandi*: like a homilist, WL had to sacrifice grace, transition, and unity, because his intention was spiritual, not literary. WL continually strives to make his point clear and he is generally painstakingly simple. *PP* is structured in two distinct ways: first, by means of the four primary divisions and a cyclical structure; second, by a continuous process of thematic linking and cross-referencing. It is doubtful that WL consciously employed a four-fold allegorization method, although he certainly wanted his audience to be receptive to multiple meanings. By the end of Passus I, we are conscious of one central message being conveyed on several levels. *PP* continually changes its allegorical depth--WL differs from most other allegorists by not maintaining a linear progression and set of consistent meanings. His manipulation of allegory reminds one less of exacting medieval exegesis than of the free, flexible procedures of the spiritual manuals.

541. Sampson, George, ed. *"Piers the Plowman* and Its Sequence." *The Concise Cambridge History of English Literature.* London: Cambridge University Press, 1941, pp. 60-64.

542. Sanderlin, George. "The Character 'Liberum Arbitrium' in the C-text of *Piers Plowman.*" *MLN*, 56 (1941), 449-53.

The C-Reviser's treatment of *Liberum Arbitrium* is sharper and more subtle than B's. In C, he teaches the Dreamer about charity. Hugh of St. Cher and John Damascene considered *Liberum Arbitrium* a universal power of the soul. In C. XVII, 173-177 he appears to be the power which chooses good over evil. This passage is an allegory of grace cooperating with free choice to defend the soul. The C-Reviser was a man of learning and theological insight.

543. Schlauch, Margaret. *English Medieval Literature and Its Social Foundations.* Warszawa: Panstowe Wydawnictwo Naukowe, 1956.

See Chapter X, section 4, *"Piers Plowman,"* pp. 213-18. The author of *PP* was generally conservative in his socio-political beliefs. His denunciation of friars and pardoners is not a direct attack on the Church, but a plea for reform from within the established ecclesiology. WL has none of the bitter hostility of Swift--his vision is essentially optimistic.

544. Schmidt, A. V. C. "Langland and Scholastic Philosophy." *Medium Aevum*, 38 (1969), 134-56.

The figures of psychological allegory in *PP* may be divided into three major categories--moral and spiritual figures, active characters, and noetic figures which personify the knowing faculties of the mind. There are two kinds of noetic figures--those that refer to both the external and internal concept of the mind (*e.g.*, Reason), and those that refer only to the internal aspect. Disagreeing with Sanderlin (542), Schmidt argues that WL's treatment of *Liberum Arbitrium* is not influenced by John Damascene--for WL, this concept is not a universal power of the soul, it is the essence of the soul. This view of *Liberum Arbitrium* ultimately derives from the Carmelite theologian Michael Ayguani of Bologna. The definition of *Liberum Arbitrium* seems to be indebted to pre-scholastic treatises on the nature of the soul. WL's philosophy is generally much closer to Augustinian thought than to scholastic philosophy.

545. _____. "A Note on Langland's Conception of 'Anima' and 'Inwit.'" *N&Q*, new series, 15 (1968), 363-64.

Schmidt discusses the probable sources of two passages in the A-text (X, 43-5 and X, 49-54). The first passage concerns the location of the soul in the body. From the *de Anima* of Cassiodorus and the *Spiritu et Anima* attributed to Alcher of Clairvaux, WL could have derived the notion that although the soul wanders throughout the body, her particular location is the heart. The second passage concerning the location of "Inwit" appears to fuse the ideas of Alcher and Cassiodorus.

546. _____. "A Note on the A Text of *Piers Plowman*, Passus X. 91-94." *N&Q*, new series, 14 (1967), 365-66.

WL uses two authorities, "goodis worde" and "holiwrit," to support his assertion that conscience is not an infallible guide to salvation. WL's source is the *Summa de Vitiis* of Jean de la Rochelle. The "holiwrit" refers to Richard of St. Victor and "goodis worde" refers to a passage from Paul which Richard glosses.

547. _____. "A Note on the phrase 'Free Wit' in the C-Text of *Piers Plowman*." *N&Q*, new series, 15 (1968), 168-69.

Liberum Arbitrium and *Anima* are the only parts of the soul given Latin names in *PP* because WL realized that English equivalents would not be precise enough. The term "Free wit" in C. XI, 51 may be an attempt to translate *Liberum Arbitrium*: WL was trying to render a difficult theological concept by mixing the terms "free wit" and "free will."

548. _____. "Two Notes on *Piers Plowman*." *N&Q*, new series, 16 (1969), 285-86.

First, in C. IV, 335-409, "mede" and "mercede" are forms of direct and indirect relation according to medieval grammar (See 189). Second, "Donum dei" (B. XIV, 275) appears to derive from Augustine's *de Patientia* where Augustine stresses the connection between patience and poverty.

549. Schoeck, R. J. "The Use of St. John Chrysostom in Six-
          teenth Century Controversy: Christopher St. German
          and Sir Thomas More in 1533." *Harvard Theological
          Review*, 54 (1961), 21-27.

     WL, like More, quotes St. John of Chrysostom from a
pseudo-Chrysostom text. Schoeck examines four parallel
passages from the *Opus Imperfectum*, the *Catena Aurea*, PP,
and John Gerson, concluding that WL was quoting the *Opus
Imperfectum* from memory in B. XV, 115 ff. and C. XVII,
271 ff.

550. Schroeder, Mary C. "The Character of Conscience in *Piers
          Plowman*." *SP*, 67 (1970), 13-30.

     All aspects of Conscience's complex character are im-
plicit from his first appearance, but each major scene
emphasizes a different aspect of his nature. Against Lady
Meed, he acts as a judge, a just arbitrator between right
and wrong. In the scene with the Doctor of Divinity, he
takes on a mystical role--this culminates in Passus XIX
when he welcomes Grace. He never oversteps the limitations
of his nature. Because of his evolution, he is the fullest
character among WL's personifications.

551. _____. "*Piers Plowman*: The Tearing of the Pardon."
          PQ, 49 (1970), 8-18.

     In the Pardon Scene, we see both an actual granting of
God's grace to Piers and a typological rendering of the change
wrought in history by the Atonement--a change from *vetus homo*
(man bound by his natural body) to the *novus homo* (man liber-
ated by divine redemption). The Pardon introduces a new dispensation by which the old law is fulfilled in the new law of
charity. Dowel is not obtainable until the end of Passus VII
when redemption through the grace of God is made possible.

552. Schweitzer, Edward C. "'Half a Laumpe Lyne in Latyne' and
          Patience's Riddle in *Piers Plowman*." *JEGP*, 73 (1974),
          313-27.

     Kaske's grammatical reading of this passage is helpful
but incomplete (408). *Ex vi transicionis* is a punning
reference to the *ex vi Paschal* (the central event of Christ's
passion), and functions as a typological reference bringing
together the Old and New Testaments and contemporary life.
Because baptism depends on passage (transitus, transitio),
its power may be best described by a punning use of the
grammatical tag *ex vi transicionis*. The "laumpe lyne"
refers to part of the baptismal liturgy when the priest
presents a lighted candle to the neophyte. Patience is
referring to the first half of the injunction and is
therefore stating that to do well is to guard one's baptism.

553. Sen Gupta, Jasodhara. *"Piers Plowman."* Essays in Criticism, 13 (1963), 201-2.

A comparison of *PP* with twentieth-century art. The rapid shifting of allegorical dimensions is somewhat similar to Durrell's "sliding panel" technique, and to Eliot's poetry. Also notes that WL's visual technique is similar to modern cinematography.

554. Shute, H. W. *"Piers Plowman, B. I. 40-1."* Archiv, 100 (1898), 155-56.

Shute provides translations of this problematic passage as it appears in all three versions. A might be translated, "for the fiend and thy flesh follow together and put thy soul to shame." C might be translated, "For the Fiend and thy Flesh follow together and that [*i.e.*, this fact] seeth the soul and telleth it thee in thy heart." In B, the problem is more complex because Skeat chose the variant "sueth" for "seeth." "Soule" should be taken as the subject. B might be translated, "For the fiend and thy flesh follow thee together. This and that seeth thy soul and telleth it thee in thy heart."

555. Sledd, James. "Three Textual Notes on Fourteenth Century Poetry." *MLN*, 55 (1940), 379-82.

Sledd provides a translation of C. VI, 65-9 which is obscured by false punctuation in Skeat's edition: "Bondsmen and bastards and beggars' children belong to labor; and lords' children should serve both God and good men according to their degree--some to sing masses, others to sit and write, to read and receive what is reasonable for them to spend."

556. Smalley, Beryl. "Problems of Exegesis in the Fourteenth Century." *Miscellanea Medievalia*, 1 (1962), 266-74.

557. Smith, A. H. *Piers Plowman and the Pursuit of Poetry*. Inaugural Lecture Delivered at the University College, London. February 23, 1950. London: H. K. Lewis, 1951.

A general review of scholarship and criticism, focusing on the contributions of Chambers, Grattan, and Kane. Smith discusses the authorship problem and provides a brief summary of the argument of the poem. Smith then describes the Chambers papers in the University College Library which include notes towards a critical text and unpublished data on the authorship controversy.

558. Smith, Ben H., Jr. "Patience's Riddle, *Piers Plowman* B, XIII." *MLN*, 76 (1961), 675-82.

According to the *Grammatica Speculativa* of Duns Scotus, "ex vi transicionis" refers to the principles of grammatical transitivity. The half-line may refer to a Psalm which contains a reference to the lamp (lumen). Smith notes four functions of the line: 1. it characterizes kind love; 2. it describes the result of the Incarnation; 3. it differentiates the two great speeches of God--the creation and the Redemption; 4. it suggests that the Father's love requires mankind's acknowledgement of His power and love.

559. _____. *Traditional Images of Charity in Piers Plowman.* The Hague: Mouton, 1966.

Discusses images of *caritas* in four major scenes in *PP*: Holy Church's speech, Patience's Riddle, the Vision of the Tree of Charity and Will's meeting with the Good Samaritan. A consistent pattern of construction is used in each of these imagistic configurations: WL extracts details of a pattern from some traditional source, then recombines them in a unique way. The imagery of Holy Church's speech is relatively simple: but the imagery of Patience's Riddle is highly complex--this reflects the thematic emphasis on the difficulty of applying charity. Will at last meets Charity face-to-face in the person of the Good Samaritan who is a type of Christ. The progression of the poem is from exposition to instruction to visionary apprehension and direct experience which culminates in the personification of charity. WL employs imagery in three different ways: 1. he evokes traditional associations of scripturally derived imagery; 2. he employs exegetical images; 3. he takes imagery that derives from neither Scripture nor exegetical tradition and weights it with exegetical overtones.

560. Smith, L. T. "English Popular Preaching in the Fourteenth Century." *English Historical Review*, 7 (1892), 25-36.

561. Smith, Macklin. *"Piers Plowman* and the Tradition of the Medieval Life of Christ." Princeton University dissertation, 1976. Abstracted *DAI*, 27: 1571A.

Smith examines medieval Franciscan visions of Christ and demonstrates WL's indebtedness to these visions--particularly their emphasis on the embodiment of spiritual ideas in the carnal and on meditation on the life of Christ.

562. Spearing, A. C. "The Art of Preaching and *Piers Plowman.*" *Criticism and Medieval Poetry*. New York: Barnes and Noble, 1964, pp. 68-95. Rptd. in *Chaucer and His Contemporaries*, ed. Helaine Newstead. New York: Fawcett, 1968, pp. 255-82.

WL's interest in preaching is demonstrated throughout *PP*. Most of the narrator's instructors appear as preachers and the poem is largely composed of sermon-like speech. The

principles of the *ars praedicandi* "may help us to read the
work in detail, as well as to grasp its *dispositio*, for
baffling transitions, changes of direction, and a use of
recurrent themes are characteristic of the poem's local
development as well as its overall structure." Like a
sermon, *PP* returns to its *thema breve*, "What good thing shall
I do that I may have eternal life?," "even though the poet
frequently digresses, and changes directions. Like St.
Bernard, WL is driven to explain and clarify points for
his audience. His commitment, spontaneity, and style indicate his close relationship with the preacher's art.
See 497.

563.   _____. "The Development of a Theme in *Piers Plowman*."
          RES, new series, 11 (1960), 241-53.

        Thematic recurrences in *PP* contribute to the development
of ideas and are part of a conscious composition process.
The ideas of hunger and bread appear in three scenes in the
C-text (VI, IX, and XVI). The C-Reviser deepens the meaning
of hunger by extending it from the realm of economics to the
moral and spiritual realms. In C. IX, Hunger uses bread as
a natural symbol for the materialist solution to economic
problems. In the *Activa Vita* scene (C. XVI) bread becomes
a symbol of the communion wafer but the images of the Hunger
episode (famine and pestilence, for example) reappear.
Activa Vita returns to Hunger's remedy for the troubles of
society, relating it to the problems of the individual--sin
is caused by too much bread.

564.   _____. *Medieval Dream Poetry*. Cambridge: Cambridge
          University Press, 1976.

        See pp. 138-51, on the A-text, pp. 152-161, on the B-
Revision. The A-text is an incomplete and inconclusive
work: its opening has much in common with other alliterative
dream visions, particularly *Winner and Waster*, but the last
four Passus present an allegorical account of the moral and
intellectual problems which prevented Langland from being
able to complete the poem. Here the dream loses its objective allegorical form and becomes a personal nightmare. In
the B-text, WL makes his personal difficulties part of the
organic form of the poem: "Plunging into the depths of
his own mind, where thoughts and impulses swirl unguided
by logic, he comes to see that he must change himself before
he can change the world" (p. 157). The "fragmentariness"
and vagueness of the poem express human attempts to apprehend transcendent realities.

565.   Speirs, John. *Medieval English Poetry: The Non-Chaucerian
          Tradition*. London: Faber and Faber, 1957.

Although he does not treat *PP* specifically, Speirs
briefly discusses the poem's mixture of realism and symbolism. See pp. 35-36.

566. Spencer, Hazelton. "Worth Both His Ears." *MLN*, 58 (1943),
        48.

Spencer suggests that the Bishop mentioned in B. Prol.,
28 should be "worthy to keep both his ears": *i.e.*, he
deserves to have them cropped. Also notes that the C-text's
description of Avarice's face (VII, 201) is superior to
B's description (V, 194); the smooth-shaven face is more
suitable for a portrait of Avarice.

567. Stillwell, Gardiner. "Chaucer's Plowman and the Contem-
        porary English Peasant." *ELH*, 6 (1939), 285-90.

In his portrait of the Plowman, Chaucer expresses the
conservative medieval ideal of the proper order of society.
According to this ideal, each individual had a God-given
position to fill. Chaucer's Plowman is similar to Piers.

568. Stock, Lorraine K. "Patience and Sloth in Two Medieval
        English Works: *Mankind* and *Piers Plowman* C." Cornell
        University dissertation, 1976. Abstracted *DAI*,
        36: 7446A.

569. Stone, George Winchester, Jr. "An Interpretation of the
        A-Text of *Piers Plowman*." *PMLA*, 53 (1938), 656-77.

Most of the social satire of the A-text is directed
toward the worldliness of the folk of the field. Personal
and historical satire is merely incidental. The *Visio* deals
with the sham in men's lives, while the *Vita* deals with the
sham in men's minds. The poem points wholly towards the
insufficiency of man unaided by divine power. The poet
explores three main themes: the idea of faith as opposed
to works, the question of predestination versus free will,
and the location of authority.

570. Strang, Barbara M. H. *"Piers Plowman* B. Prologue 132-8."
        N&Q, new series, 7 (1960), 436.

571. Strange, W. C. "The Willful Trope: Some Notes on Personi-
        fication with Illustrations from *Piers* A." *AnM*, 9
        (1968), 26-39.

The personifications of *PP* are not merely figures of
speech, but figures of thought. In the character of Lady
Meed, for example, WL discloses a genuine psychological
complexity--he portrays Meed as a creature of appetite with
a deep-rooted diabolism. She is not a mere caricature of an
abstract quality. Strange discusses the differences between
personification and metaphor. Metaphor is condensed, in-

vestigative, and tolerant, while personification refuses to
be economical. It is a metaphysical fact not merely a
rhetorical strategy.

572. Sullivan, Sister Carmeline. *The Latin Inscriptions and the
    Macaronic Verse in Piers Plowman*. Published Catholic
    University of America dissertation. Washington, D.C.
    Catholic University of America Press, 1932.

    A compilation and classification of Latin quotations and
    Macaronic lines. Sister Sullivan concludes: the difference
    in the use of Latin quotations between the three texts is
    not striking (indicating single authorship); of 619 Latin
    quotations, 514 are from the Bible; quotations have a dis-
    tinct ethical, never a merely poetical or artistic, value;
    WL is fairly accurate in his quotations considering the
    amount of Latin material he employs; WL evidently had a
    wide acquaintance with religious literature; Macaronic
    lines are often introduced to enhance alliteration; WL uses
    Latin when referring to a Book of the Bible or to a Psalm;
    he often names the parts of the mass in Latin; epithets
    for Christ are usually entered in Latin.

573. Taitt, Peter. "In Defence of Lot." *N&Q*, new series, 18
    (1971), 284-85.

    In C. II, 25-6, 27-8, WL makes Lot guilty of incest.
    In both the Vulgate and Hebrew original, Lot is not a willing
    participant in the act. Chaucer makes a similar mistake in
    The Pardoner's Tale (485-91). The source of this information
    for both Chaucer and WL may be the *Historia Scholastica* of
    Peter Comestor (Chapter LIV).

574. _____. *Incubus and Ideal: Ecclesiastical Figures
    in Chaucer and Langland*. (ElizS 44.) Salzburg: Inst.
    für eng. Sprache & Lit., Univ. Salzburg, 1975.

    Chapter II treats WL. Taitt examines WL's views of
    friars, summoners, clerks, pardoners, monastic orders,
    parsons, and parish priests. Chaucer is able to blend
    individuals with types in his appraisals of ecclesiastical
    figures: WL rarely portrays ecclesiastical figures in
    vivid human terms--most of his figures are representative
    types. WL's methods of characterization depend on his
    critical examination of specific ecclesiastical abuses.
    Compares Chaucer's and WL's uses of irony, metaphorical
    language and imagery, word play, and conventional devices.
    Includes an index of single and parallel references to
    ecclesiastical figures in *PP*.

575. _____. "The Quest Theme in Representative English
    Works of the Thirteenth and Fourteenth Centuries."
    University of British Columbia dissertation, 1974.
    Abstracted *DAI*, 35: 3703A.

576. Ten Brink, Bernard. "William Langland." *Early English Literature (To Wyclif)*. Trans. Horace M. Kennedy. New York: Henry Holt, 1883. Book IV, Chapter III, pp. 351-67.

Ten Brink believes that "Langley" may be the more correct form of the author's name. WL is compared to Richard Rolle. The poem "is much like a series of paintings whose mutual connection lies more in the intention than in actual execution" (p. 354). Concerning the relationship between WL and Wyclif: "in all practical questions, Langland and Wyclif were of the same opinion" (p. 367). But WL was never antagonistic toward Catholic doctrine.

577. Thimmesh, Hilary. "A Synoptic Reading of Central Themes in *Piers Plowman*." Unpublished Catholic University of America dissertation, 1932.

578. Thomas, G. A. "A Study of the Influence of Langland's *Piers Plowman* on Gower." Unpublished Cornell University dissertation, 1927.

579. Thomas, P. G. "*Piers Plowman* and its Congeners." *English Literature Before Chaucer*. London: Edward Arnold & Co., 1924, pp. 141-48.

Thomas discusses the late fourteenth-, early fifteenth-century poems of social complaint as descendents of *PP*. *The Parlement of the Thre Ages* anticipates *PP*. WL was a mouthpiece of the poorer classes, and he chose to write in the popular meter.

580. Tillyard, E. M. W. *The English Renaissance: Fact or Fiction?* London: Hogarth, 1952. See pp. 90-92.

581. _____. "Langland." *The English Epic and its Background*. Oxford: Oxford University Press, 1954. Part II, Chapter III, pp. 151-70.

PP emerges as the "undoubted, if imperfect, English epic of the Middle Ages." By combining a public theme with an individual tragic theme, WL influences all subsequent English works that might be termed epic, such as *The Faerie Queene*, *Arcadia*, *Paradise Lost*, and *The Pilgrim's Progress*. But although *PP* is "nobly planned," it is seriously flawed. WL let his obsession get in the way of his art. The poem has many epic ingredients, but WL tends to decrease the art of the poem by repetition and preaching. More important are the structural defects: *e.g.*, the *Vita* repeats the theme of the *Visio*--the quest for Dowel.

582. _____. *Myth and the English Mind: From Piers Plowman to Edward Gibbon*. New York: Collier Books, 1962. See pp. 126 ff.

583. Traver, Hope. "The Four Daughters of God: A Study of Versions of this Allegory with Special Reference to those in Latin, French, and English." Unpublished Bryn Mawr College dissertation, 1907. Abstracted *Bryn Mawr College Monographs*, 6 (1907), 147-52.

584. _____. "The Four Daughters of God: A Mirror of Changing Doctrine." *PMLA*, 40 (1925), 44-92.

Traver traces the evolution of the literary motif of the debate of the four daughters of God. Examines the Marcianite and Valentinian heresies, and Jewish and Christian commentary on Genesis and Psalms. Traver cannot find a likeness to WL's treatment of this motif in any source, except perhaps Bernard or Bonaventura. *PP* may have influenced the treatment of this motif in the *Castell of Perseverance* and Lydgate's *Life of Our Lady*.

585. Traversi, Derek. "Langland's *Piers Plowman*." *A Guide to English Literature*, I, *The Age of Chaucer*. Ed. Boris Ford. Baltimore: Penguin, 1954, pp. 127-45.

PP is not a purely personal creation: it represents the convergence of two distinct traditions—the popular and the theological. Agrees with Owst that the poem was influenced by the sermon arts (497). *PP* "suggests less the finality of an individual creation than a cumulative expression of a traditional conscience" (p. 134). The allegorical pattern is balanced by a "profoundly tragic view of the state of the world" (p. 139). WL is a master of the "comedy of humors": he does not present the qualities of abstractions in abstract form. His portraits are dramatic and human, and are always rendered with a moral intention.

586. _____. "Revaluation X: *The Vision of Piers Plowman*." *Scrutiny*, 5 (1936), 276-91.

Compares WL's and Spenser's use of allegory. WL is able to use allegory as a flexible and expressive instrument while Spenser's allegory is contrived and stale. Traversi also praises WL's poetic language.

587. Tristram, E. W. "Piers Plowman in Early English Wall Paintings." *Burlington Magazine*, 31 (1917), 135-40.

Tristram examines early wall paintings whose subjects are derived from, or are in some way connected to, *PP*. These illustrations frequently depict the simple peasant bearing the wounds of the crucifixion. In the church of Ampney St. Mary's near the Malvern Hills, there is a portrait of Christ represented as Piers Plowman with farm implements placed around his head in the shape of a halo.

588. Tristram, Philippa. *Figures of Life and Death in Medieval English Literature*. London: Paul Elek, 1976.

See pp. 197-201. For Will, the Harrowing of Hell is a revelation of the meaning of life. The death and descent into Hell are assimilated to the experience of every man. Piers is the human Christ: he must "like all men, seek through uncertainties, even to the suffering of death itself, for the meaning of life." The poem does not end in affirmation. The Harrowing relates to the reenactment of the Crucifixion in the mass and the pilgrimage of each man on earth--it must recur and be rediscovered.

589. Trower, Katherine B. "The Figure of Hunger in *Piers Plowman*." *ABR*, 24 (1973), 238-60.

Hunger functions on at least three levels in his scene with Piers: 1. he is actual famine; 2. he symbolizes spiritual famine; 3. in terms of salvation history he represents the period in which mankind hungered for God. Hunger's intervention occurs in the midst of a breakdown of penitential activity necessary for the folk's deliverance to Truth. Piers is said to learn "leechcraft" from Hunger-- basically, Piers learns that man must rely on Christ to sustain his physical needs. Piers may then detach himself from physical hunger and lead the folk to Truth. Hunger figures as the hungering Christ and is also Christ, the physician of souls.

590. _____. "The Plowman as Preacher: The Allegorical and Structural Significance of Piers the Plowman in *Piers Plowman*." University of Illinois dissertation, 1969. Abstracted *DAI*, 30: 712A.

591. _____. "Temporal Tensions in the *Visio* of *Piers Plowman*." *MS*, 35 (1973), 389-412.

In the *Visio*, WL dramatizes the transition in salvation history from a pre- or near-Christian period to the "sixth world age," or the age of the Church, which was initiated by the birth of Christ. Piers operates as the spearhead of this transition. He functions on three distinct yet simultaneous levels in time. He is an Old Testament representation of the just man such as Abraham or Moses. He is a type of the apostles and disciples, primarily St. Peter. Finally, he is a type of any man in the age of the Church who, in seeking salvation, imitates Christ.

592. Troyer, Howard W. "Who is Piers Plowman?" *PMLA*, 47 (1932), 368-84. Rptd. *Style and Symbolism in Piers Plowman*, ed. Blanch, 1969, pp. 156-73.

The unity of the Piers symbol lies in the humanness of all its variants. On the moral level, Piers signifies all

things man ought to be--*e.g.*, the perfect labourer, the charitable lord, the righteous magistrate, and the conscientious
pope. On the anagogical level, he is the revelation of man's
redemption through Christ. Man held a pardon from God in
the Atonement of Christ, but men have come to rely on the
pardon and not on their own good deeds. Piers tears the
document because he feels that men have made the pardon
futile.

593. Tucker, Martin. *The Critical Temper: A Survey of Modern
     Criticism on English and American Literature from the
     Beginnings to the Twentieth Century.* New York:
     Frederick Ungar, 1969.

     Tucker provides brief excerpts from major critical
     studies of *PP*. Includes selections from: 43, 274, 294,
     445, 243, 528, 557, 317, 580, 340, 462, 441, 540, 498, 604,
     209, 440, 219.

594. Tucker, Samuel. "From Walter Map to Langland." *Verse
     Satire in England Before the Renaissance.* New York:
     Columbia University Press, 1908, pp. 35-79.

     PP is the greatest medieval satire, although it is much
     more than a satire. Nonetheless, the whole complex struc-
     ture of the poem is too cumbersome for satire. Furthermore,
     allegory tends towards abstraction, while satire tends
     towards realism. In *PP* we see these modes working together:
     e.g., many of WL's characters, like Meed and Piers, are more
     than mere abstractions--they are realistically portrayed
     individuals. WL achieves a "unique adaptation of a very
     abstract method to very realistic material" (p. 72). This
     form is without precedent or subsequent influence in English
     satire. Curiously, WL lacks the "very vital feature of
     humor" (p. 79).

595. Van't Hal, Bernard. "Didactic and Mimetic Ambivalence in the
     A-*Visio* of *Piers Plowman*." Northwestern University
     dissertation, 1972. Abstracted *DAI*, 32: 5205A-06A.

     In the A *Visio*, WL regularly alternates between a
     didactic mode (commentary) and a mimetic (fictive) mode.
     He does not attempt to harmonize these modes and the nar-
     rative therefore frequently appears incoherent.

596. Vasta, Edward, ed. *Interpretations of Piers Plowman.* Notre
     Dame, Ind.: University of Notre Dame Press, 1968.

     Contents: (See separate listings)
     H. W. Wells. "The Construction of *Piers Plowman*." (604)
     G. R. Owst. "A Literary Echo of the Social Gospel." (From
     Literature and Pulpit in Medieval England.) (497)
     Nevill K. Coghill. "The Character of Piers Plowman Considered
     from the B-text." (270)

T. P. Dunning. Selections from *Piers Plowman: An Inter-*
pretation of the A-text. (316)
E. Talbot Donaldson. Selections from *Piers Plowman: the*
C-text and Its Poet. (311)
R. W. Frank. "The Art of Reading Medieval Personification
Allegory." (336)
S. S. Hussey. "Langland, Hilton, and the Three Lives."
(393)
T. P. Dunning. "The Structure of the B-Text of *Piers*
Plowman." (317)
John Lawlor. "The Imaginative Unity of *Piers Plowman*."
(440)
R. W. Frank. Selection from *Piers Plowman and the Scheme*
of Salvation. (340)
R. E. Kaske. "Patristic Exegesis in the Criticism of
Medieval Literature." (414)
M. W. Bloomfield. "*Piers Plowman* as a Fourteenth-Century
Apocalypse." (218)

597. _____. *The Spiritual Basis of Piers Plowman*. The
Hague: Mouton, 1965.

PP is concerned with the mystic's way to salvation
rather than the way to ordinary Christian perfection. The
Visio depicts Will's first conversion--here, he learns to
accept the opposite of self-love. *Dowel* depicts Will's
true conversion where the deeper manifestations of self-
love are driven out. *Dobet* concerns Will's growth in
charity, culminating in the Harrowing of Hell scene where
he obtains a "kynde knowing." In *Dobest*, Will gains a
conscious awareness of the life of grace which is contemplation. The poem describes the gradual deification of
Will's soul as he moves from perfection, to contemplation,
to final union with God. The vision of Christ functions
both historically and psychologically--this vision is granted
to Will at the peak of his soul's growth and he awakens in a
state of heightened devotion to God. Piers is the archetype
of the soul united with God--when the soul seeks Piers, it
seeks charity. Piers himself does not change significance
in the narrative--in the Pardon scene, he does not undergo
a change of heart. Rather, he seeks to initiate change
in the hearts of others. He takes on the characteristics
his followers must assume if they are to enjoy the perfection
he already knows. Piers is not identical with Christ--he
is, rather, human nature perfected.

598. _____. "Truth, the Best Treasure, in *Piers Plowman*."
PQ, 44 (1965), 17-29.

The "Truth" of Holy Church's speech to the Dreamer
refers to a spiritual condition which may be achieved in this
life. Truth in the Tower (B. I) has an ethical meaning,
referring to God's will as man's absolute rule of action.

143

Earthly truth is the type the dreamer should seek: *i.e.*, truth in thought, word, and deed.

599. Vaughan, Mícéál F. "The Tropological Context of the Easter Awakening: *Piers Plowman* B. Passus 16-20." Cornell University dissertation, 1974. Abstracted *DAI*, 34: 7205A-06A.

600. Walker, Marshall. "Piers Plowman's Pardon: A Note." *English Studies in Africa*, 8 (1965), 64-70.

When Piers tears the Pardon, he is not rejecting the Active life. The three lives begin with an active involvement in this world. Without the first stage, succeeding progress is impossible. The Priest is the antithesis of Piers. In tearing the Pardon, Piers rejects indulgences, but does not reject the meaning of the Pardon.

601. Warton, Thomas. *The History of English Poetry From the Close of the Eleventh to the Commencement of the Eighteenth Century*. London: J. Dodsly, 1774. Vol. I, Section 8, pp. 266-86.

Warton names the poet "Robert Longlande, a secular priest." *PP* is "a satire on the views of almost every profession: but especially on the corruptions of the clergy, and the absurdities of superstition. But instead of availing himself of the rising and rapid improvements of the English language, Longland prefers and adopts the style of the Anglo-Saxon poets" (p. 266). His use of alliteration "contributed also to render his manner extremely perplexed and to disgust the reader with obscurities" (p. 266-67). Warton also prints several passages from Crowley's edition.

602. Webbe, William. *A Discourse of English Poetry* (1586). Ed. Edward Arber. Westminster: A. Constable & Co., 1895.

Webbe briefly mentions *PP*: "The next of our auncient poets, that I can tell of, I suppose to be *Pierce Plouhman*, who in hys dooinges is somewhat harshe and obscure, but indeede a very pithy wryter and . . . was the first that I haue seene that observed the quantity of our verse without the curiosity of Rhyme" (p. 32).

603. Wedel, T. *The Medieval Attitude toward Astrology*. Yale Studies in English, 60. New Haven: Yale University Press, 1920.

PP demonstrates the fear of practical science coupled with the acceptance of astrological theory. Dame Study condemns astrology as an evil practice in both the A- and B-texts. In C, however, astrology appears to be condoned. This change in attitude does not indicate multiple authorship: between the composition of B and C, there was a movement toward greater trust in astrological theory (pp. 120-22). Includes a discussion of the astrologers of medieval England and astrology in Middle English literature.

604. Wells, Henry W. "The Construction of *Piers Plowman*." *PMLA*, 44 (1929), 123-40. Rptd. *Interpretations of Piers Plowman*, ed. Vasta, 1968, pp. 1-21.

The *Visio* is a study of the life of the laity as it should be, whereas the *Vita* is an account of the world as seen by the thinker who has passed through the medieval disciplines of learning and priestly responsibility. The *Vita* deals with ideas superfluous to the layman but ideas that are necessary for the "select soldiers of God." The *Visio* introduces the need for the *Vita*. In the last passus of the *Visio*, Piers states that he will change the course of his life and turn to the cultivation of his soul. The three lives represent three stages in this process of cultivation--Dobest is to rule others as a bishop guards his flock; Dobet is to rule oneself; Dowel is an advanced state of charity. The three-fold division of the *Vita* is paralleled by the Trinity: Father--Dowel, Son--Dobet, Holy Ghost-- Dobest.

605. _____. "The Philosophy of *Piers Plowman*." *PMLA*, 53 (1938), 339-49.

The three lives of the *Vita* relate to the Active, Contemplative, and Mixed states of mystical thought. The life of Dowel includes the knowledge and fear of God; Dobet includes contemplation and meditation on the passion of Christ; Dobest describes the ideal or Unitive life. Dowel is the lower stage of the Active life where man learns to rule his life by discipline and faith. Dobet is the life of devotion. Dobest presumes both of these. There is also a historical relationship among the terms: Dowel depicts the pre-Christian world which believes in God but not the Trinity; Dobet depicts the world in the time of Jesus; Dobest represents the dispensation of the Holy Spirit.

606. Wenzel, Siegfried. "Chaucer and the Language of Contemporary Preaching." *SP*, 73 (1976), 138-61.

607. _____. *The Sin of Sloth: Acedia in Medieval Thought and Literature*. Chapel Hill, N.C.: University of North Carolina Press, 1967.

The Seven Deadly Sins are not a major organizing device in *PP*: rather, they are used in several separate allegories (Passus II, V, XIII, XIV, XX). Wenzel discusses WL's portrait of Sloth, noting that the close connection of Sloth with Gluttony is not unique in Medieval Literature--the latter, in fact, usually causes the former.

608. Wertenbaker, Thomas J. *"Piers Plowman,* Prologue B. 196."
    Explicator, 34, vii (1976), Item 51.

    The problem in this line is not, as Demedis believed,
    that improper meanings have been assigned to certain words
    (302). The confusion arises from a complex grammatical
    construction and a sense-obscuring use of alliteration.
    Wertenbaker reads the lines: "For better is a litel losse
    [that we do not 'mysse a schrew'] þan a long sorwe [that
    we suffer "þe mase amonge us alle'].'"

609. Wesling, Donald. "Eschatology and the Language of Satire
    in *Piers Plowman." Criticism,* 10 (1968), 277-89.

    WL uses three types of satire--dialectic, invective,
    and apocalyptic. This last term may be used as a general
    term for the satire as a whole. There are strong disinte-
    grative tendencies in the narrative of *PP* which are mirrored
    in WL's use of language. The quest for perfection operates
    on the verbal level when the poet attempts to burnish terms
    to ultimate precision so that words and the behavior they
    describe are congruent. In the Meed scene, for example,
    linguistic confusion is a symptom of the imperfect human
    condition. Once Conscience clarifies the meaning of Meed,
    moral difficulties are resolved. Friars are distorters
    of language and the ambiguous use of words creates an
    ambiguous moral atmosphere.

610. White, Helen C. *Social Criticism in Popular Religious Litera-
    ture of the Sixteenth Century.* New York: Macmillan,
    1944.

    See Chapter I, "The *Piers Plowman* Tradition," pp. 1-40.
    Sixteenth-century readers emphasized WL's attacks on the
    wealth of friars and stressed his affinities with Wyclif.
    They apparently did not recognize WL's basic orthodoxy and
    chose to see his work as foreshadowing their own revolt. *PP*
    spawned many popular religious works: *e.g., The Praier and
    Complaynte of the Ploweman unto Christe* (1531), a sustained
    assault on the friars, as well as *Pyers Plowmans Exhortation
    unto the Lordes, Knightes, and Burgoysses of the Parlyament-
    house* (1550), Francis Thynne's *Newes From the North* (1579),
    and *I Playne Piers* (c. 1550).

611. Whitworth, Charles W., Jr. "Changes in the Roles of Reason
    and Conscience in the Revisions of *Piers Plowman."
    N&Q,* new series, 19 (1972), 4-7.

    Changes in the roles of Reason and Conscience in the B
    and C versions reflect WL's growing knowledge of theological
    distinctions, as he attempts to clarify the meanings of these
    terms. According to scholastic philosophy, conscience has
    two meanings: first, it is the moral faculty of the mind
    in general; second, it is speculative reason. In *PP,*

Reason represents the first sense, Conscience, the second. In the A-text, Conscience preaches the sermon, but in B and C, the sermon is delivered by Reason. In writing B, WL realized that it was more suitable for Reason to preach the sermon because it is the moral faculty.

612. Wilkes, Gerald L. "The Castle of Vnite in *Piers Plowman*." *MS*, 27 (1965), 334-36.

The *Ancrene Riwle* may be the direct source for both the image of the castle of Unity in B. XIX (C. XXII) and the idea that Christian unity is the best protection against the devil. Certain alliterative patterns are also parallel.

613. Wilson, R. M. *The Lost Literature of Medieval England*. London: Methuen & Co., 1952. Revised edition, 1970.

Includes two notes on *PP*: 1. p. 117, Wilson attempts to trace WL's reference to the "rymes of Robyn hood" and "Randolf, erle of Chestre," through references in Dugdale and Holinshed; 2. Notes that references to copies of *PP* occur in at least three wills: those of Walter de Brugge of York (1396), John Wyndhill (1431), and Thomas Roos (1435).

614. Wimsatt, James I. *Allegory and Mirror: Tradition and Structure in Middle English Literature*. New York: Pegasus, 1970.

PP demonstrates the range of personification allegory: WL employs not only narrative allegory, but tableaux, realistic scenes, and extensive moral lectures as well. The poem is coherent and unified--the individual visions are held together as a sequence of actions toward the salvation of the world. The poem is an allegory of the psyche. Will, the faculty which chooses, is properly the Dreamer's name. After the lessons of sense and experience are exhausted, Will must turn to learning. Slowly, he becomes dependent on supernatural powers rather than on his own reason. *Dowel* is an allegory of reason, while *Dobet* and *Dobest* constitute an allegory of revelation. See pp. 36-60.

615. Wittig, Joseph S. "The Dramatic and Rhetorical Development of Long Will's Pilgrimage." *NM*, 76 (1975), 52-76.

The B-text possesses a consistent narrative and dramatic form which was structured for a precise rhetorical purpose. In the first dream of the *Vita*, WL presents the human will's resistance to "the affective remaking of itself." The audience identifies with Will's intellectual and emotional problems and participates in his spiritual awakening in Passus XI-XII. In the remainder of the poem, WL applies Will's personal reform to the situation of every Christian and to salvation history. At the conclusion of the poem,

WL presents the problem to its potential solvers--the individual wills of the audience.

616. _____. "*Piers Plowman* B, Passus IX-XII: Elements in the Design of the Inward Journey." Cornell University dissertation, 1970. Abstracted *DAI*, 30: 5425A.

617. _____. "*Piers Plowman* B, Passus IX-XII: Elements in the Design of the Inward Journey." *Traditio*, 28 (1972), 211-80.

WL deliberately manipulates the misadventures of his persona: the episodes in which the Dreamer is involved are bound to a network of perspectives that universalize his progress. WL sympathizes with the persona but uses him to dramatize the struggle of the human will against the background of salvation history. In Passus IX-XII, Will embarks on a journey into his own psyche. The process of his conversion to faith calls each aspect of his personality into prominence. In order for Will to ascend spiritually, he must find the *Imago Dei* in himself. Passus IX-XII trace Will's progress from corporeal to spiritual knowledge.

618. Wolfe, H. *Notes on English Verse Satire*. London: L. & E. Woolf, 1929.

619. Woolf, Rosemary. "Some Non-Medieval Qualities of *Piers Plowman*." *Essays in Criticism*, 12 (1962), 111-25.

The literal level of the poem is unsteady and unsustained, unlike any other medieval allegory except de Meun's continuation of the *Roman de la Rose*. Piers functions as a multi-layered symbol and there is a "romantic uncertainty" about him that is foreign to the Middle Ages. WL maintains no visual image of Piers, yet, by a skillful accumulation of references to him, concentrates the emotional force of the poem in his character, so that he is present even when he does not appear. The use of the dream vision is also non-medieval: WL's dreams have the illogical qualities and vague backgrounds of actual dreams. The use of the dreamer-persona is also unique in *PP*. Will, unlike the personae of Chaucer and the Pearl-Poet, has such an authentically drawn personality that we feel we are party to the poet's exploration of his own mind.

620. _____. "The Tearing of the Pardon." *Piers Plowman: Critical Approaches*, ed. Hussey, 1969, pp. 50-75.

The Pardon is actually a condemnation. A genuine pardon could be granted only to those who have done good, and the people who receive the Pardon are poor and imperfect sinners. The Pardon symbolizes the decree of the Old Law which exalts justice over mercy. Piers represents Christ. When he tears the Pardon, he is not rejecting its teachings but demonstrating how Christ's divine mercy functions. The Pardon scene is a mythic prelude to the Judgement Day and Harrowing of Hell scenes.

621. Yunck, John A. *The Lineage of Lady Meed: The Development of Medieval Venality Satire*. Notre Dame, Ind.: Notre Dame University Press, 1963.

Lady Meed is the focus of WL's indictment of the world of affairs--she is the central medieval image of human venality and acts as the major obstruction in the individual's quest for salvation. She also represents dramatic social change--as the social embodiment of Antichrist, she symbolizes the difficulties of the new-moneyed economy. The framework of the Meed episode is the fundamental problem of the relationship of the City of God and the City of Man. WL's references to papal venality and episcopal simony appear perfunctory--he is clearly more interested in the influence of Meed on the life of the common man. Yunck examines the roots of WL's use of venality satire, tracing analogues to his treatment of Meed in both medieval and classical literature. WL was probably influenced by the "Roman de Carité," although it is impossible to locate specific sources.

622. Zacher, Christian K. "*Curiositas* and the Impulses for Pilgrimage in Fourteenth-Century English Literature." University of California, Riverside dissertation, 1970. Abstracted *DAI*, 30: 4429A.

623. Zeeman, Elizabeth. "Piers Plowman and the Pilgrimage to Truth." *Essays and Studies*, 11 (1958), 1-16. Rptd. *Style and Symbolism in Piers Plowman*, ed. Blanch, 1969, pp. 117-31.

Zeeman examines the influence of Hilton, Juliana of Norwich, and the author of *The Cloud of Unknowing* on WL's metaphor of the pilgrimage. The search for truth is the unifying theme of *PP* and it touches all the characters. Piers is the "Christ-element" in man. Piers is not Christ himself--he must remain separate from the divine force which operates in him. WL's ambiguous portrait of Piers as both human and divine probably resulted from WL's attempt to render the mystic's subtle arguments. Hilton's succinct paradoxes are far more paradoxical when rendered dramatically.

624. _____. "*Piers Plowman* and 'The Simonie.'" *Archiv*, 203 (1967), 241-54.

Zeeman investigates the similarities between *PP* and a short semi-alliterative social protest poem, "The Simonie," found in the Auchinleck MS, Peterhouse, Cambridge MS 104 and Bodley MS 48. The two poems are similar metrically

but, more importantly, share several thematic concerns. "The
Simonie" sets a precedent for a poem of satire and complaint
which mingles criticism with constructive advice and which
is more concerned with efficient communication than with
elegant alliteration. Both poems bitterly review secular
and spiritual ill-health.   Like *PP*, "The Simonie" indicts
the corrupt church, worldly priests, and avaricious friars.
WL's portraits of Simony and Covetousness may have their
direct source in this poem.

IV. *Piers Plowman:* Style, Meter, and Language

Langland's style and poetic expression were long considered to
be crude and unpolished. In the earliest analysis of the style
and meter of *Piers Plowman,* Thomas Warton noted that Langland chose
a distinctive but disagreeable poetic medium:

> Instead of availing himself of the rising and rapid
> improvements of the English language, Langland
> prefers and adopts the style of the Anglo-Saxon
> poets. Nor did he make these writers the models of his
> language only: he likewise imitates their allit-
> erative versification, which consisted in using
> an aggregate of words beginning with the same letter.
> He has therefore rejected rhyme in the place of
> which he thinks it sufficient to substitute a
> perpetual alliteration. But this imposed constraint
> of seeking identical initials, and the affectation
> of obsolete English, by demanding a constant and
> necessary departure from the natural and obvious
> forms of expression, while it circumscribed the
> powers of our author's genius, contributed also
> to render his manner extremely perplexed.[1]

Warton's disapproval of Langland's "archaic" style and meter was
echoed throughout the nineteenth century. Gerard Manley Hopkins
felt that the versification of *Piers Plowman* was of "degraded and
doggerel shape."[2] Although he admired certain descriptive passages
of *Piers Plowman,* W. J. Courthope conceded that "the movement of the
verse, even where the imagery is beautiful, is disagreeably monoto-
nous and lends itself to cheap tricks of alliteration."[3] Courthope
felt that the verbal artifice of the poem was, in fact, its greatest
flaw: in choosing the "rude alliterative measure," Langland
"sacrificed the claim of his work to be ranked among the master-
pieces of English poetry."[4] Recent critics have not shared this
distaste for Langland's poetic medium: in fact, Langland is now
recognized as one of the most creative and innovative poetic crafts-
men in Middle English literature. His alliterative meter is now
generally understood to be a graceful and natural mode of utterance,

well-suited to the movement of his allegorical narrative. The
fullest treatment of Langland's style, meter, and language is
Elizabeth Salter's *Piers Plowman: An Introduction* (540). Salter
compared *Piers* with other works of the Alliterative Revival, and
pointed out that although Langland adopted the basic form of the
newly revived alliterative measure, he did not partake of its
stylistic features: "At no point does Langland show an interest
in the elaborate forms of alliterative verse so extensively and
lovingly cultivated by other poets. The open delight in art for
art's sake which must explain the high rhetoric to be found in
nearly all alliterative poems, is no part of Langland's attitude
to his craft." Langland never employs the specialized poetic diction
typical of most Middle English alliterative poems: his phrasing is
generally more simple, natural, and prosaic. Following the earlier
suggestions of G. R. Owst, *Literature and Pulpit in Medieval
England* (497), and John Burrow, "The Audience of *Piers Plowman*"
(243), Salter argued that Langland deliberately avoided the stylistic
conventions of the Alliterative Revival in order to reach a wider
popular audience through a simple and familiar idiom. According to
Salter, Langland wrote in what might be termed a "plain style"; his
expression is not, however, unlearned or unsophisticated as earlier
critics had believed.

A. C. Spearing, in "Verbal Repetition in *Piers Plowman* B and C"
(664), supported Owst's contention that Langland's techniques of
expression were directly influenced by the style of the vernacular
homily. According to Spearing, Langland was uninterested in
stylistic embellishment for its own sake--he viewed the verbal
artifice of his work in strictly functional terms and avoided
stylistic devices which added nothing to the poem's meaning. Langland favored schemes of repetition, puns, and various kinds of word
play. Spearing noted that the use of these stylistic devices was
"particularly encouraged by the utilitarian ethos of the *ars
praedicandi* with its strong emphasis on the preacher's effectiveness
in relation to his audience." Langland frequently employs
adnominatio (repetition of a root word with different inflectional
endings), *contentio* (antithesis), *similiter cadens* (a balance of

words with similar endings), *commutatio* (the reversal of the order of the first half of a line in the second half) and *traductio* (repetition for emphasis).

In *"Petrus, id est, Christus:* Word Play in *Piers Plowman,* the B-text" (637), B. F. Huppé discussed Langland's use of *adnominatio* and suggested that puns and verbal repetitions function architectonically in the poem. William M. Ryan, "Word Play in Some Old English Homilies and a Late Middle English Poem" (657), studied the occurrences of *adnominatio* and "alliterating matched pairs" in the A, B, and C versions. Ryan contended that the alliterating matched pair (parallelism in word and clause) provides a "subthematic continuity" in the poem. R. E. Kaske, "The Use of Simple Figures of Speech in *Piers Plowman* B: A Study in the Figurative Expression of Ideas and Opinions" (642), examined Langland's use of simile, metaphor, metonymy, synecdoche, and simple personification.

NOTES

[1] Thomas Warton, *The History of English Poetry From the Close of the Eleventh to the Commencement of the Eighteenth Century* (London: J. Dodsly, 1774), Vol. I, Sect. 8, p. 266.

[2] In a letter to Robert Bridges, quoted by R. W. Chambers, *Man's Unconquerable Mind: Studies of English Writers From Bede to A. E. Housman and W. P. Ker* (London and Toronto: Jonathan Cape, 1939), p. 94.

[3] W. J. Courthope, *History of English Poetry* (New York: Macmillan, 1895), p. 245.

[4] Courthope, p. 243.

625. Baltzell, Jane. "Rhetorical 'Amplification' and 'Abbrevi-
     ation' and the Structure of Medieval Narrative."
     Pacific Coast Philology, 2 (1967), 32-39.

     Baltzell examines the *Ars versificatoria* of Matthew of
Vendôme, the *Poetria Nova* of Geoffrey of Vinsauf, and the *De
arte prosayca metrica et rithmica* of John of Garland in order
to discover how medieval literary critics viewed the structure
of narrative poetry. All agree that narrative poetry should
be essentially didactic--the *sententia* or central theme should
be signified both at the beginning and at the end of the poem
and it should be reiterated throughout the narrative by means
of rhetorical amplification and abbreviation. Discusses the
use of narrative schemes in fourteenth-century English poetry.

626. Bernard, Emil. *Langland: A Grammatical Treatise.* Bonn:
     Emil Strauss, 1874.

     Bernard examines the grammar of *PP*, focusing on the
origins of WL's vocabulary. WL's poetic idiom is plain and
unadorned. Unlike many poets of the alliterative revival, WL
did not frequently use Romance borrowings--his diction is pre-
dominantly Anglo-Saxon. The B-text (Skeat's Laud MS. 581) is
chosen for examination because it appears to be closest in
dialect to the poet's original. The A-text (Skeat's Vernon
MS) appears to be "southernized."

627. Brunner, Karl. *Abriss der mittelenglischen Grammatik.*
     Tübingen: Max Niemeyer Verlag, 1962. Trans. by Grahame
     Johnston, as *An Outline of Middle English Grammar.*
     Cambridge, Mass.: Harvard University Press, 1963.

628. Caplan, H. "Classical Rhetoric and the Medieval Theory of
     Preaching." *Classical Philology*, 28 (1933), 73-96.

629. Day, Mabel. "Strophic Division in Middle English Alliterative
     Verse." *EStudien*, 66 (1931-1932), 245-48.

     Day reviews Kaluza's argument concerning the possibility
that certain ME alliterative poems were originally divided into
quatrains. (See 641). Day believes that certain poems were
written in quatrains but if these quatrains were found to be
irregular, the authors eliminated the strophic divisions--
hence the passus in these poems generally contain a multiple
of four lines. Examines *Cleanness* and *Patience*. See 636.

630. Eby, James A. "The Alliterative Meter of *Piers Plowman,*
     A." University of Michigan dissertation, 1972.
     Abstracted *DAI*, 32: 3948A.

     Eby attempts to correct the traditional view of WL as a
metrically careless poet: WL's meter has long been misunderstood because of his complex and variable use of the final -e

syllable. WL actually demonstrates great metrical precision. *PP* has a more direct relationship with OE verse forms than other poems of the alliterative revival and it was the inheritor of a continuing alliterative tradition.

631. Elliott, Ralph W. V. *Chaucer's English*. London: Andre Deutsch, 1974.

Elliott focuses on Chaucer's language but frequently suggests comparisons between Chaucer's and WL's expression. On p. 241 Elliott compares WL's and Chaucer's use of oaths: the oaths of WL's characters are dictated by the requirements of alliteration rather than by the nature of the speaker. Chaucer uses a greater variety of oaths and he employs them to add irony and local color to his character portraits. Elliott also discusses the use of the exclamation "Peter!" by Chaucer, the Gawain-Poet and WL (*e.g.*, *PP*. C. VIII, 182).

632. _____. "Landscape and Rhetoric in Middle-English Alliterative Poetry." *Melbourne Critical Review*, 4 (1961), 65-76.

In ME alliterative verse, landscape description is frequently stale and conventionalized as in the *Morte Arthur*. The Gawain-Poet, however, was able to avoid the tedious use of descriptive tags, as did the poet of the *Parlement of the Thre Ages*. "The requirements of alliteration did add to the temptation of slapdash writing and many a potentially good landscape backed by the varied and often grandiose scenery of the English northwest, became a mere list of features enumerated without interest or sparkle" (p. 76).

633. Fischer, Jos. and F. Mennicken. "Zur mittelenglischen Stabzeile." *Bonner Beiträge zur Anglistik*, 11 (1901), 133-54.

634. Greg, W. W. "The Continuity of Alliterative Tradition." *MLR*, 27 (1932), 453-54.

Greg points out fallacies in the arguments of J. P. Oakden concerning the continuity of alliterative tradition in OE and ME (651). The C-type of alliteration does not survive in ME. The alliteration of consecutive lines with the same letter is rare in OE but common in ME. The repetition of the initial of the last unalliterated stressed syllable of a line as an alliterative letter of the next line does not constitute proof of continuity. Oakden answers in 652.

635. Hulbert, J. R. "A Hypothesis Concerning the Alliterative Revival." *MP*, 28 (1931), 405-22.

Hulbert extends the argument advanced by Samuel Moore concerning the existence of a special patronage system in Western and Northern England in the late fourteenth century

(See 650). Hulbert notes that many families associated with the baronial opposition were connected with the alliterative revival. The subject matter of the poems of the revival is adapted to a baronial audience. These works were designed to contribute to cultural development independent of the court and to help make the baron's castles centers of social activity. The barons wished to foster a literature which expressed English interests and traditions, in contrast to the royal court literature which was heavily influenced by French poetry. The subject matter of *PP* is "decidedly English as compared with that of Chaucer's early work" (p. 413). Perhaps *PP* is merely the culmination of a popular literature which had maintained the alliterative long line. It is also possible, however, that the "barons were clever enough to foster a poetry which would arouse the people to thought about political conditions and moral betterment and so gain aid for the baronial opposition in any attack on the corruptions and usurpations of the royal house" (p. 413).

636. _____. "Quatrains in Middle English Alliterative Poems." *MP*, 48 (1950), 73-81.

Hulbert tests Kaluza's hypothesis (641) that certain ME alliterative poems were originally composed in quatrains. Hulbert examines the A-text of *PP*, breaking up lines 1-109 into quatrains (see pp. 77-79). The A-text appears to lend itself to such structural division. The irregularity of *PP* texts is due to the carelessness of copyists who did not recognize these divisions.

637. Huppé, Bernard F. *"Petrus, id est, Christus:* Word Play in *Piers Plowman;* the B-Text." *ELH*, 17 (1950), 163-90.

Word play is an important rhetorical device for WL and it contributes to the structural coherence of *PP*. WL employs a wide variety of word play: consonance and vowel harmony is used to suggest double meanings, to enforce the effectiveness of an image, and to support rhetorical contrast. Huppé discusses how puns and verbal repetitions function architectonically in the poem. WL concentrated on the details of Will's appearance and his surroundings in such a manner as to make them constants upon which variations are played. These constants are fixed as: 1. the time and season of the year; 2. the surroundings of Will's resting place; 3. sounds; 4. Will's costume; 5. his wandering, his weariness and other references to his state of mind. WL plays on these details in describing the waking and sleeping states of the Dreamer throughout the poem. Notes that the allusive character of Piers is created by means of word play in *"Petrus, id est, Christus."*

638. Hussey, S. S. "Langland's Reading of Alliterative Poetry." *MLR*, 60 (1965), 163-70.

Hussey disagrees with critics who feel that *PP* has little in common with other poems of the Alliterative Revival. WL was certainly well-acquainted with *Winner and Wastour*, *The Parlement of the Thre Ages*, and *William of Palerne*. He could have also read *Joseph of Arimathea*, the *Alliterative Morte Arthure*, *Patience*, *Purity*, and several other alliterative poems. Both *Winner and Wastour* and *The Parlement of the Thre Ages* have openings similar to the Prologue of *PP*, although neither shares its structural complexities.

639.   Jordan, Richard. *Handbuch der mittelenglischen Grammatik*. Third edition. Heidelberg: Carl Winter Universitätis- verlag, 1968. Trans. Eugene Joseph Crook, *Handbook of Middle English Grammar: Phonology*. The Hague: Mouton, 1974. [See p. 11. Discusses Staffordshire manuscripts of *PP*, and illustrates the phonological features of the West Midlands dialect with examples from *PP*].

640.   Kaluza, Max. *Englische Metrik in historischer Entwicklung*. Berlin, 1909. Trans. by A. C. Dunstan as *A Short History of English Versification*. London: George Allen, 1911.

Kaluza divides the long-line into four members and pro- poses that there were ninety subspecies of OE alliterative verse. The OE long-line "decayed" in ME verse: "The strict laws which had regulated its structure in the Old English period were no longer observed with the same care" (p. 128).

641.   _____. "Strophische gliederung in der mittelenglischen rein alliterierenden Dichtung." *EStudien*, 16 (1892), 169-79.

Kaluza suggests that several ME alliterative poems including *Patience*, *Cleanness*, and *PP* may have originally been composed in quatrain units. Discussed by Day (629) and Hulbert (636). *PP* is discussed briefly pp. 169-71.

642.   Kaske, R. E. "The Use of Simple Figures of Speech in *Piers Plowman* B: A Study in the Figurative Expression of Ideas and Opinions." *SP*, 48 (1951), 571-600.

Kaske examines the use of simile, metaphor, metonymy, synecdoche, and simple personification as they contribute to the presentation of ideas and opinions in *PP*. There are three main categories of such figures: 1. those which express intellectual attitudes; 2. those which illustrate or support statements by means of similitude; 3. those which provide concrete substance for abstract concepts. In the first category, WL generally uses metaphor. In the second, similes are used to support and illustrate moral arguments by drawing on physical phenomena. There are five classes of abstract concepts in *PP:* 1. psychological concepts; 2. cosmic and

apocalyptic ideas; 3. political issues; 4. rules of conduct
and church doctrine; 5. spiritual concepts which lie beyond
earthly understanding.

643. Käsman, Hans. *Studien zum Kirchlichen Wortschatz des
Mittelenglischen, 1100-1350*. Tübingen: Max Niemeyer
Verlag, 1961.

644. Klapprott, L. *Das End-e in W. Langlands Buch von Peter dem
Pflüger*. Published Göttingen dissertation, 1890.

645. Leonard, William Ellery. "The Scansion of Middle English
Alliterative Verse." *Wisconsin University Studies*,
11 (1920), 58-104.

PP is discussed pp. 72-74. Leonard disputes the traditional view of ME alliterative verse as following the same
basic pattern as the OE long-line. By mixing parts of *Gamelyn*
and *PP*, Leonard attempts to demonstrate that *PP* does not contain four stresses per line: it appears to share the more
variable stress system of the metrical romances.

646. Luick, Karl. "Die englische Stabreimzeile im XIV, XV, und
XVI Jahrhundert." *Anglia*, 11 (1889), 392-443. [See section 2, "William Langley und seine schule," pp. 429-43.]

647. _____. "Zur metrik der mittelenglischen reimendalli-
terienden Dichtung." *Anglia*, 12 (1889), 437-53.

648. Manly, John Matthews. "Chaucer and the Rhetoricians."
Warton Lecture on English Poetry. *Proceedings of the
British Academy*, 12 (1926), 95-114. Rptd. Folcroft
Library, 1972; cf. Murphy, James J., "A New Look at
Chaucer and the Rhetoricians." *RES*, new series, 15
(1964), 1-20.

649. Mersand, Joseph. *Chaucer's Romance Vocabulary*. New York:
Comet Press, 1937.

See Chapter IV, "The Vocabularies of Chaucer and of His
Contemporaries," pp. 44-53. WL's vocabulary discussed p. 51.
It is impossible to conclude whether WL's or Chaucer's
vocabulary is richer, although it appears that Chaucer's
poetry has a greater proportion of Romance borrowings.

650. Moore, Samuel. "Patrons of Letters in Norfolk and Suffolk c.
1450." *PMLA*, 27 (1912), 188-207 and "Patrons of Letters
in Norfolk and Suffolk c. 1450." *PMLA*, 28 (1913),
79-105.

Moore discusses patronage in the fifteenth century,
focusing on the patrons of Lydgate. He then attempts to extend his discoveries concerning patronage in East Anglia c.
1450 to the West Midlands c. 1350. Moore suggests that the

Alliterative Revival may have been initiated by a special
patronage group. Discusses *PP* pp. 103-104. His argument is
extended by Hulbert (635).

651. Oakden, J. P. *Alliterative Poetry in Middle English.* 2 Vols.
     Manchester: Manchester University Press, 1930-35.
     Vol. I, *The Dialectal and Metrical Survey* (1930);
     Vol. II, *A Survey of the Traditions* (1935).

     Although all MSS of *PP* are scribally corrupt, it appears
     that WL's original dialect was West Midlands. Oakden briefly
     discusses the survival of OE alliterative patterns in *PP*.
     The most frequently used OE pattern was aa/ax and it is re-
     tained in *PP:* 65.2 % of the lines in the A-text follow this
     pattern (70.3 % of the B-text and 72.1 % of the C-text).
     Oakden argues that there was a continuing popular tradition
     that kept alive OE alliterative verse forms and that it was
     localized in the West, particularly the Southwest Midlands.
     "While there is no break in literary tradition, there is, in
     a real sense, a revival, a renewed poetic vitality and inspir-
     ation" (Vol. II, p. 86). There appears to have been a degree
     of rivalry between the poets of the North and West: Northern
     poets tended to make light of OE traditions while Western
     poets, particularly WL and the author of *The Parlement of the
     Thre Ages,* remained faithful to Anglo-Saxon verse forms.

652. _____. "The Continuity of Alliterative Tradition."
     MLR, 28 (1933), 233-34.

     Oakden defends his thesis (651) concerning the survival
     of OE metrical features in ME alliterative verse against the
     accusations of W. W. Greg (634).

653. _____. "The Survival of a Stylistic Feature of Indo-
     European Poetry in Germanic, especially Middle English."
     RES, original series, 9 (1933), 50-53.

     Oakden examines the stylistic device of using three names
     in sequence with the last qualified by an epithet. This
     device is used eight times in *PP:* *e.g.,* "Adam and Abraham
     and Ysay the prophete" (B. XVI, 81).

654. Olszewska, E. S. "Illustrations of Norse Formulas in English."
     Leeds Studies in English, 2 (1933), 76-84.

655. _____. "Norse Alliterative Tradition in Middle
     English." *Leeds Studies in English,* 6 (1937), 50-64.

656. Rosenthal, F. "Die alliterierende englische langzeile im 14
     Jahrhundert." *Anglia,* 1 (1878), 414-59. [*PP* is briefly
     examined pp. 418-19.]

657. Ryan, William M. "Word Play in Some Old English Homilies and a Late Middle English Poem." *Studies in Language, Literature, and Culture of the Middle Ages and Later*. Ed. E. Bagby Atwood and Archibald A. Hill. Austin: University of Texas Press, 1969.

Ryan disagrees with B. F. Huppé who noted that WL's favorite stylistic device was the rhetorical figure *adnominatio* (637). Rather, WL seems fondest of using "alliterating matched pairs": this device occurs one thousand times in the three texts of *PP*; *adnominatio* occurs five hundred times. WL frequently uses these techniques together, particularly in the C-text. The use of alliterating matched pairs is common in the works of Wulfstan and other OE homilists. WL, however, uses more of these figures than "any other medieval rhetorician-poet who wrote in English" (p. 273-74). WL does not repeat alliterating matched pairs, but constantly develops new ones. Ryan provides a partial list of alliterating matched pairs in *PP* (pp. 271-73).

658. Saintsbury, George. *Historical Manual of English Prosody*. London: Macmillan, 1910. Rptd. Schocken Books, 1966, with an Introduction by Harvey Gross.

WL is briefly discussed p. 153, p. 155. Although WL attempted to write verse without meter ("in the strict sense"), he did occasionally compose metrical lines. Decasyllables, Alexandrines, and fourteeners do occur in *PP*, but as a rule, WL "avoids them either with singular skill or with remarkable luck, and on the whole achieves a consistent medium, not so much dominated as permeated by a sort of anapaestic underhum of rhythm, but otherwise maintaining its independence" (p. 153). WL's versification is deficient in beauty and is unsuited for many of the subjects of poetry. WL represents the purely accentual phase of late fourteenth-century English prosody.

659. _____. *A History of English Prosody From the Twelfth Century to the Present Day*. Vol. I, *From the Origins to Spenser*. London: Macmillan, 1906.

See Book II, Chapter V, "Langland and Other Alliteratives," pp. 179-88. WL consciously avoids the new metrical scansion represented by Chaucer and Gower. His lines are divided into sharply separated halves. He generally employs two alliterated syllables in the first and longer hemistich and one in the second. WL chose a verse form in which rhyme is unnecessary. "The whole run and fall of the rhythm is so arranged that the ear does not in the least expect or call for rhyme" (p. 183). WL's lines are fairly regular: the average line contains thirteen syllables.

660.   Salter, Elizabeth. "The Alliterative Revival, I."
            MP, 64 (1966), 146-50.

        Salter argues against Hulbert's suggestion that the
        Alliterative Revival was initiated by the baronial opposition
        (635). Salter notes that in the fourteenth century there was
        general accord between the barons and the royal administration.
        The poets of the Revival were under the patronage of noble
        families. Salter discusses the Berkeleys, the Bohuns, and
        the Beauchamps and argues that these families helped to foster
        the development of the new alliterative poetry.

661.   _____. "The Alliterative Revival, II." *MP*, 64 (1966),
            233-37.

        Concerned primarily with the Gawain-Poet and the
        Northern participants in the Alliterative Revival. Salter
        notes that the influence of the Revival was not restricted to
        the North and West: the geographical distribution of MSS of
        alliterative poems suggests that the Revival was actually
        widespread. "The distinction of the Middle English verse is
        its power to invest an old measure with contemporary splendor
        and relevance" (p. 235).

662.   Serjeanston, Mary S. "The Dialects of the West Midlands in
            Middle English." *RES*, original series, 3 (1927), 319-31.

663.   Southworth, James G. *Verses of Cadence: An Introduc-
            tion to the Prosody of Chaucer and his Followers.*
            Oxford: Basil Blackwell, 1954. Supplement:
            The Prosody of Chaucer and his Followers. Oxford:
            Basil Blackwell, 1962.

        Southworth briefly discusses the punctuation used in
        PP MSS to indicate pauses and bar-junctures, and relates this
        usage to Chaucer's prosody. See Supplement, p. 25.

664.   Spearing, A. C. "Verbal Repetition in *Piers Plowman* B and C."
            JEGP, 62 (1963), 722-37.

        The C-poet employs repetitions to dramatize and emphasize
        his points: for example, the word "mede" occurs twenty times
        in thirty-three lines to verbally demonstrate the ubiquity
        of mede in society. C also uses a complex form of repetition
        in which two or more repetends are interlocked. Although
        verbal repetition is a common rhetorical technique in devo-
        tional writings, WL uses it in a completely different fashion.
        For WL, repetition is not decorative: it is a necessary
        instrument of thought. This use of repetition owes more to
        the *ars praedicandi* than to the *ars poetica*. Spearing
        suggests that the poem may have been designed originally for
        oral recitation.

665. Stewart, G. R. "The Meter of *Piers Plowman*." *PMLA*, 42 (1927), 113-28.

The meter of *PP* is based neither on a four stress (primary) system nor a seven (secondary and primary) stress system. The metrical pattern is dipodic--it employs a combination of these two systems. *PP* reads more melodically when not held to either a four stress or seven stress reading. Stewart concludes that: the alliterating syllable does not necessarily carry primary stress; WL did not regularly sound the final -e; before a marked medial pause or at the end of a line, there is no regular secondary stress pattern; secondary stress can fall upon either of the last two syllables. *PP* should be considered as trisyllabic dipodic verse.

666. Stobie, Margaret M. R. "The Influence of Morphology on Middle English Alliterative Poetry." *JEGP*, 39 (1940), 319-36.

Stobie disputes the assumption that French and Latin poetic forms influenced English rhythms in the fourteenth century. The changes in the English language itself naturally gave rise to the newer meters. Examines ME alliterative poetry in terms of the disappearance of inflectional endings, the lengthening of the short vowel in an unaccented syllable, and the shortening of vowels in compounds. *PP* is briefly discussed pp. 333 ff.: in *PP*, we see the increased use of prepositions and the loss of inflections.

667. Suddaby, Elizabeth. "The Poem *Piers Plowman*." *JEGP*, 54 (1955), 91-103.

A general discussion of WL's poetic method. WL uses alliteration as an instrument of argumentation--it serves to emphasize points. His similes generally have the appearance of popular wisdom--he has a strong aphoristic tendency which allows him to concentrate a great deal of meaning in a single line. WL favors vivid, connotative diction and he strives to embody abstract ideas in concrete language.

668. Swieczkowski, Walerian. *Word Order Patterning in Middle English*. The Hague: Mouton, 1962.

Swieczkowski provides a comparative quantitative analysis of *PP* and a group of ME sermons in order to determine WL's relationship to the *ars praedicandi*. He examines: 1. the relation of subject to predicate; 2. the relation of the predicate to other elements of the clause; 3. the position of the object. Swieczkowski concludes that while there are many similarities in the word order patterns of *PP* and the sermons, WL's range of syntactical patterns is considerably wider than the homilists'.

669. Teichmann, Eduard. *Die Verbalflexion in William Langly's Buch von Peter dem Pflüger*. Program der Realschule a Aacken, 1887.

670. _____. "Zur Stabreimzeile in Langland's *Buch von Peter dem Pflüger*." *Anglia*, 13 (1891), 140-74.

671. Thompson, Claud A. "Structural, Figurative, and Thematic Trinities in *Piers Plowman*." *Mosaic*, 9, ii (1975-76), 105-14.

Thompson suggests that the structure, movement, and meaning of *PP* are shaped by trinities: "its versification, its images, and its themes are dominated by triads, triplets, and triplicities which intertwine like labyrinthine trefoils in a medieval tapestry" (p. 105-6). There is a basic triplicity inherent in the metrical system of *PP*. The alliterating syllables normally occur in triads. The triple alliteration underscores the figurative and thematic trinities of the poem. "The very prosody of *Piers Plowman*, with the triple emphasis on sound in conjunction with stress, reinforces the reader's appreciation of those more elaborate triadic harmonies which dominate the poem" (p. 108).

672. Wandschneider, W. *Zur Syntax des Verbums in Langleys Vision of William Concerning Piers The Plowman*. Published University of Leipzig dissertation, 1887.

EPILOGUE

Although recent critics have discovered a great deal about the
form and meaning of *Piers Plowman*, our knowledge of certain aspects
of the poem is fragmentary and incomplete.

The most important and persistent problems in the study of
Piers Plowman relate to the poem's structure and coherence. Despite
more than forty years of scholarly study, the design of Langland's
narrative remains mysterious and elusive. Early critics attributed
the rapid shifts in time and space, digressions, and abrupt changes
in the direction of the plot to the poet's artistic ineptitude.
Langland's narrative was considered circuitous and confusing but
nonetheless simple in its basic design. J. J. Jusserand, for example, noted:

> All Langland's art and all his teaching can be
> summed up in one word: sincerity. He speaks,
> as he thinks, impetuously, recking little of
> the consequences of his words either for him-
> self or for others; they flow in a burning
> stream, and could no more be checked than the
> lava of Vesuvius. . . . Langland is unconscious
> of what he is led to: his visions are for him
> real ones; he tells them as they rise before
> him; he is scarcely aware that he invents; he
> stares at the sight and wonders as much as we
> do; he can change nothing; his personages are
> beyond his reach. There is therefore, nothing
> prepared, artistically arranged, or skillfully
> contrived, in his poem. The deliberate hand
> of the craft is nowhere to be seen.[1]

In reaction to this view, modern critics have advanced several
complex theories to account for Langland's unique use of narrative
elements, yet none has completely succeeded in dispelling the
reader's confusion over the poem's labyrinthine design. The
shortcomings of most critical approaches to *Piers'* structure are
attributable to an insistence on a clear-cut organizational plan.

But instead of providing *Piers Plowman* with a tidy structure which it does not actually possess, we might investigate the reasons behind its apparent discontinuity.

A starting point might be an examination of Langland's attempts at narrative organization. *Piers Plowman* partakes of several medieval literary forms including fabliau, exemplum, personification allegory, consolation, debate, dream vision, and sermon: but because Langland uses none of these in a sustained way, the poem's genre is indistinct.   The narrative begins in the conventional fashion of the medieval dream vision with the persona falling asleep on a May morning, "Vnder a brood bank by a bourn[e] side." In his first dream, Will meets Holy Church who responds to his questions concerning the nature of truth. The device of the dialogue provides an organizational plan for Passus I (B-text), but in the next Passus, Langland alters his narrative mode and presents a dramatic allegory depicting the role of Lady Meed in Church and State. In Passus V, the poem finds a temporary organizing principle in the pilgrimage of the folk to St. Truth, but this is terminated in Passus VII by the enigmatic tearing of the pardon. Several critics have argued that the poem is organized by the Dreamer's quest (for truth, or salvation, or perfection): actually, the quest motif contributes little to the poem's formal unity--it begins several times but never concludes, and the poem ends ambiguously with Conscience assuming Will's quest for *Piers Plowman*. Although the succession of partial organizing structures arouses conventional expectations, Langland continually abandons conventional literary forms.

The abortive or frustrated attempts at organization are relevant to the meaning of the visions. What is needed is a reassessment of the narrative's successes and failures in light of what we now know about the principles of medieval literary composition. A study along these lines was begun by Charles Muscatine in *Poetry and Crisis in the Age of Chaucer*.[2] Muscatine's approach to the problems of unity and coherence in *Piers Plowman* is based on his recognition of the poem's structural imperfections. He describes the flaws of the narrative in terms of the disintegrative tendencies of late Gothic art and argues that the form of *Piers Plowman* is "symptomatic of some sort of [cultural] breakdown." Muscatine's approach suggests interesting possibilities for future studies of the poem's narrative complexities, particularly Langland's avoidance of conventional literary forms. The critical techniques employed by Robert Jordan in his study of Chaucer's use of compositional principles might yield profitable results in the study of *Piers Plowman*. Jordan's theories concerning inorganic form in medieval narrative poetry, especially his observations on narrative discontinuity in the *Clerk's Tale*, are relevant to the structural peculiarities of Langland's visions.[3]

A comparative study of the structures of *Piers Plowman* and T. S. Eliot's *The Wasteland* might provide contexts for an understanding of Langland's design. Eliot's deliberate use of narrative discontinuity, abrupt transitions, and allusive echoes is similar in many ways to Langland's compositional technique. Both poets wrote in times of dramatic cultural change and both employed literary forms that reflect social and moral tension.

Most modern critics have focused their attention on the structure and meaning of *Piers Plowman* and few have examined its language, style, and meter. Although it has been frequently suggested that Langland's predilection for verbal repetition might be an outgrowth of the requirements of oral delivery, no one has conducted a serious investigation of this possibility.[4] The theory of oral delivery accounts for the repetitive and digressive style of much of *Piers Plowman*: for example, the iteration of the word "mede" in Lady Meed's argument with Conscience may be a result of Langland's desire to drive home a central point of his argument to an audience of listeners:

> It bicomeþ a kyng þat kepeþ a Reaume
> To yeue [hise men *mede*] þat mekely hym serueþ,
> To aliens, to alle men, to honouren hem with ȝiftes;
> *Mede* makeþ hym biloued and for a man holden.
> Emperours and Erles and alle manere lordes
> [Thoruȝ] ȝiftes han yonge men to [yerne] and to ryde.
> The Pope [wiþ hise] prelates presentȝ vnderfonge[þ],
> And *mede* men h[y]mseluen to mayntene hir lawes.
> Ser[u]aunt for hire seruyce, we seeþ wel þe soþe,
> Taken *Mede* of hir maistres as þei mowe acorde:

Beggeres for hir biddynge bidden [of] men *Mede*;
Mynstrales for hir myrþe *Mede* þei aske;
The kyng haþ *mede* of his men to make pees in londe;
Men þat [kenne clerkes] crauen [of hem] *Mede*;
Preeste þat prechen þe peple to goode
Asken *Mede* and massepens and hire mete [als];
Alle kynne craft[y] men crauen *Mede* for hir Prentices;
[*Mede* and Marchaundiȝe] mote nede go togideres;
No wiȝt, as I wene, wiþouten *Mede* may libbe.

B. III, 209-227

Beryl Rowland has noted that in order to comprehend the sense
of orally delivered verse, medieval listeners required familiar
phrasing: "They could not go back over something which they failed
to comprehend. They needed surface simplicity, a texture which was
thin or if full and ornate, was mostly in language in common use,
interspersed with formulae and synonymous doublets. They enjoyed
repetition, alliteration, onomatopoeia, and all rhythmic effects of
dramatic speech. If they were to respond to a single reading, the
poetry had to have a certain diffuseness."[5] The following passage
from the notoriously difficult riddle of Patience hardly fits these
criteria:

'Disce,' quod he, *'doce, dilige inimicos.*
Disce and dowel, *doce* and dobet, *dilige* and dobest:
[Th]us [lerede] me ones a lemman, loue was hir name.
"Wiþ wordes and werkes," quod she, "and will of þyn herte
Thow loue leelly þi soule al þi lif tyme . . . .
Kynde loue coueiteþ noȝt no catel but speche .
Wiþ half a laumpe lyne in latyn, *Ex vi transicionis,*
I bere þer, [in a bouste] faste ybounde, dowel.

B. XIII, 137-141, 150-152.

The obscure analogy and complex grammatical pattern of this passage
could not have been easily understood in an oral format. Nonetheless, a close analysis of the evidence for oral delivery would help
us to better understand Langland's style and the audience for whom
the poem was designed.

There have been few studies of Langland's rhetoric except for
some brief examinations of certain recurrent simple figures of
speech such as *adnominatio*, metaphor, and *contentio*. The traditional view of Langland as a "non-rhetorical" poet has only recently
been challenged. This deceptive generalization was based primarily
on the absence of obvious textbook formulae and ornate schemes and

tropes in *Piers Plowman*. Although Langland never employs rhetorical devices for mere beautification, we should not "fail to notice the considerable amount of rhetoric the poem does contain."[6] Future studies of Langland's rhetoric might consider the poet's use of persuasive strategies such as arguments from authority, iteration for emphasis, declamation, and arguments from analogy. Langland's unique mixture of narrative and persuasive discourse also bears investigating. Robert Payne's discussion of the influence of medieval rhetorical theory on Chaucer has implications for a study of Langland's use of rhetorical strategies and structural dispositions, particularly schemes of abbreviation and amplification.[7]

The language of *Piers Plowman* has not been closely studied for nearly a century, the primary reason being the lack of definitive texts of the three versions of the poem. Because Emil Bernard's 1878 study of Langland's diction was based on the incorrect assumption that MS Laud Misc. 581 was the poet's holograph, his conclusions are no longer very valuable.[8] When complete, The Athlone Press critical edition will provide the basis for a badly needed concordance of the three versions and for studies of Langland's vocabulary, poetic diction, syntax, and mixture of heterogeneous dialects. Furthermore, the definitive texts will make possible study of the prosodic features of *Piers Plowman*. A comparative study of the prosody of *Piers Plowman* with other alliterative poems of the fourteenth century would be of considerable interest: *e.g.*, an analysis of the differences between Langland's and the Pearl-Poet's use of alliterative meter might help us to better understand the place of *Piers* in the alliterative revival.

In his review of *Piers* scholarship from 1904 to 1938, Morton W. Bloomfield observed a tendency among scholars to discuss the poem outside its immediate historical context and suggested that future studies of *Piers Plowman* focus on "backgrounds in folklore, art, theology, homilies, religious tractates and various literatures as well as in social and economic history."[9] There has been considerable response to Bloomfield's *desideratum*: in the past forty years, scholars have demonstrated an increasing awareness of the importance of the intellectual climate of the fourteenth century

169

and its relation to the poem. A great many studies of the general backgrounds and intellectual currents of the later Middle Ages have appeared: Robert Worth Frank's *Piers Plowman and the Scheme of Salvation*, Muscatine's *Poetry and Crisis in the Age of Chaucer*, John Yunck's *The Lineage of Lady Meed*, and Bloomfield's *Piers Plowman as a Fourteenth-Century Apocalypse* provide valuable information concerning the social, theological, and ecclesiastical backgrounds of Langland's age.

Work remains to be done, however, on the political and economic backgrounds of *Piers Plowman*. In recent years, critics have deemphasized the social satire for which *Piers* was once well known and with it the cultural situations that helped to shape the poem's original purpose. Langland lived in a time of political and social upheaval: an era of uprisings, riots, and assassinations which witnessed the demise of the traditional feudal system and the rise of a capitalistic economy. A reexamination of the political and economic tensions of late fourteenth-century England will help us to understand the meaning that *Piers Plowman* held for its original audience and to evaluate Langland's use of satire and complaint. The recent facsimile edition of Robert Crowley's 1550 edition of *Piers Plowman*, edited by J. A. W. Bennett, will provide a basis for studies of sixteenth-century interpretations of Langland's satire.

We still know very little about the literary backgrounds of *Piers Plowman*. In the absence of specific sources for the poem, we need to turn to works which may have exerted some influence on Langland. Since the publication of G. R. Owst's *Literature and Pulpit in Medieval England*, it has been generally assumed that Langland was influenced by homiletic literature, although most modern *Piers* critics disagree with Owst's contention that *Piers Plowman* represents merely the culmination of the pulpit's "familiar time-worn methods of speech."[10] No one has yet closely examined the sermons to which Langland may have had access--with the exception of Thomas Brunton's sermons with which the poet was clearly familiar. A study of the relationship between *Piers Plowman* and such works as the *Gesta Romanorum* and John Bromyard's *Summa Praedicantium* might yield interesting results: these preaching manuals enjoyed wide circulation in fourteenth-century England and in them, or in similar compilations, Langland might have found ideas for his poem. Several scholars have argued that Langland's source for his story of the four daughters of God (B. XVIII) was the *Castle of Love*. However, it is more likely that he was familiar with the story of Agios's daughters in the *Gesta Romanorum* or a similar collection of exempla and tales.[11]

In the past twenty years or so, critics have emphasized Langland's use of scriptural commentaries and glosses. While it is certain that Langland was familiar with such works, we do not know the manuscripts to which he had access. A listing of patristic sources available in the Malvern area and in London in the later fourteenth century would help us to assess Langland's indebtedness to specific exegetical commentaries. Only two brief examinations of the influence of folk motifs on *Piers Plowman* have been published.[12] A profitable study might be made of the influence of folk elements on Langland's animal and agricultural imagery.

These suggestions for future studies of *Piers* are based on a recognition of the achievements of modern *Piers* criticism and not on its shortcomings. A recent critic of *Piers Plowman* commented that "modern criticism does not dispel one's sense of puzzlement but rather tends to substitute new and more complex puzzles for the old."[13] This assessment, apart from its pejorative implications, is altogether accurate. But the inadequacies of *Piers* criticism are not, by and large, due to the failures of scholars and critics but rather to the mysterious and inconclusive nature of the poem itself. *Piers* is the most difficult and controversial work in Middle English and it raises questions that have no simple answers. Dame Study's observation on the difficulties of theology applies to the problems experienced by all critics of *Piers Plowman*:

> Ac Theologie haþ tened me ten score tymes;
> The moore I muse þerInne þe mystier it semeþ,
> And þe depper I deuyne[d] þe derker me [þouȝte].
> It is no Science forsoþe to sotile Inne.
>
> B. X, 185-188

[1] *Piers Plowman: A Contribution to the History of English Mysticism*, trans. M. E. R. (New York: Russell and Russell, 1894), pp. 153-55.

[2] "*Piers Plowman*: The Poetry of Crisis," *Poetry and Crisis in the Age of Chaucer* (Notre Dame and London: University of Notre Dame Press, 1972), pp. 71-110.

[3] *Chaucer and the Shape of Creation* (Cambridge, Mass: Harvard University Press, 1967), pp. 198-207.

[4] See G. R. Owst, *Literature and Pulpit in Medieval England* (Cambridge: Cambridge University Press, 1933), pp. 376-406; J. A. Burrow, "The Audience of *Piers Plowman*," *Anglia*, 75 (1957), 373-84; A. C. Spearing, "The Development of a Theme in *Piers Plowman*," *RES*, 11 (1960), 241-53; Spearing, "Verbal Repetition in *Piers Plowman* B and C," *JEGP*, 62 (1963), 722-37.

[5] "Chaucer's Imagery," in *A Companion to Chaucer Studies*, ed. Beryl Rowland (Toronto: Oxford University Press, 1968), p. 114.

[6] Elizabeth Salter, *Piers Plowman: An Introduction* (Oxford: Basil Blackwell, 1962), p. 37.

[7] *The Key of Remembrance* (New Haven and London: Yale University Press, 1963), *passim*.

[8] *Langland: A Grammatical Treatise* (Bonn: Emil Strauss, 1874), *passim*.

[9] "The Present State of *Piers Plowman* Studies," *Speculum*, 14 (1939), 232.

[10] *Literature and Pulpit in Medieval England*, p. 228.

[11] *Gesta Romanorum*, ed. Sidney J. H. Herrtage, EETS, extra series, 33, pp. 132-35.

[12] Paul Franklin Baum, "The Fable of the Belling of the Cat," *MLN*, 34 (1919), 462-70; Dorothy Jean Burton, "The Compact with the Devil in the Middle English *Vision of Piers Plowman*, B. II," *California Folklore Quarterly*, 5 (1946), 179-84.

[13] Muscatine, *Poetry and Crisis*, p. 73.

APPENDIX: STUDIES NOT LISTED IN CHAPTER ONE
WHICH COMMENT ON THE QUESTION OF AUTHORSHIP.

Favoring Multiple Authorship.

Day, Mabel. "Duns Scotus and *Piers Plowman*." *RES*, 3 (1927), 333-4.

Dunning, T. P. *Piers Plowman: An Interpretation of the A-text*
     (1937).

Fowler, David C. "The Relationship of the Three Texts of *Piers the
     Plowman*." *MP*, 50 (1952), 5-22.

Favoring Single Authorship.

Chambers, R. W. "Long Will, Dante, and the Righteous Heathen."
     Essays and Studies, 9 (1924), 50-69.

_____. *Man's Unconquerable Mind*   (1939).

_____. "The Three Texts of *Piers Plowman* and Their Grammatical
     Forms." *MLR*, 14 (1919), 129-51.

_____ and J. H. G. Grattan. "The Text of *Piers Plowman*."
     MLR, 4 (1908-1909), 357-89.

_____ and J. H. G. Grattan. "The Text of *Piers Plowman*."
     MLR, 26 (1931), 1-51.

_____ and J. H. G. Grattan. "The Text of *Piers Plowman*:
     Critical Methods." *MLR*, 11 (1916), 257-75.

Dawson, Christopher. *Medieval Religion* (1934), p. 167.

Donaldson, E. Talbot. *Piers Plowman: The C-Text and Its Poet*
     (1949). Ch. VII, "The Poet: Biographical Material," pp. 199-
     226.

Jusserand, J. J. *Piers Plowman, A Contribution to the History of
     English Mysticism* (1894).

Mensendieck, Otto. *Charakterentwicklung und ethischtheologische
     Anschauungen des verfassers von Piers the Plowman* (1900).

Mitchell, A. G. "Notes on the C-Text of *Piers Plowman*." *London
     Medieval Studies*, I (1937-1939), 483-92.

_____ and G. H. Russell. "The Three Texts of *Piers the Plow-man*." *JEGP*, 52 (1953), 445-56.

Morley, Henry. *English Writers*. Vol. I, Pt. II (1866), pp. 557-67.

Russell, G. H. "The Salvation of the Heathen: The Exploration of a Theme in *Piers Plowman*." *Journal of the Warburg and Courtauld Institute*, 29 (1966), 101-16.

Sullivan, Sister Carmeline. "The Latin Inscriptions and the Macaronic Verse in *Piers Plowman*." Catholic University of America Dissertation, 1932.

Ten Brink, Bernard. *Early English Literature (To Wyclif)* (1883).

AUTHOR INDEX
(Numbers refer to items, not pages)